Teaching Literature

Teaching Literature

A Companion

Edited by

Tanya Agathocleous

and

Ann C. Dean

First published 2003 by
PALGRAVE MACMILLAN
Houndmills, Basingstoke, Hampshire RG21 6XS and
175 Fifth Avenue, New York, N.Y. 10010
Companies and representatives throughout the world

PALGRAVE MACMILLAN is the global academic imprint of the Palgrave Macmillan division of St. Martin's Press, LLC and of Palgrave Macmillan Ltd. Macmillan® is a registered trademark in the United States, United Kingdom and other countries. Palgrave is a registered trademark in the European Union and other countries.

ISBN 978-0-333-98793-3

This book is printed on paper suitable for recycling and made from fully managed and sustained forest sources.

A catalogue record for this book is available from the British Library.

Library of Congress Cataloging-in-Publication Data
Teaching literature : a companion / edited by Tanya Agathocleous and Ann C. Dean.
    p.   cm.
Includes bibliographical references and index.
ISBN 0–333–98792–6 — ISBN 0–333–98793–4 (pbk.)
1. English literature—Study and teaching (Higher)   2. American literature—Study and teaching (Higher)   3. Literature—Study and teaching (Higher)
I. Agathocleous, Tanya, 1970–   II. Dean, Ann C., 1967–

PR33 .T43 2002
820'.71'1—dc21

2002035530

10   9   8   7   6   5   4   3   2   1
12   11   10   09   08   07   06   05   04   03

Transferred to Digital Printing in 2011

Contents

Foreword

One of the best indications that this book will have done its work effectively would be the publication fairly soon of similar books, concerned with the problems of teaching literature, not by the Modern Language Association but, say, by the university presses of Cambridge, Oxford, Harvard, Yale or Chicago. The unlikeliness of this eventuality is a mark of this book's importance. For it undertakes directly to consider the problems of teaching literature, but in such a way that it not only contributes to our understanding of the practical problems of teaching but also enhances our appreciation of literature itself. That is, while teaching literature at the college and university level here becomes the legitimate subject it has rarely been, it does so in a way that legitimizes it as a subject – by throwing light on the literature that most of us who will be reading this book spend our professional lives teaching.

The problems this book engages apply not only to the American university classroom, but to undergraduate teaching internationally. While the American system is perhaps distinctively oriented to set classes across the entire curriculum organized for groups of varying sizes, from relatively small seminars to huge auditorium-size lectures, the problems of focusing on teaching as the fundamentally important activity of all professors extends even to the English system of tutorials. And while it is clear that 'publish or perish' has been a hallmark of the American system for a long time, it is especially interesting and saddening to note that the new English demand for research assessment, imposed nationally and formally, virtually guarantees that rewards will be distributed as they are in America, to the departments with the largest collection of long Curricula Vitae. The 'CV,' registering books, essays, reviews written, conferences attended, lectures given, manuscripts read for leading presses – that is the key to academic success virtually everywhere. And it is to the problems this creates for the crucial and creative work of teaching that this book is addressed.

That for the most part the profession (and the institutions that publish its work) has not taken teaching as the sort of 'contribution to knowledge' that makes for a major entry on the 'CV,' is self-evident. This fact is an aspect of a complicated condition that has kept the study of the teaching of literature, especially by its best and best-known teachers, a second-class part of the work of literature faculty at research institutions. If, as we know to be the case, there are some astonishingly good teachers among the stars and celebrities of literary study, we know also that they picked up their skills by virtue of a passion for teaching and a willingness to work at it and learn in spite of the absence of institutionally sanctioned instruction, and despite the absence of professional reward for the work. An English don can nod while sitting in his rooms with two undergraduates as certainly as an American professor can fail to prepare adequately for his lectures or to be sensitive to the special intellectual needs of his students. That there are so many dons and professors who give themselves intensely to their teaching is a cause for surprise given the current system, since such intensity has always gone beyond what any promotion review committee at the top of the university hierarchy has been likely to attend to seriously. We know that very few of those who are both splendid scholars and splendid teachers ever write about what is entailed in being a good teacher and none of them has made a reputation by virtue of primary devotion to teaching. This book is, I hope, a sign that the times, at last, are changing.

It is hard to write seriously about the general problems of teaching in college literary programs because virtually everything one might say, and certainly all that I have already said, has achieved the status of cliché. It is a cliché, and no less true for it, that we all know that a great deal of lip-service is paid to teaching in universities that yet reward their faculty according to research assessment: everybody knows it and nobody does anything about it. We have all heard, with a mixture of cynicism and belief, that you can't be a good teacher of literature unless you can provide real evidence that you are both abreast of the scholarship in the field and contributing to it. We might all, also, agree that the extant literature confronting the problems of teaching in practical ways seems transient and trivial in comparison to the vast literatures of literary scholarship and criticism. It is obvious, too, that literature about teaching literature is generally treated as inferior by the peers who evaluate it and certainly not adequate as evidence that might lead to tenure and promotion.

The problems are longstanding. They were obvious to me at the beginning of my now very long career in teaching literature. The passion for teaching that I and my graduate student colleagues felt when confronted, utterly unprepared, with our first freshman writing classes (a passion that still seems to be endemic among American graduate students feeling their way into the profession) had to be its own reward. Part of the reward was that by teaching freshmen how to write, I learned about writing myself. But that of course was not the reason I was assigned classes in freshman composition, and the disconnect between the teaching we actually had to do and the training we were getting was virtually absolute (and to a large extent remains so). None of my often wonderful teachers said anything to me about teaching. Occasionally, urgent self-criticisms emerged from the academy, indications that everyone really did know that graduate training for teaching trained us for anything but teaching.

But American prosperity continuing until the early 1970s ensured that the paradoxes inherent in the post-war system of higher education were not tackled. Increased enrolments entailed the greater and greater use in introductory courses of graduate assistants, which meant that universities needed more and more PhD candidates who wanted to study literature rather than to teach writing courses. Their ambitions seemed to be sanctioned by the fact that their own teachers were clearly rewarded for being brilliant scholars, not brilliant teachers (which again, by some weird accident, they sometimes were). Directors of composition programs in large state universities tended to be people who couldn't get tenure or who, having got tenure, were recognized as second-class citizens. Institutions, like community and two-year colleges, without graduate programs and with heavy 'teaching loads' (which diminished in research universities from four courses a semester to three to two and...) increasingly distrusted the PhDs who had, willy-nilly, learned that the only place to be professionally was at an institution at least as research-oriented as the ones in which they trained – and in which teaching loads were 'light.' The largest number of teachers of literature in college education teach much more and make less money and get less disciplinary recognition than those few who fill the pages of *PMLA*, *Critical Quarterly*, and dozens of small circulation (and I'm talking seriously small) journals that make tenure possible.

Obviously, there is a parallel situation in the United Kingdom, although the chronology seems to be different in that case. The growth of the redbrick universities after the war actually did produce, along with a new abundance of university teachers, some very engaged teaching, although this was made difficult, of course, by the increased volume of students to be attended to one-to-one. But in the end, the disconnect between graduate training and profes-sional teaching today is about the same as it is in America. Indeed, I have heard from young and often brilliant university teachers in England that the new pressures on extending the CV have made survival in academia virtually incompatible with the very hard and equally intellectually demanding work of teaching.

Clichés again. Nothing new here. My own career thrived because I published a lot. And if I might flesh out one of these clichés with an anecdote, I will note that at a point when my career was taking off (as we say in the trade) by virtue of a recently published book, I was offered a job at a major research institution quite well known also for the seriousness of its commitment to teaching. After a day or so of heavy interviewing, I realized that I had not seen the director of undergraduate studies or talked about undergraduate teaching with anyone. When I asked if I might talk with the director, my hosts said, of course, but why would I want to?

Yet the times they do seem to be changing – a little. And I take this book both as a valuable indication of that change and a provocation to more and better. Under the pressure of public distrust provoked in no small part by the egregious culture wars, and with a continuing series of attacks begun in the Reagan years on the lazy professoriate (the mark of a broad public discovery of the paradox of the system I have described), university after university has, at least publicly, declared its commitment to teaching. My own institution, with no sense of irony at all, declared a 'year of the undergraduate.'

But while in fact many departments made efforts to come to terms with the paradoxes of the system (trying to make teaching a serious subject as well as practice) and the concomitant injustices, the institutions themselves did very little for undergraduates – and that's a generous evaluation. Economic austerity has imposed pressures on teachers everywhere. In America, the cutting of faculty lines has forced increases in class sizes and further shifted the work of introductory teaching, now not only from regular faculty to teaching assistants but also to part-timers. Thus, while the commitment to teaching officially intensified and graduate programs began to install training programs for new teachers, a large corps of teachers – transient, temporary, inadequately compensated, with no particular allegiances to the institutions in which they worked – were turned loose in the classroom.

It has always been difficult to earn a place among the English professoriate, and as the American economy boomed through the 1990s, the job crisis did not significantly diminish. For a quarter of a century at least, since 1972, only 51 per cent of those who went looking for jobs in the first year after completion of the PhD got tenure track jobs. I don't know that things have improved much at all, despite the establishment of urgent commissions to consider cures, despite the work of some universities to diminish the shift to part-time employment, and despite the attempts by some graduate programs to cut down enrollment. The need for teachers increases. The work that teachers must do increases. Jobs do not become available. And literary scholars at research universities get promoted for publishing books on culture and literature.

One of the interesting consequences of these economic shifts has been that graduate students are now being asked to teach courses in literature at a greater rate than ever before – or so it seems from my limited experience. This volume is partly a response to this development, for while in many institutions now graduate students are directed in their teaching of writing, they are suddenly confronted with the sorts of challenges in the classroom for which they ought to be trained in literature programs – that is, the teaching of literature. And here once again, there is very little for them to go on but what they might have learned in preparing for writing courses and a thin, undervalued literature about teaching literature. This book is a significant contribution to that literature. And though it emerges from a climate in which graduate students and university culture as a whole are being forced to become much more self-conscious about the work of teaching, this initiative remains one that is likely to keep the literary editors of major university presses suspicious. There is, of course, a precedent for training in teaching, and that precedent is The School of Education.

It is partly as a consequence of that precedent that literary programs have remained wary of formal discussion of teaching and have simply refused, with some rare exceptions, to include such training in teaching in the PhD program. The notorious failure of schools of education to improve the quality of American education stands as a warning. Nobody interested in literature wants to shift the emphasis from the subject of study to the methods of teaching it if that means that method replaces the subject, becomes the subject, and as a consequence produces people who have no serious commitment to the study of literature and no real training in learning how to deal with it. Better the 'publish or perish' program of most literary departments than 'Mickey Mouse' courses (as many of my students used to call them) in education. But, of course, these need not be the options.

It is simple common sense: training in the teaching of literature ought to be part of the training of anyone who wants to make a career of teaching literature. It should be emphasized that even in the golden expansive days of literary programs – that is, about twenty years, from the end of World War II until the early 1970s – the vast majority of those who went into university teaching did not publish much, if anything. The vast majority spent their professional lives focused on the work of teaching. If in research universities it is hard to create an ethos in which teaching in an of itself is the ultimate object of one's professional life, even there it is crucial that it be understood that it is not a mark of failure if young PhDs go on to be, primarily, good teachers. The fact that university presses don't publish books about teaching literature very much and that universities don't promote good unpublishing teachers and that community colleges are wary of hiring PhDs is related to the fact that there is little serious and adequate literature about teaching literature. There is little such literature because universities and departments do not yet genuinely believe in the importance of the teaching they insist on.

So the critical questions emerging from the debris of these disheartening clichés is whether it might not, after all, be possible, to begin to produce a serious literature about the teaching of literature, one that would, within the profession, achieve something of the prestige of literary scholarship and criticism and would do so by genuinely engaging the dominant literary and cultural interests of faculty, genuinely adding to knowledge, both of teaching and of literature, genuinely exploring the ways in which teaching literature tests our theories of literature and our sense of what it is we do when we do criticism, genuinely engaging an audience untrained in our disciplines' language and professional style. What is a reader-response theory without engagement with real readers? What is cultural theory if its creators cannot find a way to see their own students as parts of the culture being studied? What are the answers scholars and critics might provide when confronted with those terrifying and fundamental questions that smart and not-so-smart undergraduates are likely to ask? How, in fact, if we are right about the value of literature and of criticism, is it possible to lead young people to come to recognize it or challenge it intelligently? These are not minor questions, even for 'distinguished' literary scholars. A literature that could begin to struggle with them seriously might deserve serious consideration when departments and colleges and universities came down to making tenure decisions.

Teaching Literature marks a significant contribution to this crucial enterprise. It attempts to move between the theoretical and the practical, from the actual work of the classroom to its theoretical underpinnings. In effect, in ways that should help push discussion of critical and cultural questions in new directions, it tests out the ideas that, as students of literature rather than as teachers, we have learned. In exploring the problems students have with literature, it is forced to lay out with clarity the assumptions about literature and literary criticism that drive the books we write for university presses. While these essays do try to give quite practical advice, provide syllabuses and reading lists, and sample exercises, these are not mere 'how-to' essays; rather, they are confrontations with our most intractable critical problems, challenges to our critical assumptions and to our powers of articulating them. Of course, there is no way that any set of essays, or any volume, can cover the full range of possibilities within the realm of literary study, but by working selectively, following, as it were, the lines of interest of the outstanding teacher/scholars contributing to this volume, the book provides both a set of models for the ways in which writing about teaching can also be writing significantly about literature, and a heuristic for further such explorations.

That is to say, this book provides models for the way in which we can, at last, begin to restructure the system of paradoxes and self-contradictions that have made the teaching of literature such an oddly anomalous activity – the work we faculty get paid to do, but the work that remains, in the structures of university compensations, most ignored institutionally. It might help to further the work of instituting required training in teaching for graduate students, showing how both the practical problems of teaching and the intellectual problems of finding a way to talk about literature to non-professionals can open up important new areas of thinking. And it can do this by at last demonstrating the intellectual richness of a genre that desperately needs development: the literature of the teaching of literature. Only when such a genre is successfully established and rewarded will there be real indication that the teaching of literature in the academy – at the level of the community college, at the level of advanced graduate work – will be accorded the dignity it deserves. And with that dignity would come our chance for a reform in the anomalous system that has at last, in recent years, evoked the sort of disapprobation from within and from outside the university that it has richly deserved for decades.

GEORGE LEVINE

Acknowledgements

We would like to thank all the teachers and mentors who have provided us with the experiences from which this book was built, as well as Bernardo Feliciano and Chris O'Brien for their help and support as we put the book together.

Some of the chapters have been published elsewhere, and we are grateful to the editors and copyright owners for permission to reprint. Altieri, Charles. "Taking Lyrics Literally: Teaching Poetry in a Prose Culture" was originally published in *New Literary History* 82: 2 (2001): 259–281. © The University of Virginia; reprinted by permission of the Johns Hopkins University Press. Miller, Richard. "Schooling Misery: The Ominous Threat and the Eminent Promise of the Popular Reader" was originally published in *Writing on the Edge* 9: 2 (1998): 63–77 Spring–Summer; reprinted by permission of the author. O'Brien, John. "Grub Street: The Literary and the Literatory in Eighteenth-Century Britain,' originally appeared in the 1998 volume of *Teaching in the Eighteenth Century*, published by the American Society of Eighteenth-Century Studies; reprinted by permission of ASECS.

Notes on the Contributors

Charles Altieri is Professor of Literature at University of California at Berkeley. He is the author of several books on poetry including the recent *Postmodernisms Now: Essays on Contemporaneity in the Arts* and the forthcoming *An Aesthetics of the Affects*.

Suzy Anger is Assistant Professor of English at the University of Maryland, Baltimore County, where she teaches courses in Victorian literature, literary theory and literature and ethics. She has published articles on nineteenth-century literature, is editor of *Knowing the Past: Victorian Literature and Culture*, and author of a forthcoming book on Victorian interpretation.

Michele Birnbaum is Associate Professor of English and African-American Studies and Director of Women's Studies at the University of Puget Sound. She has published articles on racial representation in the late nineteenth century in *American Literature, African American Review* and elsewhere, and is the author of *Race, Labour and Desire in American Literature, 1860s–1930s* (2002). Her forthcoming work concerns mixed-race studies and the production of American literary history.

Glenn Burger is Associate Professor of English at Queen's College and the Graduate Center of the City University of New York. He is the editor of *A Lytell Cronycle*, Richard Pynson's translation of Hetoum's *La Fleur des histoires de la terre d'Orient* and coeditor (with Steven F. Kruger) of *Queering the Middle Ages*. His book, *Chaucer's Queer Nation*, is forthcoming.

Susan Jaye Dauer is Professor of English, Valencia Community College, Florida. Her recent essay, 'Cartoons and Contamination: How the Multinational Kids Help Captain Planet to Save Gaia', will appear in a volume on ecocriticism and children's literature, and she has presented conference papers at NCTE and NISOD on teaching with computers.

Philip Davis is Professor of Literature, University of Liverpool. He has teaching and research interests across the curriculum. He recently published *Sudden Shakespeare* and *Real Voices: On Reading*. Other publications include *Memory and Writing: From Wordsworth to Lawrence, In Mind of Johnson, The Experience of Reading* and an edition of Ruskin's selected writings. He is currently writing the volume on the Victorians in the *Oxford History of English Literature* series.

Jillana Enteen is Visiting Assistant Professor of Literature at Northwestern University. She teaches and writes about the Internet, postcolonial literature and theory, cultural studies, and theories of gender. She has published essays about the use of English-language terms for sexualities and genders in the urban cultures of Thailand.

Nancy Henry is Associate Professor of English, SUNY Binghamton. She teaches nineteenth-century British and American literature, women's studies, colonial and postcolonial studies and Judaic studies. She has authored a number of articles on Victorian literature and her current project, *George Eliot and the British Empire*, is forthcoming.

Richard E. Miller is Associate Professor of English and Associate Director of the Writing Program at Rutgers University. His recent book, *As if Learning Mattered: Reforming Higher Education*, discusses the history and future of educational reform.

Steven F. Kruger is Professor of English at Queen's College and the Graduate Center of the City University of New York. He is the author of *Dreaming in the Middle Ages* and *AIDS Narratives: Gender and Sexuality, Fiction and Science*; he has coedited, with Deborah R. Geis, *Approaching the Millennium: Essays on 'Angels in America'*, and, with Glenn Burger, *Queering the Middle Ages*. His book in progress is *The Spectral Jew: (Dis)embodiment and the Dynamics of Medieval Jewish/Christian Interaction* (forthcoming).

George Levine is Kenneth Burke Professor of English and Director of the Center for the Critical Analysis of Contemporary Culture at Rutgers University. A member of the MLA Commission on Professional Employment, he has written frequently on educational matters, most recently in 'Saving Disinterest: Aesthetics, Contingency, and Mixed Conditions' (*ELH*, Autumn 2001), and 'Aesthetics and Ideology Revisited' (*Contemporary Literature*, Winter 2000). His latest book is *Dying to Know: Scientific Epistemology and Narrative in Nineteenth Century England* (forthcoming).

John O'Brien is Assistant Professor of English at the University of Virginia. He is completing a book entitled *Entertaining Culture: English Pantomime and the Emergence of Entertainment in Britain, 1690–1760*.

Rob Pope is Professor of English Studies at Oxford Brookes University and a UK National Teaching Fellow. He has taught at universities in Wales, Russia and New Zealand, and led curriculum and staff development programs in America, Australia, South East Asia and Central Europe. His publications include *Textual*

Intervention: Critical and Creative Strategies for Literary Studies (1995) and *The English Studies Book* (2nd edn 2002). He is currently writing *Creativity* and coediting *English Language, Literature & Culture: a Critical and Historical Source Book* (forthcoming).

Carolyn Williams is Associate Professor of English at Rutgers University and Co-Director of the Center for the Critical Analysis of Contemporary Culture. She specializes in nineteenth-century British literature and culture. Her book, *Transfigured World: Walter Pater's Aesthetic Historicism*, was publish recently. Another, on Gilbert and Sullivan, is forthcoming. She received the Metcalf Award for Excellence in Teaching at Boston University and the Susman Award for Excellence in Teaching at Rutgers.

Editors

Tanya Agathocleous is currently a fellow at the Center for the Critical Analysis of Contemporary Culture at Rutgers University. She works on Victorian and colonial literature and culture and Commonwealth literature; she has published articles on nineteenth-century literature and written a biography of George Orwell.

Ann Dean is Assistant Professor of English and Director of College Writing at the University of Southern Maine. She teaches about writes about eighteenth-century Anglo-American writing and composition studies.

Introduction

Tanya Agathocleous and Ann Dean

What do you want your students to learn? What do you want them to *do* in your class? What do they do instead? How do you respond?

As graduate student teaching assistants in the early 1990s, the editors of this book began teaching literature courses at the university level. We found ourselves asking each other and everyone we knew the questions above. Though our department did not have a pedagogy in place to advise graduate students how to teach literature, we had both taken a required course on teaching composition and had been exposed there to the burgeoning literature on that subject; we therefore went to the library looking for equivalent books on teaching literature to help us through those difficult first classes. What we found instead were impassioned polemics about what should be on or off university syllabuses (the culture wars were raging). Other accounts of teaching described particular readings of texts, and often included sentences with assertions such as: 'the students came to see that...'. But, we asked each other, *how* did the students come to see it? How did the teacher know that they had come to see it?

This book is a response to that experience, one that we know is shared by many college and university teachers. Some instructors, like us, begin their teaching careers as graduate students, fortunate to have early experience but still developing expertise and confidence as scholars. Others teach very little in graduate school and enter the classroom as faculty with little experience but with the sense that they ought to know how to teach already. We have all read intensively and spent hours in our apartments or in cold libraries writing and rewriting, then found ourselves in front of groups of people: either as graduate student teaching assistants, first-year professors, or part-time teachers earning some money while we work on a novel. All of us ask ourselves: What do we say to these people in front of us? What do we wear? Why do they keep looking at us like that?

Since we first wished for a book like this in the early 1990s, a number of notable institutional changes have placed a new emphasis on the value of

1

teaching at the postsecondary level. In the US, the Carnegie and Pew foundations have funded a number of campus initiatives to improve teaching in all the disciplines, and organizations such as the American Association of Higher Education (AAHE) and the American Association of Colleges and Universities (AAC&U) now hold frequent conferences on assessing student learning and on the scholarship of teaching. In the UK and Australia, some institutions have begun to offer certificates in higher education teaching, and many centers for teaching offer access to research on educational methods and standards (for instance, those at Bristol and Hull). In the fall of 2000, the English Subject Centre was founded at Royal Holloway, University of London in order to make teaching and assessment central to the funding of higher education in the UK. Everywhere, hiring committees are beginning to ask for, and critically examining, teaching portfolios from candidates; some departments are also using these portfolios to aid in tenure and promotion decisions. Accreditors are also more likely to prompt for information about teaching methods and effectiveness than they were in the past. Correspondingly, the literature on teaching at the college and university level has begun to grow. New journals, such as *The Journal of the Scholarship of Teaching* and *Pedagogy*, provide accounts of the theory and practice of teaching, while the number of MLA panels on teaching has increased dramatically in the last few years.

Until very recently, however, any focus on teaching has largely been isolated from the discipline of literary and cultural study, and especially from the training of many graduate students. There are two reasons for this isolation. One is the fragmentation of the university. When administrators or faculty members attend a conference on assessment or launch an initiative to improve teaching, they often do so in the context of undergraduate education, working with tenured faculty who teach undergraduates. Graduate students and adjuncts are frequently excluded from such work, either because they are seen as peripheral or transient workers, or because they rarely have the extra time or energy the project would require.

A second reason is that many people in literary and cultural studies find discussions of assessment and quality unappealing, for both aesthetic and political reasons. Writers in the assessment movement, particularly, often borrow the language of management and of quality from business. Many scholars, however, identify more with labor than with management, and others value the beautiful over the efficient – the discourse of 'learners' and 'educational outcomes' is thus repellent to both groups. The fact that teaching can seem to be the more 'conservative' aspect of our work as academics – in the strictest sense of conserving, and passing on, a received body of knowledge (even though teaching is, of course, usually creative and innovative as well) – may also have contributed to literary scholars' reluctance to theorize their teaching practices. Research, on the other hand, might be seen as an inherently 'progressive' enterprise: again, in the literal sense that it adds to, and advances, existing bodies of knowledge as opposed to reiterating them. Aesthetically, moreover, the experience of teaching poses a unique challenge. While research is often a 'private' conversation between scholars, with a recognizable language and cadence, teaching is a conversation with the public: one that is therefore necessarily more awkward, unpredictable, and heterogeneous.

This gulf between scholarship and teaching creates a strange effect: many of us are influenced by work we have never studied or even read. Paulo Freire's liberatory pedagogy and John Dewey's constructivist educational theories have filtered into English departments though composition studies, teacher education, and campus events associated with the student activism of the 1960s and 1970s. Younger scholars, even when they have not read Dewey or Freire themselves, have often been educated by teachers who have experimented with collaborative group work in the classroom, or informal discussions, or interdisciplinary projects, or experiments with vernacular language. Liberatory, constructivist, and learning-centered approaches have not, however, come into contact with scholarly *writing* in literary studies, even when they have informally influenced teaching and learning *experiences* in literature departments. It is difficult to find an academic article that cites both Freire and John Guillory, or Freire and Henry Louis Gates. Scholarly work on cultural studies, canon formation, and disciplinarity, then, has been isolated from the hallway- and mailroom-conversations and classroom experiences of pedagogy in literature departments.

In his investigation of the concept of cultural capital, Guillory claims that 'to decline the theoretical and practical labor of analyzing pedagogic structures in their institutional sites is to cede everything to the imaginary, to play the game of culture without understanding it' (37). This book takes on the 'labor of analyzing pedagogic structures in their institutional sites,' in order to combat the isolation that such analysis has, until now, entailed. Guillory makes this argument in the context of the canon debate, but it can be made about questions of the 'learner-centered classroom,' the place of writing in the university classroom, questions of policy about grading and plagiarism, or the presence, absence, and quality of 'class participation.' College and university teachers make decisions about all of these questions each semester and each week. All of these questions or problems relate to Guillory's 'pedagogic imaginary': an imagined space of rational discussion, an imagined perfect paper, college student, or educated public.

What would it look like to analyze such pedagogic structures in their institutional sites? Guillory himself never discusses undergraduate education specifically – his twentieth-century examples all have to do with graduate study. Other theoretical approaches to the question of what it is we do in the literature classroom, such as Robert Scholes' *The Rise and Fall of English*, also offer powerful reflections on the state of the field and the question of what it is we should be teaching. Rather than arguing about which texts we should be focusing on, for instance, Scholes calls for a 'canon of methods' and brings together the pedagogical aims of literature and composition. Few, if any, of these important discussions of the teaching of literature, however, provide new teachers with both a discussion of our theoretical aims and also with practical applications of them: with a much-needed sense, in other words, of how teachers have dealt with the contingencies of the classroom.

We are interested in examining these practical questions alongside the theoretical aims of our field. In helping to counter the isolating experience of this work, we hope to assist new instructors in what can often be a very anxious and difficult situation. As graduate student teaching assistants, or as first-year assistant professors, or as part-timers or adjuncts on the margins of institutions, many people experience their first few semesters as overwhelming. The workload is enormous; the sense of exposure is painful. Questions of authority charge the atmosphere, but the anxieties of both students and teachers make them difficult to address. Teachers are called upon to put together a structure for their class, to contend with the diversity of their students' past learning experiences, and to make a number of decisions about things ranging from what to put on their syllabuses, to how late a 'late paper' is, what the difference between a C+ and a B– is, and what it means when a student falls asleep in class. The contributors to this book consider such questions in the context of analyses of their disciplines, their universities, and the texts they read, rather than in the context of projected or imaginary plenitudes of students who 'come to see' precisely what the teacher hopes they will.

We do not want, however, to present a series of narratives about how one or another nifty teaching tip brought our students from the darkness into the light, although we also never turn up our noses at nifty teaching tips, having found them indispensable on numerous occasions. But the trouble with teaching tips is that they are context-dependent. They don't address either the anxieties teachers experience or the kind of analysis Guillory or Dewey recommend. In describing how they teach, then, the contributors to this volume do not shirk political and theoretical questions by taking refuge in the practical. Instead, our contributors take new positions in relation to questions of canon, theory, and practice; Burger and Kruger, for example, discuss the centrality of questions of 'queerness' to teaching Chaucer; Birnbaum delineates the problems of segregating African-American writing from discussions of literary realism and means of combating this segregation, and Davis writes of the usefulness of acting out Shakespeare passages to deepening students' understanding of 'implicit' literary meaning.

Our authors also address the theoretical foundations for their practical decisions, and the material conditions that influence both. Rather than accounting for all periods of literary study and all problems that arise when teaching, our contributors present intellectual frameworks and modes of inquiry that will be useful and stimulating to readers who teach in any literary field. Similarly, these accounts of how teachers theorized their decisions should be relevant to people working in quite different institutional contexts: universities and polytechnics in the Commonwealth countries as well as community colleges, small colleges and universities in the US. Williams, for instance, shows us how 'autobiography' can be a flexible organizing principle for courses with a range of topics – from 'women writers' to 'coming-of-age narratives' – and a range of formats – from a small class with frequent writing assignments to a large lecture class directed toward a final exam or paper. The range of activities and approaches she suggests all have the pedagogical benefit of continually drawing students' attention to form and its material and historical significance. Pope's method of having students 're-write' literary texts – through experiments with imitation, adaptation and parody – to perform critical analysis and research can be adapted to the teaching of any period or genre.

The following essays, then, are not examples of pedagogical 'techniques' or an ideologically uniform set of theories about teaching in the twenty-first century, but accounts of how individual teachers have analyzed their teaching and their experience of it in the classroom. By assembling them here, we hope to begin the process of replacing Guillory's 'pedagogic imaginary' with a field knowable through a new set of terms, or old terms understood in new ways; we also hope to widen the current conversation about teaching just beginning to take place and to bring our 'private' research and 'public' teaching selves into dialogue.

Now that literary studies is being conceived of, and practiced as, a globalized field of study, openly in conversation with a number of other disciplines, it makes sense to have conversations about pedagogy that cross borders as well. In this book, therefore, you will find specialists in a variety of literary fields and genres, as well as teachers who see their work as applying to a variety of national and local contexts. An American community college professor, for instance, can find relevance in a British university lecturer's account of helping students engage with Shakespeare. You will find a range of teaching styles: advocates for in-class writing, for theoretical language, for close reading in the plain style, for the traditional canon, against the traditional canon. Miller asks his students to examine and question different kinds of reading practices, including those of popular fiction, while Altieri describes and theorizes a particular method of reading that is both immediate, because students can experience it bodily, and alien, because of its complexity and because the texts are those of 'high' literary culture. Reading the two together suggests that the definition of 'reading' may differ widely from class to class, and can help us think about how to teach students to experience, theorize, and name different sorts of reading.

These writers are unified not by their theoretical or political positions, then, but by their interest in what students can really learn in a semester of English and how teachers can challenge and help them. Their work allows us to consider the questions facing us all as scholars in terms of the questions facing us all as teachers. Taken together, these essays make up a widely varied account of the daily labor of teaching literature: one that ranges from the experience of professors at large private universities to lecturers at small liberal arts colleges and from public institutions to alternative adult schools, in order to account for the immensely diverse classroom experiences that new teachers face.

This is not to say that every essay will speak to your individual experience. This book will be most helpful if used flexibly, with an eye to adapting and incorporating the ideas therein into a framework specific to your needs. Some essays may be useful to you in setting up a class because of the theoretical frame they use; others, outside your period, may suggest approaches to knotty problems that come up in all periods – directing students' attention toward form, negotiating long texts, providing historical context. Dauer's suggestions for how to maintain order and inspire student dialogue in the online, off-site classroom, for instance, are adaptable to any web-based classroom experience and even to the traditional classroom in some cases; Henry's advice for how to encourage students to read lengthy, difficult texts and to think rigorously about historical context is applicable not only to those teaching the Victorians, but also to instructors helping students with Milton and Shakespeare, or Ellison and Pynchon. Similarly, while some of the appendixes offer suggestions for teaching particular classes and texts, most provide pedagogical strategies that can be appropriated for different classes and contexts.

To make this volume as adaptable as possible, we have divided our essays into two sections that break down the tasks we face when we set out to teach. 'Fields of Study in the Twenty-First Century Classroom,' the first section, tackles the teacher's task of mediating between a discipline – a dynamic body of continuing work – and a classroom, where students are new to the discipline's texts, its methodologies and its history. O'Brien's essay, for instance, addresses two current concerns of scholars of eighteenth-century literature: the development of authorship as a historically constructed category and the relationship between print culture and the public sphere. His course makes the most recent questions and issues of the field accessible and comprehensible, both for the students and for the teacher who must organize the readings, discussions, papers and exams. Similarly, Anger's essay helps students think between disciplines and suggests how teachers can provoke, encourage, and grade such thinking.

Our second section, 'Classroom Rituals, Old and New,' demonstrates how teachers might rethink the rituals and conventions of the classroom in a critically informed way. Agathocleous and Enteen, for instance, describe the ways in which the Internet can help to address the challenges of teaching a subject as dispersed and nascent as 'World Literature in English'; Dean discusses putting newer forms of criticism in dialog with more traditional ones in the classroom as a means of challenging students' preconceived readings of literary texts. Apart from the appendixes at the end of contributors' essays, we have also included a bibliography of print sources that will help provide pathways through the growing field of scholarship on teaching literature; in addition, a bibliography of web resources lists some of the most important sites on literary scholarship and teaching currently available. The number and variety of both print and web sources is encouraging; a sign, we think, of a new field of inquiry in literary studies and a move, we hope, towards the institution of a literary pedagogy in graduate schools. As we become more articulate about our ideas and experiences as teachers, the profession as a whole will benefit; this book opens a conversation we encourage its readers will continue and extend.

Fields of Study in the Twenty-First Century Classroom

1
Teaching Autobiography

Carolyn Williams

Having taught many different courses on autobiography during the past 25 years, I'm increasingly convinced of their pedagogical versatility. The focus on auto-biography has an immediate appeal to those undergraduate students who have little interest in the technical aspects of literary analysis, while at the same time opening the way for a wide range of historical, philosophical, theoretical and literary-historical questions of interest to more adept readers, majors and graduate students.

I'll assume in the background of this essay three basic models of a course on autobiography: a general course, made up of highly readable texts for a group of non-majors; a course on the history of autobiography; and a period course on Victorian autobiography. Both of the latter are adaptable to all degrees of difficulty (suitable, in other words, for non-majors, majors, or graduate students, depending on the level of classroom discourse). Sample syllabuses will be found in Appendix A. But the range of possible courses is much wider than these three models could ever suggest, for the study of autobiography invites thematic treatment. Several times, for example, I've oriented the course around gender and sexuality; several times I've focused only on women's autobiograph-ies; several times I've concentrated on 'coming-of-age narratives', or narratives of 'coming into voice'; sometimes I focus on 'the turning-point' and consider exemplary changes such as conversion, deconversion, serious illness, marriage, or coming out; sometimes I look at modern and postmodern experiments with autobiography, especially their attention to cultural diversity, bilingualism, and the perceived multiplicity of the self. In every case, however, I make attention to form the primary motive of the course.

This essay chiefly describes the conceptual framework within which any of these courses might be taught. I will pay particular attention to setting up the course and getting it going, for I know that individual teachers will choose various reading lists according to their own interests and that each course will spend most of its time discussing those individual texts. So my focus on form should not be misleading; I know that most class time will be spent considering the details of the life stories on the syllabus. My point is simply that form can and should be an organizing principle, to which any discussion of a particular story can always be returned.

In Appendix B, I'll offer a few writing exercises that have worked extremely well in my experience. These exercises are definitely not 'paper topics'; that is, they are not meant to guide the close academic analysis of any particular texts. I value and teach close reading, and I try to design all my paper topics to encourage its practice. I always assign extremely specific paper topics, in an effort to focus students on the concepts developed in our course and to steer them away from the Internet paper mills and their old-fashioned equivalents. But Appendix B offers something else instead, a set of writing exercises that are meant to encourage more thoughtful comprehension of the points I try to make about autobiographical form. Therefore they should be useful for any class, no matter what particular texts are on the syllabus. These writing exercises are meant primarily for use in an undergraduate class. But I've found them useful in graduate courses as well, where mentioning possible writing exercises – even if students are not asked to do them – can provide vivid conceptual illustrations, making difficult theoretical points practical for the nonce, even in the most advanced discussions.

Form matters

'Form matters.' This axiom argues that the consideration of form needn't be – and shouldn't be – reductively treated as 'mere' or 'empty' formal*ism*. It's a challenge for all teachers of literature – now more than ever, at a time when 'formalism' is so widely disparaged – to demonstrate that the consideration of form is *not* the opposite of, but is an integral part of any consideration of social, cultural and historical issues. Form *matters* most of all because literary form has material and historical significance. This is not the place to discuss the long-standing debate about the relation of form to content or form to matter, though in passing I want to note that the axiom 'form matters' helps to unsettle the notion of 'content' as prior to and separable from 'form.' I should note that I tacitly distinguish in this essay between autobiography and other forms of first-person writing – such as lyric poetry, diaries and journals, essays and letters – though it can also be pedagogically useful to question this distinction, as I do persistently in my graduate class. For the purposes of this essay, however, the term 'autobiography' will be taken to indicate the story of a person's life, written by that person.

There are several ways of considering autobiographical form. I begin by introducing rhetorical or grammatical figures of self-reflection, and then move rapidly toward the consideration of narrative structure; finally, I emphasize form as it relates to genre. Every course begins with a short discussion of self-reference. I ask: 'What is an autobiography? How do you know an autobiography when you see one?' Various good answers to this question include: it tells the story of a whole life; it says so on the cover or on the title page (see Lejeune). I make sure that all three parts of the word are covered: *auto*, *bios*, *graphein* (see Olney, 'Some Versions'). I wait until someone says that it is written in the first person, and I pause to stress the odd consequences of this fact.

I want students to become immediately sensitive to pronouns and especially to the way they establish the position of the subject: I/me/mine. 'I will even venture to say that I am like no one in the whole world. I may be no better, but at least I am different.' 'Call me Ishmael.' 'Like most people I lived for a long time with my mother and father.' 'I hadn't so much forgot as I couldn't bring myself to remember.' During this consideration of the initial assertion of the first person, I ask them to do a brief exercise (5–10 minutes): 'Write a first sentence for your own autobiography.' This will get a good class discussion going. In class we can explore this principle of self-assertion from its most absolute to its most skeptical versions. One Hebrew name for the monotheistic deity (YHWH, Yahweh) is often translated 'I am,' while Samuel Beckett's assertion is made in the face of radical doubt: 'I say I unbelieving.' (When I ask students to think of exemplary moments of self-assertion, someone inevitably mentions Popeye's 'I yam what I yam and that's all what I yam.') After a while, I turn the discussion back to the notion of the grammatical assertion of subjectivity: how is it done? I try to get students to understand the reflexivity of the linguistic point that 'I' refers to the one who says 'I.' As Benveniste emphasized, it is 'in the instance of discourse in which *I* designates the speaker that the speaker proclaims himself as "the subject"' (Benveniste, 226).

I tell students to look out for the deictic markers that organize space and time around the subject (this, that, here, there, now, then, and so forth). Pointing words like these help to orient the subject within a world. *Jane Eyre*, for example, opens with the sentence: 'There was no possibility of taking a walk that day.' (We don't know much at that point, but we do know how important '*that* day' will turn out to be.) I tell them to look out for figures of self-reflection, those moments when the self is distanced from itself and seen as other, or when another is seen as a reflection of the self: moments, for example, when an autobiographical narrator looks in a mirror, or when she sees the face of her mother, or when he sees his name written on a tombstone. These figures of self-reflection provide the basis for scenes of blatant identification and disidentification, when the autobiographical narrator determines how she or he is like and unlike the significant other. (These figures also may be treated as figures of de-facement, as in the notable essay by De Man.) I point out the pun on 'reflection,' the way it means both a process of thoughtful rumination and also a mirroring image; this double meaning of 'reflection' suggests the blending of subjective and objective views characteristic of autobiography. Sometimes I discuss these terms, 'objective' and 'subjective,' trying to get students to see that those words modify kinds of statements, and that a 'fact' is a construction every bit as much as a 'fantasy' is. By the end of this discussion we have on the table a good basic vocabulary: first person, self-reference, subjectivity, identity, deictic markers, figures of self-reflection, and identification. 'OK,' I say. 'What happens when presentation in the first person is extended over the course of a life narrative?'

The structure of retrospection

I always offer a diagram illustrating the structure of first-person retrospective narration (see Figure 1.1). I use this diagram to illustrate several features of the conventional retrospective autobiography. For example, using this diagram, students can see how the relations between present and past are organized through the narrating 'I,' a figure that seems to be divided between 'now' and 'then.' This seeming self-division is, of course, itself a grammatical effect, generated by the disparity in verb tenses. The best discussion of these matters is by Jean Starobinski, who locates the crucial 'style' of autobiography in this 'double deviation,' the deviation in the time and in the identity of the 'I.' It is on the 'now' of writing that these deviations depend. This figure of doubled deviation, when it is extended, precipitates a certain narrative structure.

Most important, at the beginning of any course, is the notion that retrospection originates in and is formed by 'I-now,' the perspective of the subject in the present moment of writing. The 'arc of retrospection' can reach back to the beginning of memory – or to the beginning of life (or even beyond, to imagine time before 'I' was born). It is important to get students to realize that the

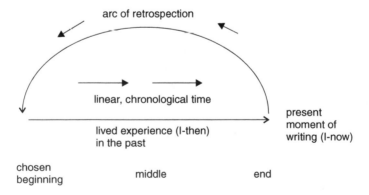

Figure 1.1

beginning is not 'a given,' but is a choice, chosen from the perspective of 'I-now' (see Writing Exercise 1). From this chosen beginning, according to the diagram, the narrating 'I' works its way forward in linear, chronological fashion, telling a story of development over the life-course, from the chosen beginning, through the conflicts of the middle, to the end. The end of the autobiography – both its closure and its goal – is the 'I' in the present moment. The story explains how 'I' got to that point. Thus, the structure revealed in this diagram is self-referential and therefore circular in its logic: the story reaches into the past and then moves toward its own present, in order to demonstrate the unique becoming of a particular 'I.'

Looking together at this diagram makes a productive beginning for a course. But soon it must be further complicated. The first complication involves representations of autobiographical change. (You might pause to ask your students what sorts of radical changes can happen during the course of a life. Using the blackboard to organize these answers will help the class pause long enough to think about how difficult change can be, and how some life changes seem to open a chasm in identity.) Autobiography presents an interesting example of a familiar conundrum: how can something change and still be regarded as the same thing? This is, of course, a philosophical conundrum not only in autobiography, but in all historical thinking; autobiography merely presents an unusual case of this conundrum, for it represents the past 'I' as if it were an objectified, historical entity. Over the history of autobiography, the radical change called 'conversion' (in which the subject subscribes to a transcendent authority) is eventually replaced by other sorts of change, and the structure of radical, once-and-for-all-time change is often replaced by a series of gradual, episodic or periodic changes. This change – or these changes – within the 'I' must be represented in such a way as to emphasize both difference and continuity.

I usually use the blackboard at this point, in order to sketch out many different models for representing autobiographical change, some involving one turning-point or 'right-angled' change (Abrams), a once-and-for-all-time change (see Figures 1.1a and 1.1b); some involving many points of change or epiphanic realization, arranged as rising or falling action (see Figure 1.1c); some involving an elegiac conclusion, in which the narrator expresses regret for a lost, happier past, and others involving an older-but-wiser conclusion, in which the narrator is more or less happy to be past the struggles and conflicts of the younger and middle years (see Figures 1.1d and 1.1e) (Starobinski, 82–3). But eventually I want to suggest a model that represents change as a blank in the linear, chronological development, a gap that must somehow be bridged, a break in identity that must be repaired, a difference between 'before' and 'after' that is difficult to comprehend (see Figure 1.2). With this model, students can see that the very identity (or sameness) of the 'I' over time is in

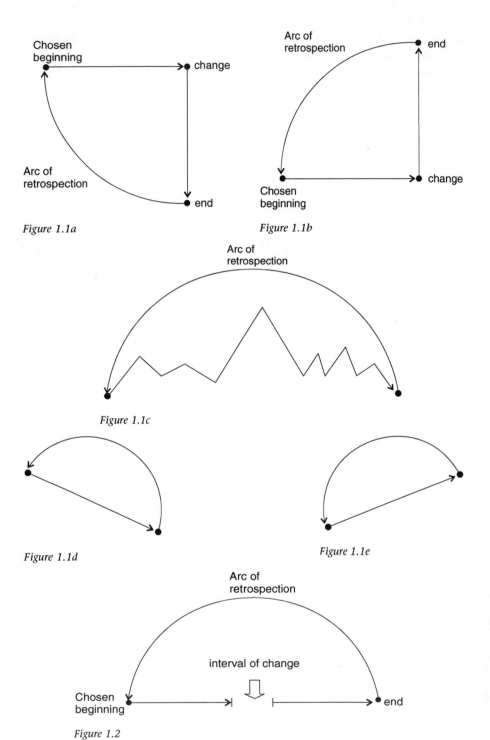

Figure 1.1a

Figure 1.1b

Figure 1.1c

Figure 1.1d

Figure 1.1e

Figure 1.2

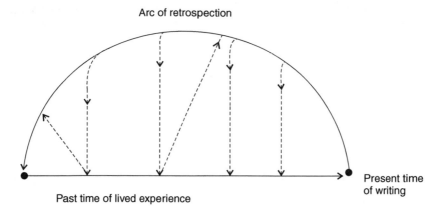

Figure 1.3

an important sense created by – or is an effect of – the activity of retrospection. The 'arc of retrospection' is the imaginative form of comprehension that encompasses and covers over the radical discontinuities in the 'I'; it is the form of identity and continuity, seen specifically *as a form* – and also as a fiction, an aesthetic artifact, a made thing.

The second complication of the initial diagram involves representing the autobiographical narrator's freedom of access to two temporalities sim-ultaneously. At any moment of narration, in other words, the narrator can suddenly move from 'now' to 'then' or from 'then' back to 'now.' Furthermore, each of these temporalities is itself infinitely expandable and divisible; there are as many moments written from the position of 'I-now' as the writer wishes, and likewise as many moments of past – many different 'nows' and many different 'thens.' The broken vertical lines (see Figure 1.3) connecting the arc of retrospection to the linear, chronological unfolding of lived experience are meant to show that the retrospective narrator has access, at every moment, both to the present and to any moment in the past. Some of the most moving effects are produced when first-person narration of the past suddenly shifts into the present tense. The fabric of one temporality bursts, revealing another. Like a zoom lens, the autobiographical narrator leaves the past behind and zooms into the present, after time has passed and changes have been absorbed.

It is no wonder that these moments of autobiographical narration can be so 'moving,' for they literally move the reader backward and forward in time with a sudden, wrenching effect. To illustrate the autobiographical narrator's freedom of movement between temporalities, I tell the story of Jane Eyre and give students a handout containing two particular passages from the novel. The first occurs in Chapter 2, while Jane is locked up in the red room: 'What a consternation of soul was mine that dreary afternoon!...Yet in what darkness, what dense ignorance was the mental battle fought! I could not answer the ceaseless inward question – *why* I thus suffered; now, at the distance of – I will not say how many years – I see it clearly.' In that sudden 'distance of – I will not say how many years,' we are simultaneously made to feel both the child's utter incomprehension and the adult's calm, retrospective comprehension of exactly '*why* I...suffered'. The second passage on the handout is the conclusion to Chapter 9, when Jane is just finishing her narration of the death of Helen Burns:

> a day or two afterward I learned that Miss Temple, on returning to her own room at dawn, had found me laid in a little crib; my face against Helen Burns's shoulder, my arms round her neck. I was asleep, and Helen was – dead.
>
> Her grave is in Brocklebridge Churchyard: for fifteen years after her death it was only covered by a grassy mound; but now a gray marble tablet marks the spot, inscribed with her name, and the word '*Resurgam*'.

All of a sudden, at the switch-point between paragraphs, the tenses shift – from 'was' to 'is' – and we are no longer in the narrator's past, but suddenly in the writer's 'now.' The parting of bodies – live from dead, friend from friend – is an almost unbearably significant moment for this narrator, whose fraught identification with Helen must now be internalized if it is to be carried into the future. This sudden temporal shift feels like relief. Time has passed, and Helen is still preserved within Jane's memory; now a memorial 'tablet marks the spot, inscribed with her name,' something like autobiography itself, the way it memorializes what's lost as time passes. In the present moment of writing, that inscribed marking-stone holds out the promise of a future to which Helen's life had been dedicated: the promise that 'I will rise.' But Jane's 'I,' meanwhile, unfolds in secular time.

This wonderful effect needs a better name than any I've found in the critical literature ('temporal shift' or 'temporal juxtaposition'? 'interruption' or 'intrusion'?) In fact it is a useful exercise to ask students to invent a name for a formal effect such as this one. The creativity of the critical enterprise is intensified if students realize that their close attention to the text may (and should) result in critical generalization. But they should also be made aware that this (grammatical and structural) narrative movement between temporalities works against the assumption of linear unfolding (or development) in the life story. Modernist and postmodernist autobiographies will work against the supposition of linear unfolding, highlighting instead temporal disjunctions and gaps, as well as epiphanic and discontinuous awareness in the present moment. But these more recent forms depend upon the rhetoric of self-reflection and the structure of retrospection for their radical effects.

What I've described so far is the introductory set-up of the course. In an undergraduate course, I try to cover this introductory material in a couple of class periods, knowing (and promising) that we will return to these ideas again and again over the course of the semester. When the discussion threatens to become too abstract, I tell stories to illustrate important points: stories (with handouts) about famous autobiographical choices for beginning paragraphs are particularly fun and helpful; stories about disruptive changes or conversions within the life course, how they took place, and what problems they solved (or caused) are also good at this point, helping to concretize the notion of radical change within identity; but though I discuss beginnings and middles at this point in the course, I save the discussion of autobiographical endings for later, during the discussion of each individual text (see Writing Exercise 3).

It is important, I feel, to present these diagrams very explicitly as learning tools only. Students must not be led to believe that writers are following some sort of floor plan or 'how-to' kit; nor that critics are looking to see whether such a plan has been strictly followed; nor that their own course papers should be accompanied by strange diagrams! I feel that they should be told frankly that these diagrams are simply a way to get us going, to get a lot of ideas out on the table in a hurry. Tell your students that despite the fact that you've given them this diagram of 'the structure of retrospection,' the course will con-centrate on the ways that each particular autobiography might or *might not* pattern itself on that structure. In fact, the 'structure of retrospection' is the *fiction* that traditional retrospective autobiographies convey, the formal creation of the integrity and causal logic of identity, a narrative demonstration of why 'I am who I am.' (Some students will get this point – without immediately reducing it to the notion that the autobiographer is lying, or that 'the self' is *only* a fiction – and others never will.) In other words, the textual process of figural positioning and deviation, construction and dissolution *forms* the 'I' over the course of narrative time.

Beyond structure: forms of social life

The necessary dialogic grammatical relation of 'first' and 'second' persons (no 'I' without a corresponding 'you') points to the irreducibly social *nature* of human *culture* (Benveniste, Horkheimer and Adorno). This second dimension of the conceptual framework for the course involves the relation between the subject of autobiography and his or her cultural context. The way this part of the course is handled can vary a great deal depending on the special interests of any particular teacher. Some teachers will want to concentrate on one aspect of the relation – on the way gender norms are learned, for example, or on gen-erational conflict, or on histories of literacy and reading; other teachers will have theoretical views – feminist, Marxist, or psychoanalytic, for example – about how the relation is formed between any individual and his or her ambient culture. Autobiography looks at the world from the inside out, so to speak, but its view is never merely personal. The crucial thing is that the relation of an individual life to a cultural or historical context is also a matter of form. In other words, the question of how the individual subject is formed by – and, in turn, transforms – the surrounding world, large or small, can only be answered by looking at the theories, models, and representations of that relation as they take textual form.

These days, the easiest way to begin discussing these issues is by raising the topic of cultural difference. What are cultural norms? And how are they perpetuated? Does the subject of the autobiography attempt to express how he or she was formed and shaped by the expectations of others? Does the form of the autobiography comment on, argue against, or imitate those social and cultural norms? Or does the subject differ – or try to differ – from them, rebelling against them or working to change them? Then: if the subject differs from certain norms, is the form of the autobiography therefore also different? In literature courses, the best way to capture sociocultural difference is to grasp it as it is embodied in the shaping choices involved in writing. The identity politics of class, race, gender, sexuality, nationality, ethnicity, and language-use are particularly heightened as issues when students are considering subject-formation, but turning these issues toward matters of literary form will make them more, not less, historically resonant.

As James Olney pointed out in the introduction to his landmark collection of essays consolidating the field, the study of autobiography within literature departments is a phenomenon characteristic of the second half of the twentieth century and the opening of the canon, directly related to the rise of women's studies, African-American studies, gay and lesbian studies, and postcolonial studies (Olney). Indeed, important work on cultural difference constitutes a great deal of the field, and a simple bibliographical list of all the good work arguing that particular groups of subjects must write against conventional forms of autobiography would be much longer than this essay. (This work also reveals the fact that conventional autobiographical form is defined in many different ways – not only as 'the structure of retrospection' that I've advanced here.) Feminist studies of autobiography put emphasis on affiliation rather than individualism, on the differences entailed in restriction to the domestic rather than the public sphere, and on attempts to write more immediately from the body (Mason, Stanton, S. Smith, Brodzki and Schenck). Sex and gender may be seen systematically in relation to socioeconomic class (Gagnier, Corbett). Studies of slave narratives, one of the most important subgenres of autobiography, focus attention on violent forms of enforced depersonalization, including bodily suffering and destruction of the family, on the inverse relation between the liberal subject's ownership of property in his own person and the slave's status as property, and on struggles to assert a subjectivity, to constitute a safe body, home and family, and to achieve literacy (Gates, V. Smith). In lesbian and gay studies, the 'coming-out' story has been powerfully described as a recent turn on the model of conversion (Cohen). Critics concerned with colonialism and postcolonialism have focused on the performative mimicry inherent in the colonial relation and the patchwork aesthetic that results from the cultural hybridity conditioned by voyages of discovery and exploration, imperial conquest, and global capitalism (Lionnet).

Thus, the opening of the canon may be seen in at least three aspects: attention to a wider variety of kinds of writing (including autobiography among the kinds of non-fictional prose that may be read as literature); attention to a wider variety of writers; and self-conscious attention to the formation of what we study, which involves the realization that the canon – as well as the sort of thinking that organizes various forms of social life into 'kinds' – are themselves changing, historical artifacts. The opening of the canon to the 'marked' subjectivities of sociocultural identity-groups that have not yet received sufficient representation, in other words, also entails attention to the fact that this sort of group-thinking has a historical life of its own.

The nineteenth century, which is the historical period I know best, is a time when varieties of this sort of thinking dominate the discussion. Thus, I feel, discussions of cultural identity and identity politics can be treated as literary-historical discussions, and the study of autobiography – which several decades ago was an instrument in the assertion of multicultural difference – can now, if handled with care, complicate and transform that discussion. In addition to the discourses on class consciousness, gender difference, and nationality that are significantly consolidated in the nineteenth century, we can highlight several particular forms of drawing the relation between an individual life course and its social, cultural or historical context. For example, our habit of conceptualizing a figure within and against its social ground or field of influences can be seen as a nineteenth-century phenomenon; 'context,' defined this way, is a synchronic affair, more or less spatially conceived. This attention to what many nineteenth-century writers called 'conditions' – that is, to the shaping forces of the 'environment' (a word whose modern usages arise in the nineteenth century) – alerts us to the development of sociological and anthropological ways of thinking about 'culture' in the period (for the disciplines of sociology and anthropology – as well as the concept of culture – are also nineteenth-century developments). The idea of 'development' itself, for that matter – the form of change-within-continuity or continuity-despite-change, the form of historical identity – is largely a nineteenth-century phenomenon; and this is one of the ways of understanding why the nineteenth century is the great age of biography and autobiography, two forms of examining the historical development of an individual, during the age of bourgeois individualism. One nineteenth-century biological fantasy of development – the idea that 'ontogeny recapitulates phylogeny' – imagined that individual development mimics the development of the species; and this model was often translated from bio-logical into sociohistorical discourses, with the role of the species replaced by the notion of a historically developing culture (Gould, Dever). Work on the *Bildungsroman* repays attention in this context, for this form of the novel – like the nineteenth-century efflorescence of autobiography – exemplifies the desire to relate the individual life course to its cultural context diachronically, as a matter of unfolding time. Advanced students of Victorian literature will certainly be interested in the idea that the form of 'development' may be studied philosophically, historiographically, biologically and psychologically as a period artifact; but even beginning students will be fascinated by the idea that 'development' is a recent historical model, and not a sempiternal truth.

But the main point here is not that any one of these models needs to be taught in any particular course. The point is simply that historical and cultural contextualization of the individual life course may be fruitfully studied as a matter of form. Questions of social determination may be treated this way as well. After years of trying to steer students toward analytical language more productive than the high school formulation of a debate about 'free will vs determinism,' I have found myself recently working against the too-broad and too-vague terminology of the search for 'agency.' I try to set up the discussion so that students will realize that every form of social life involves constraints and that these forms of restriction are themselves the forms within which any individual transformation or transformative action must be performed. It's not, of course, that the search for 'agency' is not a good agenda – in a way, it's too good, and it's certainly too big, too broadly construed. I try to make the point that we should come at these questions more obliquely and more specifically.

Take, for example, John Stuart Mill, whose opening autobiographical thesis is his utter determination by his father. Mill's view is historically complex; he realizes that his father was himself conditioned by specific historical forces and that he, in turn, was conditioned by his father's theories and practices of education. But exactly what discourses and practices did Mill's father employ in the education of his son? Which texts, and which subjects of study informed the young Mill's subjectivity? (The cultural specificity of pedagogical attention to classical languages and to logic will interest students, especially if introduced as a strange feature of cultural difference.) And then, once having recognized the particular formative, shaping forces that made him, how does Mill go about re-making himself? Does Oedipal rebellion amount to 'freedom'? Does a 'conversion' to romantic poetry and romantic love leave Mill utterly changed? What stories and figures of speech does he use to describe his new-found sense of greater self-determination? What discourses and practices become the vehicle for this sense of greater freedom? Does he hope to change the world around him? In what particular ways, and by what means? Even if they read only excerpts from chapter 1 and chapter 7, along with the whole of the 'crisis in [his] mental history,' the turning-point narrated in chapter 5, students will be able to see that Mill's new-found commitments to emotional feeling and romantic love do not change his practice of philosophical and political argument with and against his peers. His commitment to feminism, too, may be seen both as a rebellious, creative change and also as an extension of his father's (and Bentham's) utilitarian principles.

This brief discussion of Mill is meant only as an example of the way an individual subject's relation to historical and cultural context can be treated as a matter of form. The example of Mill also makes the obvious point that other cultures – even those seemingly unmarked or close to our own time – can be distanced and seen as historical formations (seen, that is, in their aspect of heightened cultural difference). These days it is especially important to see that the question of cultural difference – and its vital relation to questions of form – is *not* a specifically contemporary concern. I've suggested that the culture described in Mill's *Autobiography* can be made strange, and that his (and his father's) wish to differ from the conventions of their own age can be appreciated as their (liberal) commitment to greater diversity of representation.

Beyond structure: genre

Augustine's *Confessions* is usually seen as the foundational text in the history of a genre (see Spengemann, for example); and indeed, any course in the history of autobiography has to take account of the genre's important original ties to Christian routines of introspection, commitments to historicity and individuality, and conceptions of radical change or 'conversion' (see Gusdorf). The secularization of this model is the crucial event in the history of autobiography, an 'event' which took several centuries and which may be roughly aligned with modernity itself. It is helpful, for conceptually marking literary-historical change, to refer to particular texts as turning-points. Thus, to illustrate the early modern (or 'Renaissance') moment of secularization, it is helpful to think of Dante, whose dream-vision may be discussed as his individualistic internalization of cosmic justice, as the story of his conversion through romantic love, and as his grand project of reconciling the literature of classical antiquity with Christian history. The essays of Montaigne illustrate a later moment – and another dimension – of early modernity, for their personal and 'inconsistent' representation of drifting and scattershot mental life shows the beginnings of the modern sense of the self's unruly multiplicity long before Freud discovered the unconscious and even longer before people began to assume that this sense of multiplicity was a postmodern realization. In literary history, the addition of the essay as a fourth 'radical of presentation' (added to the classical Aristotelian trio of epic, lyric, and dramatic forms) may be seen as a vivid marker of modernity (Guillén). This important form of first-person writing, and the fact of its consolidation in the early modern period, marks an epoch in intellectual history as well as in literary history. (Victorian studies, which used to concentrate more than it does now on the period's 'intellectual prose,' has a long history of attending to this sort of writing; and these days, that concentration can be effectively retrieved and revised through the consideration of autobiography.)

The later-modern (or 'Romantic') phase of secularization dates from the late eighteenth and early nineteenth centuries. In fact, the term 'autobiography' itself also dates from that crucial era, signaling a recognition that the process of secularizing the confession (and spiritual autobiographies that turned on conversion) had reached a point that demanded a new term, a term that took account of the 'autotelic' or self-referential mandate of the form in its later, partially secularized manifestations. Noting that Rousseau aims his *Confessions* at his fellow man rather than addressing them to God and that he describes a life course with many episodic turning-points, seemingly endless in their potential for beginning again, we can appreciate the force of his secularizing inventiveness. His narrative – like that of Wordsworth, who marks a similar moment in English literary history – is famously elegiac in its thrust, dwelling on the fall from an edenic childhood, and demonstrating not only the residual ties of the form to the scriptural story, but also its prefiguration of psychoanalysis. The nineteenth century is the culminating moment of this long transition, and many – if not most – of its great autobiographers invent forcefully secularizing strategies, finding the old forms still availing though the content (of conversion and confession) has been evacuated and transformed. Thus Mill converts to poetry; Carlyle converts from Byron to Goethe, from the 'everlasting No' to the 'everlasting Yea'; and Gosse deconverts from his father's Christianity, turning instead to literature; Florence Nightingale in *Cassandra* adopts a prophetic voice that conjoins classical and Christian resonances; and Mrs Oliphant confesses not to God but to her beloved dead daughter.

After the nineteenth century, by and large, the Christian model of the conversion narrative becomes less relevant, and therefore the concept of secularization is also less frequently invoked – though it may still be relevant in some instances (see Williams). While it is ongoing, the process of secularization is always incomplete and ambivalent; any secularizing text will exhibit *both* its adherence to the earlier, religious models *and* its strategic distance and difference from them, its treatment of them *as forms*. When secularization is more complete, the model seems merely absent; but it is not. The Christian resonance of the narrative form will no longer be felt, though the form itself lives on.

Only when we take the long view in order to posit a certain continuity in form can we see and grasp the significance of historical changes within that form. To put the same point another way: When seen as a genre, autobiography becomes itself a historical category whose identity can be confirmed only because of internal differences. As with any genre, the specific historical phases cut like slices through the transhistorical persistence of form.

Appendix A: sample syllabuses

Autobiography: Sample syllabus for undergraduate non-majors
Autobiographical novels appear in square brackets.

* Very brief excerpts from Augustine, Montaigne, and Rousseau (suggestions: Augustine, Book I part 6; Montaigne, 'Of the inconsistency of our actions'; Rousseau, Book I, page 1.
* [Charlotte Brontë, *Jane Eyre*]
* Harriet Jacobs, *Incidents in the Life of a Slave Girl, Written by Herself*
* Frederick Douglass, *Narrative of the Life of Frederick Douglass, an African Slave*
* Maya Angelou, *I Know Why the Caged Bird Sings*
* [Alice Walker, *The Color Purple*]
* [Anzia Yezierska, *Bread Givers*]
* Frank Conroy, *Stop-Time*
* Susanna Kaysen, *Girl, Interrupted*
* Maxine Hong Kingston, *The Woman Warrior*
* Audre Lorde, *Zami: a New Spelling of My Name*
* Jeanette Winterson, *Oranges Are Not the Only Fruit*
* Rigoberta Menchú, *I, Rigoberta Menchú: An Indian Woman in Guatemala*

History of autobiography: sample syllabus for undergraduate or graduate students
* Augustine, *Confessions*, Books I–IX and brief selections from Book X (suggestion: sections 1–4, 7–8,13–16, 19)
* Dante, *Inferno* cantos 1–5, *Purgatorio* canto 30, *Paradiso* canto 33
* Montaigne, 'Of the inconsistency of our actions,' 'Of cannibals'
* Rousseau, *The Confessions*, at least Book I
* John Bunyan, *Grace Abounding to the Chief of Sinners*
* Delarivier Manley, *The Adventures of Rivella*
* Charlotte Charke, *A Narrative of the Life of Mrs. Charlotte Charke*
* James Boswell, *London Journal*
* Fanny Burney, *Journals*
* Benjamin Franklin, *Autobiography*
* William Wordsworth, *The Prelude*, Books 1–2, 6–7, 12–13
* Thomas De Quincey, *Confessions of an English Opium Eater*
* John Stuart Mill, Autobiography, chapters 1, 4 and 7

- [Charlotte Brontë, *Jane Eyre*]
- Harriet Jacobs, *Incidents in the Life of a Slave Girl, Written by Herself*
- Frederick Douglass, *Narrative of the Life of Frederick Douglass, an African Slave*
- [Proust, opening of *Swann's Way*]
- [Joyce, *Portrait of the Artist as a Young Man*]
- Virginia Woolf, *Moments of Being*
- Gertrude Stein, *The Autobiography of Alice B. Toklas*
- Zora Neale Hurston, *Dust Tracks on a Road*
- Richard Wright, *Black Boy*
- Maxine Hong Kingston, *The Woman Warrior*
- Audre Lorde, *Zami: a New Spelling of My Name*
- Jeanette Winterson, *Oranges Are Not the Only Fruit*
- Rigoberta Menchú, *I, Rigoberta Menchú: An Indian Woman in Guatemala*

The Victorian First Person: Sample Syllabus for Graduate Students

- William Wordsworth, *The Prelude, or Growth of a Poet's Mind: an Autobiographical Poem*
- Alfred Lord Tennyson, *In Memoriam AHH*
- Thomas Carlyle, *Sartor Resartus*, Book I chapters 1–5, Book II chapters 1–2, 6–9, Book III chapters 3, 5–8
- John Stuart Mill, *Autobiography*, chapters 1, 4 and 7
- Thomas De Quincey, *Confessions of an English Opium Eater*
- John Henry Cardinal Newman, 'History of My Religious Opinions to the Year 1833,' from *Apologia Pro Vita Sua*
- [Charlotte Brontë, *Jane Eyre*]
- [Charles Dickens, *David Copperfield*]
- [Charles Dickens, *Bleak House*]
- Mary Prince, *The History of Mary Prince, A West Indian Slave, As Related by Herself*
- [Elizabeth Barrett Browning, *Aurora Leigh*]
- Mrs. Oliphant, *The Autobiography of Margaret Oliphant*
- Hannah Cullwick, *Diaries of Hannah Cullwick, Victorian Maidservant*
- Florence Nightingale, *Cassandra*
- Anthony Trollope, *An Autobiography*
- Edmund Gosse, *Father and Son*
- Beatrice Webb, *My Apprenticeship*
- 'Walter,' *My Secret Life*
- Sigmund Freud, *Fragment of an Analysis of a Case of Hysteria (Dora)*

Appendix B: writing exercises

1 'Formative' experience/autobiographical beginnings

I ask students at the beginning of a class session to choose an early, 'formative' moment or event from their own lives, an event with which they might open an autobiography. I ask them to write about that moment, to tell what happened and to interpret its significance. I give them only 15–20 minutes, so the writing will be rough, but a lot of conceptual work gets done. The rest of the class period is spent discussing the reading assigned for that day. But then, there is a follow-up assignment: students must take the writing they've done in class and make a list of ten later events or moments from their own lives that might form the focus of later chapters of their autobiography, following from and relating to the opening moment they had chosen to write about in class. These later events may develop (by repeating with various differences) or overturn (by shifting the life course away from whatever was implied by) that early moment. Thus they will feel, in the practical effects of plotting their life stories, how a 'formative' experience is formative both in psychological and narrative terms.

But the assignment doesn't end there. At the beginning of the next class, they repeat the thought-experiment. They are asked to choose *another* early, formative moment, and to imagine it *instead* as the opening chapter of their autobiographies. And again, for the homework assignment, they must make a list of ten later events or moments that relate to (and overturn, or bear out the promise of) that beginning moment. Several points become clear: First of all, an autobiography can begin anywhere; but the beginning exerts a shaping force on the rest of the story. Second, both autobiographies (should they ever be written) would be 'true,' but they would be different; each would tell a different story, portray a different set of significances, a differently-formed life course, and a (slightly or very) different representation of self.

2 The issue of autobiographical 'truth'

This set of exercises follows logically from the first, to explore further the difficult notion discovered at the end of Exercise no. 1: that two different autobiographies of the same person can both be true, but that autobiographical truth is a psychological relation. I-now is a 'subjective' witness to an 'objectified' I-then; but I-then can be objectified and remembered differently, depending on the situation of I-now. The important point here is that 'truth' in autobiography is significantly related to the present moment of retrospection – it's the truth *now* – and that's why it can change, for the writer's interpretation of a past event can change radically over time. (A great short story by Dorothy Canfield, 'Sex Education,' brilliantly deals with the changing nature of a person's serial re-interpretations of the past.) Lived experience is messy; retrospection gives it shape, and the effort to find that shape can sometimes make things seem more orderly in retrospect than they were at the time. And besides, students can explore the notion of a spectrum of truth/ falsehood that ranges through a lot of ambiguous territory from factual reporting, slanting the story toward the self, embellishing the story for the self's greater glory, interpreting other people's motives (or other versions of telling about things that cannot be known), to blatant lying. For all these reasons, autobiographical 'truth' is a vexed issue. These exercises are all designed to get students to think more precisely about this issue:

(a) Ask students to write about the conceptual differences among the following three oppositions: 'objective' vs 'subjective' statements, 'fact' vs 'fiction,' and 'fact' vs 'fantasy.' What we want students to realize is that factuality is a creation (or 'construction') every bit as much as fiction is. The writer can choose to step back and hide, foregrounding the observational objectivity of the third person, or the writer can come forward as 'I.' But in either case, the writer exerts the shaping function. *Bleak House* is a great text for considering the relations as well as the differences between 'objective' (third-person) and 'subjective' (first-person) narration. And even if you don't have time to read *Bleak House* together, you can tell your students about it. *The Woman Warrior* is a great text for considering the 'real' (causal, determining) blend of fact and fantasy in lived experience.

(b) Because I emphasize form, many of my courses examine both autobiographies and autobiographical novels. Ask students to write about the following question: How can you tell the difference between a fictional and a factual autobiography? (The answer: sometimes you have access to extra-textual verification of the subject's life, and sometimes you don't; when you don't have access to extra-textual verification, sometimes you *can't* tell the difference. Students will enjoy talking about autobiographical hoaxes.) Another version of this writing exercise: How can you tell that *Jane Eyre* is an autobiographical novel? (The answer: the blatant coincidence of her wandering out into the wilderness and stumbling upon the only people in England who are related to her shows the exertion of a novelist's 'moral design.' Besides, at the beginning of chapter 11 she acknowledges in passing that she is writing a novel. And of course, she addresses her 'Dear Reader' throughout.)

3 Autobiographical closure

This exercise is meant to turn students' attention to some of the ways that autobiographical closure can work – or not work. It is often noted that the one thing an autobiographical narrator can't do is to narrate his or her own death. Therefore, the end must do something else instead; and it often substitutes something else for the death of the narrator – the death of another character, for example. Sometimes the ending is meant to be a sort of summary, an intensified representation of 'the structure of retrospection,' in which the goal of the story is to show how 'I' has come to be the writer of this autobiography. Does the ending try to sum up and tell us the meaning of the story? Does it try to leave us 'in the present moment,' by vividly making that moment clear to us, and placing us there? Does it establish the feeling that everything is now settled and that nothing else is going to happen? (Marriage and other forms of 'happy endings' often suggest that nothing else will ever happen; your students will readily see that this is a strange notion of happiness.) Finally: does the closure actually work as a good ending for this particular story? Why or why not? Are there threads left hanging as well as the ones that are tied up? Where does the 'closure' begin (in the last chapter, the last third of the text, the last paragraph)?

At the end of the discussion of each text in the class, ask your students to open the book – or hand out a photocopy of the last paragraph(s) of the text – and ask your students to describe and evaluate the closure of each particular autobiography.

4 Different ways of reading

This exercise is designed to turn students' attention to some of the differences between a literary reading and other ways of reading. Choose a text that could have documentary value within another disciplinary framework. I've often used *The Diaries of Hannah Cullwick, Victorian Maidservant* for this exercise (and, of course, that text also enables discussion of the differences between a diary and an autobiography), but any autobiographical writing by a figure whose life illuminates a historical period, a social class, gender, sexuality or race, an ethical problem, or a geographical region would do well for this exercise. Ask students to write a one- or two-page essay discussing what it would mean to give the work a literary reading; at least one paragraph should take up the question in general, and at least one other paragraph should perform an exemplary close reading of a chosen passage. Then: ask them to write another one- or two-page essay discussing how to read the work as a document offering historical (or some other form of) evidence about a certain period, milieu, class, family, or locale. A class period spent discussing the differences between these ways of reading will be lively and illuminating. Students will learn not only about disciplinary differences (and their different standards of evidence), but they might also perceive that disciplines themselves are historical entities. A discussion of the question 'What is literature?' might (or might not) be too difficult, depending on the group of students. But it should be possible to point out that what's included in 'literature' does change; that autobiography has only relatively recently been included; and that many sorts of texts (even non-literary texts) can be given a literary reading.

5 The group autobiography

This is a project for a whole semester (or longer). Each week, set aside 20–30 minutes in one class period for writing. Students will agree on a topic, and all will write on the same topic. What they write in class will be used as the first draft of a finished short essay (one or two pages, double-spaced) that they will bring to the next class. Each set of essays forms one chapter of the group autobiography. At the end of the semester, the local copy center can 'publish' it as a book, by binding photocopies in a plastic spiral binder (or something more substantial, if there's a fund for this sort of thing at your college or university – or if students are willing to pay for their bound copies). Students are welcome to add photos or other illustrations, if they wish. (Interpreting a photo can be a great exercise for this sort of writing.)

A word on the selection of chapter topics: Students should brainstorm together about what the topic for each week should be, and then various suggestions should be put to a vote. The topics that work best, I've found, are highly concrete and a bit oblique: 'an early illness or injury,' 'an important female influence, not your mother,' 'the family dinner table,' 'pets,' 'a lie I once told,' 'a place I like to hang out,' 'a book that made a difference to me,' 'a friend who disappointed me,' 'a physical challenge,' and so forth. The book will need a beginning chapter – 'my earliest memory,' 'where I'm from,' 'how I ended up here (at this particular college or university),' 'what I'm sure of and what I'm confused about,' and so forth – and an ending chapter – 'a fantasy of the future,' 'where I stand now,' 'how things have not turned out the way I expected,' and so forth.

Though this is an enjoyable project – and it most certainly will help students develop more fluidity and confidence in their writing – it is also useful for initiating theoretical discussions about the possibilities, paradoxes and conflicts inherent in the concept of a group autobiography.

Works cited

Abrams, M.H. *Natural Supernaturalism: Tradition and Revolution in Romantic Literature* (New York: Norton, 1971).

Benveniste, Émile. 'Subjectivity in Language,' in *Problems in General Linguistics* (Coral Gables, FL: University of Miami Press, 1971), pp. 223–30.

Brodzki, Bella and Celeste Schenck (eds). *Life/Lines: Theorizing Women's Autobiography* (Ithaca: Cornell University Press, 1988).

Canfield, Dorothy. *The Bedquilt and Other Stories*, ed. Mark J. Madigan (University of Missouri Press, 1997).

Cohen, Ed. 'The Double Lives of Man: Narration and Identification in Late Nineteenth-Century Representations of Ec-centric Masculinities,' in Sally Ledger and Scott McCracken (eds). *Cultural Politics at the Fin de Siècle* (Cambridge: Cambridge University Press, 1995), pp. 85–114.

Corbett, Mary Jean. *Representing Femininity: Middle-Class Subjectivity in Victorian and Edwardian Women's Autobiographies* (Oxford: Oxford University Press, 1992).

De Man, Paul. 'Autobiography as De-facement,' *Modern Language Notes* 94 (1979): 919–30.

Dever, Carolyn. *Death and the Mother from Dickens to Freud: Victorian Fiction and the Anxiety of Origins* (Cambridge: Cambridge University Press, 1998).

Frankfurt Institute for Social Research. 'The Individual' and 'The Group,' in *Aspects of Sociology*, preface by Max Horkheimer and Theodo Adorno (Boston: Beacon Press, 1972), pp. 37–71.

Gagnier, Regenia. *Subjectivities: a History of Self-Representation in Britain, 1832–1920* (Oxford: Oxford University Press, 1991).

Gates, Henry Louis (ed.). *The Classic Slave Narratives* (Penguin/Mentor,1987).

Gould, Stephen Jay. *Ontogeny and Phylogeny* (Cambridge, MA: Belknap, Harvard University Press, 1977).

Guillén, Claudio. 'On the Uses of Literary Genre,' in *Literature as System: Essays Toward the Theory of Literary History* (Princeton: Princeton University Press, 1971), pp. 107–34.

Gusdorf, Georges. 'Conditions and Limits of Autobiography,' in Olney (ed.), *Autobiography*, pp. 28–48.

Lejeune, Philippe. 'The Autobiographical Pact,' in *On Autobiography* (Minneapolis: University of Minnesota Press, 1989), pp. 3–30.

Lionnet, Françoise. *Autobiographical Voices: Race, Gender, Self-Portraiture* (Ithaca: Cornell University Press, 1989).

Mason, Mary G. 'The Other Voice: Autobiographies of Women Writers,' in Olney (ed.), *Autobiography*, pp. 207–35.

Olney, James (ed.). *Autobiography: Essays Theoretical and Critical* (Princeton: Princeton University Press, 1980).

Olney, James. 'Autobiography and the Cultural Moment: a Thematic, Historical, and Bibliographical Introduction' and 'Some Versions of Memory/Some Versions of *Bios*: the Ontology of Autobiography' in Olney (ed.), *Autobiography*, pp. 3–27, 236–67.

Smith, Sidonie. *A Poetics of Women's Autobiography: Marginality and the Fictions of Self-Representations* (Bloomington: Indiana University Press, 1987).

Smith, Valerie. 'The Loophole of Retreat,' introduction to *Incidents in the Life of a Slave Girl/Harriet Jacobs* (New York: Oxford University Press, 1988).

Sommer, Doris. '"Not Just a Personal Story": Women's *Testimonios* and the Plural Self,' in Bella Brodzki and Celeste Schenck (eds), *Life/Lines: Theorizing Women's Autobiography* (Ithaca: Cornell University Press, 1988), pp. 107–30.

Spengemann, William C. *The Forms of Autobiography: Episodes in the History of a Literary Genre* (New Haven: Yale University Press, 1980).

Stanton, Domna C. 'Autogynography: Is the Subject Different?' in *The Female Autograph: Theory and Practice of Autobiography from the Tenth to the Twentieth Century* (Chicago: University of Chicago Press, 1984), pp. 3–20.

Starobinski, Jean. 'The Style of Autobiography,' in Olney (ed.), *Autobiography*, pp. 73–83.

Taylor, Charles. 'Our Victorian Contemporaries,' in *Sources of the Self: the Making of Modern Identity* (Cambridge, MA: Harvard University Press, 1989), pp. 393–418.

Williams, Carolyn. '"Trying to Do Without God": the Revision of Epistolary Address in *The Color Purple*,' in Elizabeth C. Goldsmith (ed.), *Writing the Female Voice: Essays on Epistolary Literature* (Boston, MA: Northeastern University Press, 1989), pp. 273–85.

Wollheim, Richard. *The Thread of Life* (Cambridge, MA: Harvard University Press, 1984).

2
Queer Chaucer in the Classroom

Glenn Burger and Steven F. Kruger

Although Monica McAlpine's 'The Pardoner's Homosexuality and How It Matters' appeared in *PMLA* in 1980, the same year as John Boswell's *Christianity, Social Tolerance, and Homosexuality*, it was not really until the 1990s that gay/lesbian/queer studies began to have a major impact on medieval literary criticism.[1] And here, probably Chaucer studies has been in the forefront of queer approaches, as shown by the work of John M. Bowers, Glenn Burger, Catherine Cox, Carolyn Dinshaw, Steven F. Kruger, Karma Lochrie, Susan Schibanoff, Robert S. Sturges, and others.[2] The most important queer theorists for this reconsideration of Chaucer studies and sexuality have been Jonathan Dollimore (*Sexual Dissidence*), Eve Kosofsky Sedgwick (*Between Men, Epistemology of the Closet, Tendencies*, and 'Queer Performativity'), and Judith Butler (*Gender Trouble, Bodies That Matter*).[3]

The initial focus of this queer Chaucerianism has been largely on representations of 'queer' sexuality, and particularly on figures who, from a contemporary perspective at least, might be seen as somehow like modern gay men and lesbians. Thus, queer theory, if and when it has entered the Chaucer classroom, has done so largely in relation to the Pardoner, and to a lesser extent in relation to other clearly sexualized figures and their tales (the Summoner, the Wife of Bath, *The Man of Law's Tale*). In this move to focus attention largely on deviant *persons*, queer has often been conflated in the reading of Chaucer's texts with the contemporary identity terms of 'gay' and 'lesbian,' and in this sense, much recent work has been, at least in part, a continuation of McAlpine's and the debate about the Pardoner's 'homosexuality' that her article set off – involving such prominent Chaucerians as Donald R. Howard, C. David Benson, and Richard Firth Green.[4] Intertwined with the focus on sexual identity is a tendency to equate the queer with the politically resistant in an overly simplifying way, producing once again a narrowing of queer inquiry to a limited set of characters that might be seen as resistant to 'heteronormativity,' and thus either demanding a transgressive Chaucer who creates such characters to interrupt social norms, or reinscribing a conservative Father Chaucer who creates such characters only to put them back in their place within the stable hierarchies of medieval society.

We ask here whether queer theory can be used otherwise pedagogically. Queer theory, after all, has departed from gay and lesbian studies in its emphasis not on identity or identity politics, not on a stable gay/lesbian community and history that can be uncovered in the present or recovered from the past, but on the unstable relations between normative social categories and complexly lived experiences. 'Queer,' in Judith Butler's influential formulation, 'raises the question of the status of force and opposition, of stability and variability':

> If the term 'queer' is to be a site of collective contestation, the point of departure for a set of historical reflections and futural imaginings, it will have to remain that which is, in the present, never fully owned, but always and only redeployed, twisted, queered from a prior usage and in the direction of urgent and expanding political purposes.[5]

As Glenn Burger has suggested in a more specifically Chaucerian context:

> The term 'queer' has emerged in recent popular culture as an attempt to insist upon alternative, more inclusive and less knowable, ways of self-identifying within a sometimes narrowing post-Stonewall identity politics... Queer as a term has... tried to resist nominalization, functioning more often as an adjective, adverb, even verb, stressing epistemology rather than ontology.[6]

In our work on Chaucer, and specifically in the Chaucer classroom, we ask ourselves whether a queer theory thus conceived can be one means by which we call into question the set of relations between our current positions as readers of Chaucer and medieval constructions of sexuality and identity, constructions that might contain within them certain of the possibilities of modern sexuality/ identity and that might, at the same time, be understood to be radically different from our own. What would a thoroughgoingly queer reading of Chaucer look like, and how might it facilitate a form of teaching that is rigorously historicist and yet urgently attentive to the current moment?

Furthermore, if queer theory is to be useful pedagogically, it must not simply work to carve out for our inquiry a realm of sexuality seen as distinct from other socially significant realms such as gender, race, religion, and class. It must, that is, disturb and reconfigure not just a sexuality conceived as the 'proper object' of queer inquiry[7] but the intersections and interimplications of sexuality and other categories of identity, in relation to both the medieval archive and postmodern lived situations. We have begun to recognize in our own moment the inadequacy of such terms as 'woman,' 'gay,' 'white' for describing complex social formations; race makes a difference to sexuality, sexuality to race – not just now but also, perhaps in very different, non-congruent ways, in the Middle Ages.[8] In reading, for instance, *The Prioress's Tale* or *The Man of Law's Tale*, where religious (and perhaps racial) difference is explicitly at issue, might the introduction of questions about sexuality – the celibacy of the Prioress; the two quite differently articulated marriages of Constance, as well as the close homosocial relations in which she is implicated in *The Man of Law's Tale*[9] – help us see more fully what is at issue in the tales' deployment of religious/racial categories of identity? In the tales of the marriage group, are ethnic differences – the setting of the tales variously in Britain, Brittany, and Lombardy – more significant to the working out of the thematics of love and marriage than has usually been recognized by the critics? To what extent is ethnic/racial/religious difference significant to the Pardoner's sexually disruptive performance as he carries relics explicitly associated with Jewishness and tells a tale set in a Flanders that is one of England's main late-medieval economic rivals?[10]

An approach like that Judith Bennett has recently demonstrated in deploying the category 'lesbian-like' to describe certain aspects of medieval women's lives[11] can be effective in acknowledging the urgency of contemporary identity positions in our approach to history – we *need* in the present to construct a history of lesbian experience, even if we acknowledge that lesbianism in its current configurations is a modern phenomenon – while at the same time resisting the presumptive force of modern heterosexuality and its oppressive binaries and hierarchies. The historically questionable conclusion to the argument that gay and lesbian are wholly modern categories is too often that, therefore, heterosexuality is the only category with which we can safely approach premodern sexuality. Of course, however, hetero- like homosexuality, is a thoroughly modern category. To approach the past asking whether we can identify 'lesbian-*like*' lives, behaviors, expressions, keeps the need for a lesbian history in play while preventing the simple imposition of a contemporary category on a very different social/cultural moment, and it allows us to explore and give representational force to the 'queerness' of medieval otherness: for example, the agency associated with identification as a single woman or with participation in a community of women, each of which might have been in part a position of power resistant to patriarchy and yet not necessarily a position standing simply in opposition to medieval norms and hierarchies.[12] Or a contemporary queer subject's investigation of medieval family organization – recognizing the *non*-heterosexual operations of the reproduction of social hegemonies – may open up the otherness and differences of the medieval experience.

A thoroughgoingly queer reading of Chaucer must further call into question the opposition of medieval/modern upon which so much of our understanding of Chaucer depends.[13] The more we historicize the development of Chaucer's author function from his first editors and transcribers to the present, the more we can see its imbrication in the development of modern regimes of gender, sexuality, class, and an English, Christian identity. But a queer reading of Chaucer should also help us re-member what has been forgotten, occluded, left behind in the construction of a coherent social and literary history of hetero-sexuality. This may occur by unearthing specific 'unofficial' histories and voices – here, we touch again on the kind of work that has been done around the Pardoner. But it is not enough simply to find modern homosexuals in the *Canterbury Tales*, or to project a modern situation (a queer resistance to hetero-sexuality) back onto the *Tales*. Rather, what queer theory might enable is an excavation, that is also a fantasizing, of what came *before* modern sexuality – before heterosexuality and heteronormativity – as a specific historical con-struction; it thus might also enable a productive (that is, a political) vision of what might come *after* heterosexuality. In seeing modern heterosexual norma-tivity as not a necessary or natural consequence of medieval sexualities, but as only one of many possibilities, something that emerged through a particular course of historical contingencies, we might also begin to see a contingent future emerge that will not simply reproduce the constructions and exclusions of the present. Bringing queer Chaucer into the classroom in these ways might enable us to focus students' attention on the consequences for the present, the past, *and* for possible futures of a historical study that neither accepts the past simply 'in its own terms' – since those terms are always somehow also our terms – nor simply finds in the past a specific history that might be picked up as a tool for our own current projects, but instead navigates complexly among past, present, and future.

Up to this point, we have presented in quite general terms some of the directions in which a serious engagement between queer theory and medieval studies might push our pedagogical engagement with Chaucer. In the remain-der of this essay, we want more pragmatically to focus attention on two specific sites in the *Canterbury Tales* susceptible to queer teaching but not often thought of as queer – the 'marriage group' and 'Chaucer the pilgrim.'[14] Each of these is a construction that has been subjected to extensive discussion and critique in the scholarly literature, and yet each maintains a certain powerful grip on our pedagogy – in part because we as teachers tend to reproduce our experiences as students, and in part because both the 'marriage group' and the idea of 'Chaucer the pilgrim' *do* stimulate productive discussion in our classrooms.

Queer theory might enable us to rethink 'Chaucer the pilgrim' as something other than a naïve, roly-poly disguise for the worldly 'customs clerk' and canny author that is the 'real' Chaucer. We might, indeed, move to examine with our classes precisely what the figure of 'Chaucer the pilgrim' has enabled for criticism – the construction of a plenitudinous Chaucer 'the poet' and 'man' over against his other, 'the pilgrim.' In this sense, 'Chaucer the pilgrim' operates uncannily like the queer Pardoner, whose ultimate silencing allows both the assertion of a particular masculinity (embodied in the Host) and the reconstitution of a unified pilgrimage body (presided over by the Knight). But queer work, in recognizing such movements, also begins to call them into question, enabling us to see how the Pardoner might be not just an empty space against which the masculine and communal body attains its fullness but also a presence irremediably disturbing community and masculinity. Similarly, our recognition of how the pilgrim's emptiness (for instance, as naïve observer of the other pilgrims in the *General Prologue*, or as 'unsuccessful narrator' of his own tales) works to construct a Chaucer who is the modern author in complete control of his poem also might lead to a troubling of such a construction, to seeing an incoherence in the author figure that is echoed in the fragmented/inorganic (medieval) structures of the *Canterbury Tales*, in some ways becoming 'the body without organs' described by Gilles Deleuze and Félix Guattari.[15]

A queer approach to the 'marriage group' would not *deny* its power as an organizing principle for a reading experience of the *Canterbury Tales*; rather, it would interrogate that power. Making the theme of marriage central to this group of tales, as innumerable critics and teachers have done, following the lead of George Lyman Kittredge, enables us to project an image of modern heterosexuality back onto the tales and thus to see a representation of the prehistory of modern sexuality. Might we come to recognize, with our students, the stake modern critics have had in finding such a prehistory, and come, with them, to see other, non-modern and queer, potentialities in the 'marriage group?' That the argument over class (nobility, 'gentillesse') in these tales is not something separate from their consideration of sexual matters is obscured by a focus on 'marriage' as the *Tales*' primary theme: queer theory, in calling our attention to the inextricability of sexual identity from not just gender, but also race, religion, ethnicity, and class, would ask us to think about what is obscured in the tales by making them be 'about marriage.' It would call us to excavate the specific social complexities of each of these tales' construction of 'marriage,' and to recognize the privileging of a certain understanding of heterosexuality that inheres in the decision to include certain tales – *The Wife of Bath's Tale*, *The Clerk's Tale*, *The Merchant's Tale*, *The Franklin's Tale* – but not others – *The Knight's Tale*, *The Miller's Tale*, *The Man of Law's Tale*, *Melibee*, *The Nun's Priest's Tale*, *The Manciple's Tale* – in the group. We also might begin to recognize with our classes how the construction of a 'marriage group' allows for the isolation of a certain range of femininity – stretching from the Wife of Bath to Griselda (in *The Clerk's Tale*) via May (in *The Merchant's Tale*) and Dorigen (in *The Franklin's Tale*) – from other women's gendered positions, including those of Emily and Hippolyta in *The Knight's Tale*, Constance in *The Man of Law's Tale*, Prudence in the *Melibee*, the Prioress and Second Nun, St Cecilia in *The Second Nun's Tale*, the mother of *The Prioress's Tale*, Apollo's wife in *The Manciple's Tale*, and Zenobia in *The Monk's Tale*. Recognizing the full range of these positions, including not just more or less recalcitrant wives but also warrior women and queens, virgin martyrs, chaste mothers, would de-heterosexualize our notions of medieval women, and would make it impossible to place all the women of the *Tales* on a *single*, gender and/or sexual, continuum like that the marriage group, traditionally conceived, might seem to imply. We could, of course, do something similar with men, interrupting the construction of a coherent group of 'husbands' and 'lovers' more or less 'free' or generous/magnanimous in their sexual relations – as Chaucer precisely does with the inclusion of the Pardoner, Friar, and Summoner in the heart of the 'marriage group,' an inclusion that might indeed be seen not as an interruption but as intimately necessary to these tales' exploration of sexuality and gender.

The Chaucer course most often taught at undergraduate institutions, whether focused exclusively on the *Canterbury Tales* or taking up Chaucer's 'major poetry,' and thus including alongside the *Tales Troilus and Criseyde* and perhaps one or more of the dream poems (not to mention the other contexts in which parts of the Chaucerian corpus might be taught – that is, the survey of British literature), already requires that teachers do a demandingly and dauntingly various kind of work. They must introduce students to the language of Chaucer's Middle English poetry; bring them into contact with the Middle Ages – its history and culture – knowing that, for many students, this course will be their only encounter with medieval material; engage with religious ideas, cultural practices, historical specificities distant from (post)modern experience and foreign to the (post)modern eye; and negotiate the difficulties of Chaucer's notoriously complex, recalcitrant poetic constructions. We do not, therefore, advocate a simply *additive* approach to using queer theory in the classroom; queer theory and the history of sexuality do not represent just one more kind of material we need to try to squeeze into an already overpacked semester. Neither do we advocate introducing queer perspectives only in relation to a putatively queer character like the Pardoner – just as we would not present feminism as pertinent only to the Wife of Bath, or a racially/ religiously-informed criticism only in relation to tales like the Man of Law's and Prioress's. It is in order to forestall such a 'minoritizing' approach that we have emphasized here queer theory's pertinence especially to what have been seen as the central, guiding principles of Chaucer's Canterbury project – the negotiation of a complex authorial persona, the vexed thematics of marriage.[16]

Queer theory, like feminism, and like a historicism attentive to medieval social and political institutions and changes, might be thoroughly integrated into the concerns of the Chaucer course, conditioning (along with feminism and historicism) the kinds of question asked about *all* the tales. To facilitate this work, of course, we might need to add certain materials to our syllabus, building into the course, alongside Chaucer's text, theoretical and critical formulations like those referred to in the first paragraph of this essay; excerpts from historical treatments of sexuality – Boswell's work on the Church and homosexuality; Mark Jordan's excavation of the 'invention of sodomy'; Dyan Elliot's treatment of 'chaste marriage'; the extensive and growing literature on medieval conjugality;[17] other medieval texts in which sexuality is at issue – Peter Damian's *Liber Gomorrhianus*; the allegorical poetic tradition represented by Alain de Lille's *Plaint of Nature* and Guillaume de Lorris's and Jean de Meun's *Romance of the Rose*; as well as Lollard, anti-Lollard, and other texts that bring together ideas about heresy and sodomy.[18]

Moving in these directions, however, does not mean turning our attention away from gender or race or religion; as we've suggested above, a queer approach should push us to consider these all in conjunction with, rather than separation from, each other. Neither does it mean not attending to the complexities of Chaucerian poetics, the architectonics of the Chaucerian text, and its intertextualities – with, for instance, the allegorical tradition noted above or with the work of Dante, Petrarch, Boccaccio, and the developing Italian 'renaissance.' Rather, queer questions should be part of such investigations, making a central concern of the Chaucer course the extent to which the development of Chaucerian poetics in the *Canterbury Tales*, and the broader medieval traditions in which Chaucer's poem takes its place, depend upon a particular thematics of sex and sexuality. From the generative, springtime opening of the *General Prologue*, where folk 'long' to go on pilgrimage, to the somber, penitential *Parson's Tale* and *Retraction* with which the *Tales* end, the nature of human desire ('longing') is at the center of the Canterbury project, and a contemporary, queer approach calibrated to questions of desire can only enrich the work of the Chaucer classroom – and the negotiation between the contemporary and the medieval that necessarily occurs there.

Notes

An earlier version of this work was presented in a session organized by Elaine Tuttle Hansen and sponsored by the Chaucer Division at the Modern Language Association Conference in San Francisco, December 1998. We thank our fellow panelists and the audience of that session for their many helpful comments and suggestions.

1. Monica E. McAlpine, 'The Pardoner's Homosexuality and How It Matters,' *PMLA* 95 (1980): 8–22; John Boswell, *Christianity, Social Tolerance, and Homosexuality: Gay People in Europe from the Beginning of the Christian Era to the Fourteenth Century* (Chicago: University of Chicago Press, 1980).
2. John M. Bowers, 'Queering the Summoner: Same-Sex Union in Chaucer's *Canterbury Tales*,' in R.F. Yeager and Charlotte C. Morse (eds), *Speaking Images: Essays in Honor of*

V.A. Kolve (Asheville, NC: Pegasus Press, 2001); Glenn Burger, 'Kissing the Pardoner,' *PMLA* 107 (1992): 1143–56, 'Queer Chaucer,' *English Studies in Canada* 20 (1994): 153–69, 'Erotic Discipline . . . Or "Tee hee, I like my boys to be girls": Inventing with the Body in Chaucer's *Miller's Tale,*' in Bonnie Wheeler and Jeffrey Jerome Cohen (eds), *Becoming Male in the Middle Ages* (New York: Garland, 1997), pp. 245–60, 'Doing What Comes Naturally: *The Physician's Tale* and the Pardoner,' in Peter Beidler (ed.), *Masculinities in Chaucer* (Cambridge: D.S. Brewer, 1998), pp. 117–30, 'Mapping a History of Sexuality in *Melibee,*' in Robert Myles and David Williams (eds), *Chaucer and Language: Essays in Honour of Douglas Wurtele* (Montreal: McGill-Queens Press, 2001), pp. 53–62, 190–5, 'Shameful Pleasures: Up Close and Dirty with Chaucer, Flesh and the Word,' in Glenn Burger and Steven F. Kruger (eds), *Queering the Middle Ages* (Minneapolis: University of Minnesota Press, 2001), pp. 213–35, and *Chaucer's Queer Nation* (Minneapolis: University of Minnesota Press, forthcoming 2002); Catherine Cox, '"Grope wel bihynde": the Subversive Erotics of Chaucer's Summoner,' *Exemplaria* 7 (1995): 145–77; Carolyn Dinshaw, 'Chaucer's Queer Touches / A Queer Touches Chaucer,' *Exemplaria* 7 (1995): 75–92, and *Getting Medieval: Sexualities and Communities, Pre- and Postmodern* (Durham, NC: Duke University Press, 1999); Steven F. Kruger, 'Claiming the Pardoner: Toward a Gay Reading of Chaucer's *Pardoner's Tale,*' *Exemplaria* 6 (1994): 115–40; Karma Lochrie, *Covert Operations: the Medieval Uses of Secrecy* (Philadelphia: University of Pennsylvania Press, 1999); Susan Schibanoff, 'Worlds Apart: Orientalism, Anti-Feminism, and Heresy in Chaucer's *Man of Law's Tale,*' *Exemplaria* 8 (1996): 59–96; Robert S. Sturges, *Chaucer's Pardoner and Gender Theory: Bodies of Discourse* (New York: St Martin's Press, 2000). For collections of essays that address more broadly the significance of sexuality for medieval culture, see Jacqueline Murray and Konrad Eisenbichler (eds), *Desire and Discipline: Sex and Sexuality in the Premodern West* (Toronto: University of Toronto Press, 1996); Louise Fradenburg and Carla Freccero (eds), *Premodern Sexuality* (New York: Routledge, 1996); Karma Lochrie, Peggy McCracken, and James A. Schultz (eds), *Constructing Medieval Sexuality* (Minneapolis: University of Minnesota Press, 1997); and Glenn Burger and Steven F. Kruger (eds), *Queering the Middle Ages* (Minneapolis and London: University of Minnesota Press, 2001).

3. Jonathan Dollimore, *Sexual Dissidence: Augustine to Wilde, Freud to Foucault* (Oxford: Clarendon Press, 1991); Eve Kosofsky Sedgwick, *Between Men: English Literature and Male Homosocial Desire* (New York: Columbia University Press, 1985), *Epistemology of the Closet* (Berkeley: University of California Press, 1990), *Tendencies* (Durham, NC: Duke University Press, 1993), 'Queer Performativity: Henry James's *The Art of the Novel,*' *GLQ* 1 (1993): 1–16; Judith Butler, *Gender Trouble: Feminism and the Subversion of Identity* (New York: Routledge, 1990), and *Bodies That Matter: On the Discursive Limits of 'Sex'* (New York and London: Routledge, 1993).

4. Donald R. Howard's response to McAlpine was given most fully in his unpublished 1984 MLA paper 'The Sexuality of Chaucer's Pardoner,' presented at a session in which both McAlpine and C. David Benson participated; see also the briefer comments in Howard, *Chaucer: His Life, His Works, His World* (New York: E.P. Dutton, 1987), pp. 488–92, esp. p. 489 and the notes on p. 614. Benson and Richard Firth Green published back-to-back articles arguing for the Pardoner's heterosexuality or 'sexual normality': C. David Benson, 'Chaucer's Pardoner: His Sexuality and Modern Critics,' *Medievalia* 8 (1985 [for 1982]): 337–46; Richard Firth Green, 'The Sexual Normality of Chaucer's Pardoner,' *Medievalia* 8 (1985 [for 1982]): 351–57. For a more recent development of Green's position, see 'The Pardoner's Pants (and Why They Matter),' *Studies in the Age of Chaucer* 15 (1993): 131–45.

5. Butler, *Bodies That Matter*, pp. 226 and 228.

6. Burger, 'Introduction,' *Chaucer's Queer Nation*.

7. Judith Butler, 'Against Proper Objects,' *differences: A Journal of Feminist Cultural Studies* (Special Issue: 'Feminism Meets Queer Theory') 6.2–3 (1994): 1–27.

8. For treatment of the complex interrelations of religious/racial, gender, and sexual categories in the context of medieval Jewish–Christian interactions, see Steven F. Kruger, 'Conversion and Medieval Sexual, Religious, and Racial Categories,' in Lochrie, McCracken, and Schultz (eds), *Constructing Medieval Sexuality*, pp. 158–79, and 'Becoming Christian, Becoming Male?' in Wheeler and Cohen (eds), *Becoming Male in the Middle Ages*, pp. 21–41.

9. On female same-sex love in *The Man of Law's Tale*, see Allen Frantzen, *Before the Closet: Same-Sex Love from Beowulf to Angels in America* (Chicago: University of Chicago Press, 1998), pp. 259–63.

10. See David Wallace, 'In Flaundres,' *Studies in the Age of Chaucer* 19 (1997): 63–91, for a discussion of how the tale's Flemish setting might resonate with the Pardoner's supposed counterfeiting of nature, his sterility, and his modernity.

11. Judith Bennett, '"Lesbian-Like" and the Social History of Lesbianisms,' *Journal of the History of Sexuality* 9 (2000): 1–24. Bennett's argument was first presented as one of the plenary addresses at the Queer Middle Ages conference, sponsored by CUNY and NYU, 5–7 November 1998, where it stimulated spirited discussion; 'lesbian-like' was later the subject of a panel discussion at the International Congress on Medieval Studies at Kalamazoo, Michigan, May 2000.

12. For medieval singlewomen, see Judith M. Bennett and Amy M. Froide (eds), *Single-women in the European Past, 1250–1800* (Philadelphia: University of Pennsylvania Press, 1999); for communities of women, Judith M. Bennett, Elizabeth A. Clark, and Jean F. O'Barr (eds), *Sisters and Workers in the Middle Ages* (Chicago: University of Chicago Press, 1989).

13. For a fuller discussion of the ways in which queer theory might help problematize the opposition of medieval to modern, see Burger and Kruger, 'Introduction,' in *Queering the Middle Ages*, pp. xi–xxiii, as well as the essays by Kathleen Biddick, Glenn Burger, Garrett P.J. Epp, Steven F. Kruger, and Larry Scanlon published in Part III of that collection.

14. For the most influential early formulation of ideas about the marriage group, see George Lyman Kittredge, 'Chaucer's Discussion of Marriage,' *Modern Philology* 9 (1912): 435–67, and *Chaucer and His Poetry* (Cambridge, MA: Harvard University Press, 1915). 'Chaucer the pilgrim' is E. Talbot Donaldson's influential phrase; see 'Chaucer the Pilgrim,' *PMLA* 69 (1954): 928–36, reprinted in Donaldson's *Speaking of Chaucer* (London: Athlone Press, 1979; reprinted Durham, NC: Labyrinth Books, 1983), pp. 1–12.

15. Gilles Deleuze and Félix Guattari, *A Thousand Plateaus: Capitalism and Schizophrenia*, trans. Brian Massumi (Minneapolis: University of Minnesota Press, 1987):

> The B[ody] w[ithout] O[rgans] is the *field of immanence* of desire, the *plane of consistency* specific to desire (with desire defined as a process of production without reference to any exterior agency, whether it be a lack that hollows it out or a pleasure that fills it)...We come to the gradual realization that the BwO is not at all the opposite of the organs. The organs are not its enemies. The enemy is the organism. The BwO is opposed not to the organs but to that organization of the organs called the organism...The organism is not at all the body, the BwO; rather, it is a stratum on the BwO, in other words, a phenomenon of

accumulation, coagulation, and sedimentation that, in order to extract useful labor from the BwO, imposes upon it forms, functions, bonds, dominant and hierarchized organizations, organized transcendences... But who is this we that is not me, for the subject no less than the organism belongs to and depends on a stratum? Now we have the answer: the BwO is that glacial reality where the alluvions, sedimentations, coagulations, foldings, and recoilings that compose an organism – and also a signification and a subject – occur... The judgment of God uproots it from its immanence and makes it an organism, a signification, a subject. It is the BwO that is stratified. It swings between two poles, the surfaces of stratification into which it is recoiled, on which it submits to the judgment, and the plane of consistency in which it unfurls and opens to experimentation. (154, 159)

16. The term 'minoritizing' is borrowed from Sedgwick's *Epistemology of the Closet.*
17. Boswell, *Christianity, Social Tolerance, and Homosexuality,* and *Same-Sex Unions in Premodern Europe* (New York: Villard Books, 1994); Mark Jordan, *The Invention of Sodomy in Christian Theology* (Chicago: University of Chicago Press, 1997); Dyan Elliott, *Spiritual Marriage: Sexual Abstinence in Medieval Wedlock* (Princeton, NJ: Princeton University Press, 1993). For medieval conjugality, see Michael M. Sheehan, *Marriage, Family, and Law in Medieval Europe,* ed. James K. Farge (Toronto: University of Toronto Press, 1996); Erik Kooper, 'Loving the Unequal Equal: Medieval Theologians and Marital Affection,' in Robert R. Edwards and Stephen Spector (eds), *The Olde Daunce: Love, Friendship, Sex, and Marriage in the Medieval World* (Albany: State University of New York Press, 1991), pp. 44–56; Andrew Galloway, 'Marriage Sermons, Polemical Sermons, and *The Wife of Bath's Prologue*: A Generic Excursus,' *Studies in the Age of Chaucer* 14 (1992): 3–30.
18. Peter Damian, *Book of Gomorrah: an Eleventh Century Treatise against Clerical Homosexual Practices,* trans. Pierre J. Payer (Waterloo, Ontario: Wilfrid Laurier University Press, 1982), or, for another translation, *Letters,* trans. Owen J. Blum (Washington, DC: Catholic University of America Press, 1989–98); Alain de Lille, *The Plaint of Nature,* trans. James J. Sheridan (Toronto: Pontifical Institute of Mediaeval Studies, 1980); Guillaume de Lorris and Jean de Meun, *The Romance of the Rose,* trans. Charles Dahlberg (Princeton, NJ: Princeton University Press, 1971). Dinshaw discusses Lollard and anti-Lollard polemics in relation to questions about sexuality; see Dinshaw, *Getting Medieval,* Chapter 1, 'It Takes One to Know One: Lollards, Sodomites, and Their Accusers,' pp. 55–99. Lochrie's work in progress on female sodomy, extending the treatment presented in *Covert Operations,* Chapter 5, 'Sodomy and Other Female Perversions,' pp. 177–227, takes up similar material.

3
Grub Street: the Literary and the Literatory in Eighteenth-Century Britain

John O'Brien

Since at least the eighteenth century, literary history has had a lot invested in the concept of the author. Despite the well-publicized death of the author at the hands of poststructuralist theorists such as Michel Foucault and Roland Barthes, authors remain the heroes of most of the stories we tell and many of the courses we teach; we admire their genius, lament their neglect, use historical and biographical contexts to illuminate new facets of texts that we call their 'works.' We frequently name courses after them. The purpose of 'Grub Street: The Literary and the Literatory in Eighteenth-Century Britain' is to interrogate the concept of author by placing it into the context of the industries of print publication and literary criticism as they emerged in Great Britain during the first half of the eighteenth century. My intention in this course, which I have taught both to advanced undergraduates and to graduates, was to help students recognize that many aspects of authorship as we now understand them are historical inventions. Why, for example, are authors, rather than patrons or publishers, the first individuals we typically associate with literary works? And how did it happen that some texts have been valued as being literary, of high artistic merit, while others are thought of as vulgar and common, as popular diversion rather than serious art – in short, as the product of the 'literatory,' the term that *The Grub Street Journal* coined to identify printing shops like that of the bookseller and publisher Edmund Curll. That *The Life and Strange Surprising Adventures of Robinson Crusoe*, for example, was seen by some contemporaries as a product of the literatory but is now ranked as a literary classic demonstrates that these categories are not absolute but subject to negotiation and revision.

This course engages an extremely active area of scholarship. In the last two decades, scholars such as Mark Rose, Margaret Ezell, Martha Woodmansee, Roger Chartier, Catherine Gallagher, Dustin Griffin, Adrian Johns, and Paulina Kewes have done extraordinary archival work into the history of institutions like publication, printing, patronage, and authorship, enormously extending our knowledge of the way these institutions functioned in the period, and reconceptualizing an entire field of study in the process. 'Grub Street' brings some of that research into the classroom, sometimes directly, by means of secondary readings drawn from their work, but more broadly by taking its cue from the radical rethinking of authorship that such works permit: their collective desire to dislodge the Romantic conception of the author as a unique inspired genius in favor of a conception of authorship that was partly constructed as an effect of transformations in factors like technology, the class system, gender roles, state censorship, economic activity – in sum, the social systems within which seventeenth- and eighteenth-century English men and women expressed themselves in writing.

There can be no doubt that the recent interest in early modern conceptions of authorship and publication owes something to the emergence and proliferation of electronic and digital media: e-books, digital libraries, and the Internet. Because we are witnesses to such revolutionary changes in the way that information is composed, owned, organized, and disseminated, we are uniquely positioned to engage sympathetically as well as critically with the equally revolutionary changes of the seventeenth and eighteenth centuries. And such a realization teaches an important lesson in itself; that we, too, are historical subjects, situated in a particular moment in human culture, a position that confers both blindness and insight into the ways that other people responded to the possibilities of their own time.

The proliferation of recent scholarship on early modern authorship means that there is far more to say, read, and study than can possibly be included in a single semester. Even to focus on the concept of the author is already to narrow the scope of inquiry to one of many possible foci for constructing such a course, and I can imagine courses that would be oriented more directly around the history of the book, or the emergence of literary criticism as a discipline. But authorship proves to be an excellent category to interrogate, as it is flexible enough to touch upon a wide variety of issues, and is familiar enough to students that it provides a useful bridge to more abstract concepts. What I describe below is a version of this course that I have taught successfully to advanced undergraduates; I have also taught a version of the course, with a heavier reading load, to first-year graduate students. The syllabus addresses three main issues, each of which is the subject of a three- to four-week unit: 'authors and authority,' 'theater and performance,' and 'genius versus dunce.' Each unit forms a case study, focusing in large part on a single major text and author to get at the issues raised by a specific mode of writing: fiction, drama, or poetry.

The course's first unit introduces the concept of authorship, situating the early modern author in the context of manuscript coteries, systems of patronage, and commercial print publication. This unit is designed to give a sense of the complicated and precarious position of 'the author' in the marketplace of print in the early eighteenth century: on the one hand, authors were trying to claim a degree of respectability for their profession; on the other hand, they were caught between a declining patronage system and an emergent and cut-throat commercial system. At the same time, they were subject to attack for running afoul of the norms and standards that were encoded in the law. We approach authorship from several directions, for example performing close readings of dedications to tease out the details of the author–patron relationship, and also reading the first number of Addison and Steele's *Spectator* series, a journal that derives considerable 'authority' from the fact that its writer remained anonymous.

More comprehensively, this part of the course tries to build a bridge between the seventeenth and eighteenth centuries by focusing on what Margaret Ezell has dubbed 'social authorship,' the practice of manuscript coterie writing, in which 'publication' constitutes circulating a text among a circle of family, friends, and affiliates, with the goal not of making money or achieving fame, but of strengthening the bonds that knit the group together. Social authors like Katherine Philips, Jane Barker, and the young Alexander Pope distributed their writings widely in manuscript, actively seeking advice, feedback, and dialogue; to them, writing was a way of reinforcing the identity and cohesion of the group, which is one of the things that made it appealing to writers who felt themselves to be underrepresented by the voices of the dominant culture, such as women, Dissenters, Jacobites, and Catholics. Because their imagined audience was typically known in advance, social authors sometimes experienced publication as a kind of fall, as writings intended to be shared within a defined group were now available to anyone willing to buy them. The most prominent example of such a writer in this course is Jane Barker, a Catholic and Jacobite writer whose poetry, circulated in manuscript form, reached print at times without her knowledge or approval, a concept that seems odd to us, accustomed as we are to thinking that print is the logical destination of all significant writing. Her most important book, *A Patch-Work Screen for the Ladies* (1723), now available in a paperback edition edited by Carol Shiner Wilson for the Women Writers in English series from Oxford University Press, is a fascinating hybrid text: defining itself as a 'novel' and comparing itself to other such works that have succeeded in the marketplace, *A Patch-Work Screen* (and its sequel, *The Lining of the Patch-Work Screen*) weave in poems that were originally included in some of the manuscript collections of poetry that Barker had earlier 'published' among her friends and fellow Jacobites. Barker's texts, combining fiction, poetry, memoir, and instruction, superbly illustrate the different and, at times, conflicting desires of an author who negotiated the worlds of coterie and print publication.

We turn next to the early eighteenth-century novel itself, reading Daniel Defoe's *The Life and Strange Surprising Adventures of Robinson Crusoe*. One of the reasons for choosing *Robinson Crusoe* was that it occupies such a prominent place in the culture, one that goes far beyond the 1719 book (which was published anonymously) in which the character of Robinson Crusoe himself was introduced to the world. In that spirit, the class also reads the introductory material to the two sequels that Defoe himself undertook. I also ask the students to look at some other popular representations of *Robinson Crusoe* from the eighteenth century – illustrations, chapbooks, abridgements, translations, and so on. Finally, the students read some of the eighteenth-century biographies of Defoe – the short biography by Theophilus Cibber (or, appropriately enough, more likely someone writing under his name), printed in the 1753 compendium *The Lives of the Poets of Great Britain*, and excerpts from George Chalmers' 1787 *Life of Defoe*, the first full-length biography, as well as the first attempt to come up with a canon of Defoe's writings. These are the books that first describe Defoe as an 'author,' a figure of significance in English literary history, rather than as a political journalist or hack writer.

The second unit focuses on the eighteenth century's understanding of William Shakespeare, who is somehow both the most characteristically English *and* the most original of all authors in the English literary tradition. My goal here has been to try to show some evidence for what I think a lot of students have always suspected – that the Shakespeare they were made to read in high school is not some magical entity who transcends space, time, and situation, but a cultural construction. We begin by reading Shakespeare's *King Lear* in a modern edition. My goal in doing this at the outset of the unit is to help us gain a reasonably solid handle on the play as it looks to us in order to demarcate a baseline from which to talk about how eighteenth-century readers and theatergoers thought about it. I chose the Cambridge edition in large part because it does a fairly responsible job of discussing the well-known problem of the differing texts of this play as we have them from Shakespeare's own lifetime. The idea that the very text of a Shakespeare play can be an object of critical dispute is a good lesson in itself, one that is fairly new to most students. I do not want generally to spend a whole lot of time on the question – much less to mislead students into thinking that our goal is to *solve* the problem of the multiple texts – but I do want to let students know that even today the question of determining what Shakespeare actually wrote is an ongoing subject of debate. Next, we read the Nahum Tate adaptation of Shakespeare's *King Lear*, first produced in 1682. This was the version of the play that was generally performed on stage in Britain during the eighteenth century, and is most notable for the fact that Tate spares the lives of Lear and Cordelia, an outcome that contemporary theater audiences and critics largely approved of. I have tried to play devil's advocate here and to argue that Tate's version has its advantages, particularly with respect to Cordelia, who is sacrificed at the end of Shakespeare's play arguably for no good reason. My students, however, tend to be truly ruthless, and are generally quite willing to let her die.

We also read some of the eighteenth-century criticism of Shakespeare, specifically the prefaces to two editions of Shakespeare's collected works: Pope's edition of 1725 (the target of Lewis Theobald's attack in *Shakespeare Restored*) and Samuel Johnson's magisterial 1765 edition. These are among the hardest texts for undergraduate students to make sense of, but they are extraordinarily important in helping them get a purchase on the different things that 'Shakespeare' has meant to English writers, as well as the different standards of judgment that eighteenth-century critics and editors used – Pope's practice of 'improving' Shakespeare's occasional uneven prosody or to smooth lines garbled by previous editors contrasts sharply with Johnson's attempts to recover the words that Shakespeare himself wrote – and to see how different these are in turn from contemporary practice. And all of these exercises work, I hope, to demystify and therefore to make more accessible the writings of the figure who has for all intents and purposes come to emblematize the author in the English-language tradition.

The final unit of the course is devoted to that central document of eighteenth-century Britain's culture wars, Alexander Pope's *The Dunciad*. This text began, as is well known, as Pope's response to Lewis Theobold's criticism of Pope's edition of Shakespeare, but it grew to encompass a much broader attack on popular culture, sweepingly categorizing its purveyors as Dunces gleefully destroying the nation at the behest of the goddess Dulness. My hope is that by the time we get to *The Dunciad*, students are able to identify for themselves some of the issues at stake, and I am generally gratified to see that this is indeed the case for at least some members of the class. I start by having the students read Pope's *Essay on Criticism*, a poem in which the young Pope makes the case that criticism is something that should be performed by authors themselves rather than mere critics. We also return to some of the questions of the first weeks of the course by reading some of the manuscript poems that Pope exchanged in correspondence with Lady Mary Wortley Montagu. In particular, the three works that came to be known as *Court Poems* demonstrate how coterie writing persisted well into what we think of as an era of print. These satirical poems, written for and in a small circle of friends and attributed by various critics to Pope, Montague, and John Gay (and probably in effect a collaboration by all three), were published illicitly by Edmund Curll, an act that so angered Pope that he famously gave Curll an emetic in revenge.

The centerpiece for this unit, and in many ways the climax for the class as a whole, is a mock trial, held in class. History records that Pope sued Curll over the issue of Curll's unauthorized publication of Pope's letters. But we also know that Pope himself manipulated Curll into publishing these letters in order to boost demand for a fully 'authorized' edition. In the alternate history posited for the sake of our class, Curll sued Pope for libel and defamation of character, and the students, separated into rival teams representing the plaintiff and the defendant, prepared briefs for their chosen client. The issues involved are extraordinarily complicated and tangled, and not simply because Pope himself was not above using deception, trickery, and chemistry to get the better of Curll. It is easy for us to see that Curll was acting without authority by printing poems, letters, and other material for which he had neither paid nor received permission. But, as Curll himself asked Pope, 'Who gave *you* the authority of punishing *me*?'

My great fear each semester has been that nobody would volunteer to participate in this trial, but that has turned out not be the case. This is perhaps in part because I offer an incentive; students who are willing to take part in the trial as participants do not have to produce the written 'brief' that is required of those who do not. But students generally enjoy this exercise, which breaks the frame of the classroom and gives them a great deal of autonomy in how to proceed. I break the class into two groups, representing each side, with students playing the parts of Curll, Pope, their attorneys, and also some expert witnesses able to address the issues in the trial that we have been examining in class. I generally sit as the judge, and the rest of the class constitutes itself as a jury.

The trial has always been a great and gratifying success. The students prepare for the trial carefully, are generally able to articulate the issues in great detail and complexity, and, when the opportunity comes, are often able to cross-examine each other shrewdly. I typically permit members of the jury to pose questions as well, and they usually have good contributions to make to the proceedings. In one instance, the jury returned a particularly splendid and appropriate verdict, finding both men capable of wrongdoing, and sentencing them to be placed in the stocks within spitting distance of each other. Such a verdict suggests that at some level the students understand that the many conflicts between the author, the publisher, the critic, and the reader are never truly resolved. Rather, these conflicts are negotiated anew over and over again; every age comes to a different accommodation based on its own needs and desires.

Appendix

Reading list and schedule for 'Grub Street: the Literary and the Literatory in Eighteenth-Century Britain'

Texts

Jane Barker, *The Galesia Trilogy and Selected Manuscript Poems of Jane Barker* (ed. Carol Shiner Wilson)
Daniel Defoe, *The Life and Strange Surprising Adventures of Robinson Crusoe*
William Shakespeare, *King Lear*

Alexander Pope, *Complete Poems*
Marc Rose, *Authors and Owners: The Invention of Copyright*

Reading schedule

I Approaching the literatory: authors, patrons, printers, critics

Week one

Introduction to course
John Dryden, 'Epistle Dedicatory' to *Marriage à la Mode*
Aphra Behn, dedication to *The Emperor of the Moon*
'G.J.,' dedication to *The Widow Ranter*
Henry Fielding, dedication to *Tom Jones*
Samuel Johnson, letter to Lord Chesterfield
Dustin Griffin, 'The cultural economics of literary patronage' from *Literary Patronage in England, 1650–1800*

Week two

Joseph Addison, *Spectator*, issue 1
Jonathan Swift, *The Battel of the Books* (1710)
Michel Foucault, 'What is an Author?'
Roland Barthes, 'The Death of the Author'
Terry Belanger, 'Publishers and writers in eighteenth-century England,' from Isabel Rivers (ed.), *Books and Their Readers in Eighteenth-Century England*
Mark Rose, *Authors and Owners*, chapters one and two

Week three

Barker, *A Patch-Work Screen for the Ladies* and selections from 'The Galesia Manuscript'
Margaret Ezell, 'The Social Author,' from *Social Authorship and the Advent of Print*

Week four

Defoe, *The Life and Strange Surprising Adventures of Robinson Crusoe* (1719)

Week five

Defoe, prefaces to *The Farther Adventures of Robinson Crusoe* and *Serious Reflections of Robinson Crusoe*
Charles Gildon, 'The Life and Strange Surprising Adventures of Mr D___De F__'*
Theophilus Cibber, from *Lives of the Poets* (1753)
George Chalmers, from *Life of Defoe* (1787)
Chapbook and other versions and adaptations of *Robinson Crusoe*
Pat Rogers, 'Classics and Chapbooks,' from *Books and their Readers in Eighteenth-Century England*
Rose, from *Authors and Owners*, chapter 3

II The True History of William Shakespeare

Week six

William Shakespeare, *The Tragedy of King Lear*

Week seven

Nahum Tate, *The History of King Lear*
Laura Rosenthal, '(Re)Writing Lear,' from John Brewer and Susan Staves (eds), *Early Modern Conceptions of Property*

Week eight

Alexander Pope, preface to *The Works of Shakespear* (1725)
Lewis Theobald, from *Shakespeare Restored* (1726)
Samuel Johnson, preface to *The Plays of William Shakespeare* (1765)
Gary Taylor, '1709' from *Reinventing Shakespeare*

III Pope and other Dunces

Week nine

Alexander Pope, *An Essay on Criticism* (1711)
Lady Mary Wortley Montagu *et al.*, *Court Poems* (1716)
Alexander Pope, *Three Attacks on Edmund Curll*
Maynard Mack, *Alexander Pope, a Life*, excerpt on Pope's relationship with Montagu

Weeks ten and eleven

Alexander Pope, *The Dunciad Variorum* (1729)

Week twelve

Mock-Trial – *Edmund Curll vs. Alexander Pope*
Maynard Mack, *Alexander Pope, a Life*, excerpt on the maneuvering concerning Pope's letters
Edmund Curll, preface to *Mr. Pope's Literary Correspondence*
Alexander Pope, *A Narrative of the Method by which the Private Letters of Mr. Pope have been procur'd and publish'd by Edmund Curll* (includes Curll's rebutting notes)
Mark Rose, chapter four and appendix to *Authors and Owners*

Week thirteen

Student presentations of final research projects

4
Teaching the Victorians Today

Nancy Henry

'Charles Dickens was paid by the word.' Many of today's undergraduates have never read a Victorian novel; nonetheless they *know* that the daunting length of *Bleak House* and *Little Dorrit* is a consequence of this perverse and antiquated form of payment without which they would be spared many a laborious description and extraneous character. The belief that Dickens was paid by the word persists with the tenacity of urban myth and carries an implicit rebuke to the teacher of Victorian literature: is it fair that we should suffer because Dickens had so many pages to fill and Victorian readers so little else to do? *Interesting frame*

Truly, it is a lot to ask of today's busy students to absorb, much less enjoy, the great multi-plot monsters of the mid-nineteenth century. If teaching Victorian literature sometimes seems like plying so many undergraduate stomachs with cheese in order to remedy a gastric weakness which prevents them from digesting it, we may, as George Eliot proposes, change the metaphor. Tom Tulliver was shaken and demeaned by his painfully undigested education at Mr Stelling's school, but reading novels as long and difficult as *The Mill on the Floss* and *Middlemarch*, I tell my students, is like running a marathon. Pace yourself: it takes hard work and discipline, but the rewards and sense of satisfaction can be tremendous. Even if you never do it again, you can be proud you did, and you might just become addicted.

This essay will address some of the intellectual and practical challenges of teaching a survey of Victorian literature. I will refer to my experiences teaching undergraduate surveys at a state university in the US. While the students and class sizes vary from institution to institution, I believe that I can offer some helpful suggestions for new teachers who are planning courses in Victorian literature and culture.

Introductions

Why teach a survey? What purpose does it serve as part of a liberal arts education today? By its nature a survey is designed not only to train students to read, think and write, but to impart some knowledge. Surveys may be criticized as superficial, but I believe that they provide scope and perspective. They give students a foundation from which to pursue their personal, specialized interests. Yes, frustrations are inherent. The current trend in scholarship and criticism is to consider broad social questions and to read literature in the context of other fields such as science, political economy or art history. Yet in a survey, we cannot always do justice to the interdisciplinarity of our own research. It may be impossible to introduce students to Victorian 'high' culture, popular culture, and material culture, as well as political and social history. If you are to consider today's pressing topics of race, class and gender, you may not have time to look at issues that were central to the Victorians, like Tractarianism, Chartism or electoral reform. In an introductory survey, the traditional approach of teaching literary texts in historical sequence is still useful, as are the basic categories – industrialization, reform, Darwinian science, religious doubt, and imperial expansion.

American teachers of Victorian literature confront the challenge of explaining cultural as well as historical differences. In contrast to students in the UK, American students will come to an introductory course with limited knowledge about British literature, British history, and even contemporary Britain. It is helpful to talk about what 'Britain' and 'Britishness' mean. Project a good, clear map on screen and put one in their hands. Point out the geographic boundaries of England, Scotland, Wales and Ireland. It will be helpful to return to this map over the course of the semester to point out the places referred to in the works you are reading. If you are teaching Gaskell's *North and South*, for example, you will want to explain the difference between the south of England and the industrialized north. Show them where London sits in relation to the rest of the nation and provide a map of London itself.

In any class, you face challenges in helping students to develop the skills of reading, writing and conducting research. A survey adds the additional challenge of providing historical perspective. You cannot fill all the gaps in their historical knowledge, but you can emphasize that history matters and that literature is neither written nor read in a vacuum. The potential for confusion cannot be underestimated. Students may, for example, show a tendency to confuse Queen Elizabeth and Queen Victoria. In one of my first nineteenth-century survey courses, despite what I thought had been an adequate effort to historicize the texts, I received a paper arguing that Shelley's 'Ozymandias' represented the devastation of World War I. In the early years of teaching, such an episode occasions self-flagellation: how could it happen in my class? There will always be clueless students, but I realized that I had failed to emphasize frequently enough the difference between the nineteenth century and the 1900s. Ever since, I have striven to part a few of the historical clouds in which many students wander. To eliminate the vagueness evident in phrases like 'in her time period' or 'in the time when she wrote,' I ask them to be specific about periodization and to use dates: 'in the early Victorian period,' or 'at the end of the nineteenth century,' or even 'at the time the novel was published in 1860.' Despite the occasional objection (as when one student rejected dates on the grounds that they 'spatialized history'), such simple steps can help most students conceptualize and differentiate the vast blank spaces of the past.

I begin a course or a section on the Victorian period by asking the class to free-associate on the word 'Victorian.' When I started teaching, I was surprised to learn that some of the assumptions I set out to challenge simply did not exist: today's undergraduates do not assume that the Victorians were sexually repressed. They are more likely to associate 'Victorian' with an ornate and frilly style of architecture – their notion of the Victorian house. Foucault's rebuttal of the 'repression hypothesis' comes as no shock. When I teach *The History of Sexuality* (vol. I), it is necessary to introduce students to the clichés against which that book works in order that they may understand its significance.

Setting the texts

The canon wars of the 1980s that have shaped our syllabuses and the anthologies from which we teach are ancient history to our undergraduates. When it comes to historical periods about which they know so little, they are unlikely to have strong views about being indoctrinated into the canon. You may even discover a desire for cultural literacy. Students taking an eighteenth-century survey told me that, while they did not particularly like *Robinson Crusoe*, they were glad to have read it, to know what it was because they had always heard of it. At the same time, most students welcome the experience of reading works of which they have never heard. I do not force-feed them great works, but rather introduce them to the historical processes by which particular texts have been validated or disparaged. They may be gratified to learn that the Edwardians rejected their predecessors – that the canonical status of authors like George Eliot and Elizabeth Barrett Browning have their own particular critical history and distinctively twentieth-century construction.

For a survey class, many teachers find it most convenient to fall back on the anthology. This is certainly a reasonable option and may solve your problem with respect to selections of poetry, short stories, essays and even complete plays. In a survey of Victorian literature, you will want to supplement the anthology with one or two novels at least. But which anthology and which novels? Evaluating the anthologies requires some advance planning. If your department receives sample copies, it will have them on hand, and your library too should help you to do this basic research. You may, and should, request review copies from the publishers. Get to know your local sales representatives and keep up with what publishers are offering.

Competition has forced publishers such as Norton and Longman to make available 'splits' of their larger anthologies, so that if you are teaching Victorian literature, it is possible to order only the Victorian literature segment – a significant saving for the students. For my eighteenth- and nineteenth-century survey, I routinely have Norton 'bundle' the last third of their first volume and the first two-thirds of their second volume for a course covering the whole of the eighteenth and nineteenth centuries. Recently, Harcourt has published a Victorian literature anthology with an emphasis on historical contexts, while others, such as the *Oxford Anthology of English Literature (Victorian Prose and Poetry)*, are being revised and updated.

Do you want to have dictated to you what you teach? Is the accidental national curriculum, shaped by the availability of texts, one behind which you can stand intellectually? The canon, which reflects the pedagogical and research interests of a new generation of scholars and teachers, is even broader and looser than it once was, but you will still have trouble finding editions of works that have not been incorporated into it. A combination of ideological and market forces make the canon today such as it is. Ideally, you set texts that suit your goals for the course and then find the books, but your choices will be determined by availability, and some great ideas for an original, non-canonical syllabus may be thwarted by the unavailability of the books in question.

Most novels that anyone would want to teach in a survey will be in print; however, availability is established by academic publishers who are skittish about publishing anything not likely to sell. You will find multiple editions of novels by Dickens and George Eliot, but perhaps only one by Margaret Oliphant or Benjamin Disraeli. Many texts published by Virago and Pandora in the 1970s and 1980s are no longer in print. My own experience as an editor of critical editions has been that publishers want to produce new editions only of those works that already exist as critical editions: they need evidence of a market, but if no edition exists, what evidence can there be? I was lucky to find a publisher for George Eliot's neglected book, *Impressions of Theophrastus Such* (of which there was no critical edition at the time), but have had proposals for other books, such as Harriet Martineau's *The Hour and the Man* (of which no critical edition exists), rejected because there was no way to measure demand. Conversely, I have had no trouble with proposals for books of which there are already several editions. Encouragingly, Broadview Press has recently taken the risk of publishing lesser-known works – a positive step toward breaking the vicious circle that reinforces canonicity.

I advise against using the cheapest editions – the ones with no introductions or historical annotation – because, while they save the students money, in the long run they encourage the sense that historical explanations for obscure words and references are unimportant. Students are better able to understand what they are reading when they have this context available as part of the textual apparatus. Internet databases provide some full texts, but I have found it impractical to assign long works that are available only in this form: it poses problems for reading and discussion.

Even before you grapple with the question of availability, you must factor in the length of the novel and the time needed to teach it when planning your syllabus. When faced with *Vanity Fair, Middlemarch, The Way We Live Now,* and *Our Mutual Friend,* is it any wonder teachers seek refuge in works like *Silas Marner, The Warden,* and *The Mystery of Edwin Drood*? The flight to shorter works, I believe, has had an impact on the canon, that is, on the availability of texts and on scholarship. Thackeray is out. *Hard Times* and *Jane Eyre* are in. I understand the impulse to shorter works, simply because they allow you to include more and to avoid the inevitable grumblings and recourse to *Cliffs Notes*. Still, I believe that reading at least one long novel is an important experience for students being introduced to Victorian literature. I can only suggest pacing (not overloading them with reading) and variety: find different ways to illuminate the text: cultural context, aesthetic considerations, basic close reading, and plenty of short writing assignments to check the students' progress.

While we may regret that our students do not come to us with more background knowledge about the texts we are teaching, we can try to make the most of what they do know. You can count on their facility in using the Internet and you may want to set up a chatroom or a listserv on which students can ask questions and exchange ideas about their readings. Many professors post the syllabus, assignments and study questions on a website. One problem faced by teachers today is that of acquiring permission to reproduce copyrighted material for educational use. When I was in college and graduate school from the mid-1980s through the mid-1990s, it was routine for professors to provide coursepacks of critical articles to supplement the books assigned in a course. Then, it was simply a matter of providing the local copy center with articles and book chapters. Costs were kept to the minimum of copying expenses. Today, companies such as Kinko's as well as university copy centers will not reproduce material without acquiring and paying for the right to reproduce any copyrighted text.

Many universities now provide a service that obtains the necessary permissions, produces a traditional coursepack and passes the costs along to the students. In response to new restrictions, however, a convenient alternative has emerged: the online coursepack. Several publishers now offer the option of self-designed or authored coursepacks. The advantage is speed of preparation, simplicity of distribution and reasonableness of cost. You may enter their databases, review their authored coursepacks and adapt them to your reading list while monitoring a running tab of how much this will cost the students. It is reasonable to ask students to read such shorter, supplemental material online and they may print or email the articles to themselves. You must be careful to select articles that are not too focused, that do not veer off into highly academic arguments or that do not depend on theoretical knowledge that you cannot provide in your course. The drawback is that the available journals are limited and book chapters are not included, but the databases are expanding all the time and the online coursepack remains a useful option.

Assignments

You will want to design writing assignments that develop the skills you are emphasizing in your course. Unfortunately, plagiarism has become a problem for all teachers. The best strategy is to stop plagiarism before it starts by giving some thought to the matter as you plan your assignments. Some approaches that have worked for me include daily response paragraphs. There are many advantages to this method. Students develop good habits by learning to think about what they are reading every day. In reading their paragraphs, you will come to know their writing styles and their strengths and weaknesses. They will have the satisfaction of knowing that their grades are cumulative, rather than depending solely on a final paper or exam. One variation on the open topic response paragraph is to ask students to identify a word that is unfamiliar to them in their day's reading. I ask them to look up the word in a dictionary (either traditional or online), to provide a definition, to quote the passage in which the word occurs and to provide a brief explanation of how the word is used in context. This encourages them to develop the habit of looking up words they do not know and challenges them to think about the author's use of language. (See the suggested sample assignments in the Appendix at the end of this chapter.)

I recommend balancing daily assignments with longer papers and exams. Concerns about plagiarism have led me away from the open topic paper. Many students like assigned topics, but others may feel constrained. I therefore provide a series of paper topics from which they may choose, and allow for some flexibility for those who want to pursue an individual topic and are willing to meet and discuss their interests. Unusual combinations of texts and topics that directly reflect class discussions are effective ways to discourage plagiarism and promote creative thought.

In the classroom

If you want to be sure that students have read and understood, you will need to test them. No one likes tests. Students may be accustomed to a 'no wrong answers' approach to literature. Yet tests are not punitive; they are useful for the student as well as the teacher. Confusions that may be concealed in discussions, in-class writings and even term papers, are revealed in a simple, short answer quiz. Such exercises test memory, note-taking skills and basic comprehension. They also eliminate concerns about plagiarism. Such a quiz early in the term can identify problems of reading comprehension, for example, in the interpretation of poetry. I have frequently used 'identification' exams. Presenting substantial, representative quotations from works that have been assigned, I ask the students to identify the author, and text, and briefly to explain the context. Some students dislike this kind of question, but when they have been adequately prepared, they should be able to recall what they have read, and if they cannot, it may be a problem to address. Tests should not be the only basis for grading, but a series of straightforward examinations combined with daily assignments and longer papers insures that you are evaluating a variety of skills in your students.

The challenges of teaching a Victorian survey are similar to those of teaching the literature of any historical period. The basic strategies for composing a syllabus, devising assignments and evaluating students' progress are the same as those for teaching any course. The key is to know the material and to convey your knowledge to the students while remaining aware of the difficulties they may encounter in digesting works that are long, complex and unfamiliar. You may never dislodge the belief that 'Dickens was paid by the word,' but perhaps you can coach them through the marathon of reading as the Victorians read, helping them to find the personal pleasure and satisfaction of entering another world and another time.

Appendix

Sample reading list

An anthology of Victorian literature including selected poems and prose by:

- Thomas Carlyle
- Emily Brontë
- Christina Rossetti
- Elizabeth Barrett Browning
- Robert Browning
- Alfred, Lord Tennyson
- Charles Darwin
- Thomas Hardy

Elizabeth Gaskell, *Ruth*
George Eliot, *Middlemarch*
Olive Schreiner, *The Story of an African Farm*
Rudyard Kipling, 'The Man Who Would be King'
Oscar Wilde, *The Picture of Dorian Gray*

- Online coursepack of critical articles

Books to help you:
Victorian Britain: An Encyclopedia, ed. Sally Mitchell (New York: Garland Publishing, 1998).
A Companion to Victorian Literature and Culture, ed. Herbert F. Tucker (Maldon, MA: Blackwell, 1999).
The Cambridge Companion to the Victorian Novel, ed. Deirdre David (New York: Cambridge University Press, 2001).
The Cambridge Companion to Victorian Poetry, ed. Joseph Bristow (New York: Cambridge University Press, 2000).

Sample daily assignments

- For each day's reading, students provide a one-page (typed, double-spaced) response to an issue of interest to them and to the class. These papers should be thoughtful and carefully written. They are exercises in language, style and expression: practice essays that may also provide a basis for discussions about writing. Students should be prepared to read their responses in class to facilitate discussion.
- From each day's reading, students select a word that is unfamiliar to them. Using a dictionary, they provide a definition of this word and a brief explanation of how it is used, making sure to indicate where the word appears in the text. These papers may be read in class to facilitate discussion about an author's word choice and its implications. Vocabulary words discussed in class may appear on the mid-term and final examinations.
- Variation: you may ask for these assignments to be turned in once a week rather than every day.

Sample essay questions or paper topics

- Mr Bradshaw in *Ruth* and Mr Bulstrode in *Middlemarch* are representative of 'new' money, of middle-class men who have come to prominence through business and banking. Both men are pious and believe that their financial power authorizes them to exert a moral influence in their societies. Using the examples of Bradshaw and Bulstrode, consider how Eliot and Gaskell treat the relationship between money/ social standing and religion/morality.
- *The Story of an African Farm* (1883) and 'The Man Who Would be King' (1888) portray simultaneous, yet dramatically different aspects of the nineteenth-century British colonial experience. The role that British men played in various parts of the far-flung empire is considered by both Schreiner and Kipling. Concentrating on the characters of Gregory Rose and Daniel Dravot, explore the two contrasting representations of masculinity represented in these works.
- The theme of the divided self appears in a number of Victorian novels. The narrator of *Middlemarch* says of Lydgate: 'he had two selves within apparently, and they must learn to accommodate each other and bear reciprocal impediments.' Internal division often leads to external division, 'the double life,': 'It was true that Bulstrode found himself carrying on two distinct lives...' (503). In *The Picture of Dorian Gray*, the divided self and the double life are carried to their logical extremes. Dorian's soul

resides in his portrait, which represents his corruption in all its gruesome ugliness. His body remains young, presenting to the world an image of untainted beauty. Selecting one example from *Middlemarch* and one from *Dorian Gray*, contrast the authors' presentation of and attitude toward the divided self. You need not choose one of the examples above. Other possibilities include Mr Casaubon and Sibyl Vane.

5

Towards Desegregating Syllabuses: Teaching American Literary Realism and Racial Uplift Fiction

Michele Birnbaum

'We must write these realities.'

Ida B. Wells-Barnett, *A Red Record* (1895)

Despite recent critical re-evaluations of American literary realism placing 'race' at the center of realist projects at the turn of the century, current institutional guides to teaching this field tend to reproduce the historical segregation of genre by race. The provocative notion that race in addition to – and, at times, in lieu of – literary form constitutes a generic feature is first and most forcefully advanced during the era of Jim Crow in the US; analyzing the critical legacy of this incorporation of 'race' (understood variably at the time as essentialist and/ or experiential) as an aesthetic component carries wide political implications for the teaching not only of American and African-American Studies, but also postcolonial, diasporic and circum-Atlantic literatures.

In 1896, William Dean Howells' influential review of Paul Laurence Dunbar's *Majors and Minors*, his introduction that same year to Dunbar's *Lyrics of the Lowly*, and his 1901 review of Charles Chesnutt's fiction in the *North American Review*, all argue for a kind of 'race literature.' He bases his argument upon the assumption that the peculiar 'race traits' of African-Americans – 'the simple, sensuous, joyous nature of [Dunbar's] race,' as he put it – were best represented in the vernacular and on explicitly racialized themes. Howells' assessment carried formidable weight; a respected author, influential editor, and the so-called 'Father of American Realism', his views have shaped not only the discourses about race and literary production at the turn of the century; they indirectly continue to inform the modern critical impulse to identify white authors of period as 'realist,' 'naturalist,' 'local color' or 'regionalist' in contrast with the contemporaneous work of African-American authors, which is most commonly marked (off) as 'racial uplift.' The effect is the perception that the respective

58

literatures operate within separate but equal genres or literary traditions. Simply put, Pauline E. Hopkins, Sutton E. Griggs, Frances Ellen Watkins Harper, Anna Julia Cooper, Charles Waddell Chesnutt, Alice Moore Dunbar Nelson, Booker T. Washington, W.E.B. DuBois, James Weldon Johnson, Charlotte Forten Grimke, Ida B. Wells-Barnett, and James D. Corrothers, for example, are not represented as intellectually mingling with their historical and literary contemporaries, Charlotte Perkins Gilman, Horatio Alger, Kate Chopin, George Washington Cable, William Dean Howells, Henry Adams, Edith Wharton, Henry James, Frank Norris, Stephen Crane, Mark Twain, Theodore Dreiser, among others.

The contemporary legacy of critical separation of writers by racial identification by African-American scholars is, of course, distinct from Howells' project, and understandable in part as a corrective to the long history of dismissive criticism of black-authored literature as merely derivative. Yet what one might call a racial anxiety of influence by both blacks and whites tends to disavow the complex ways both traditions at times mutually inform each other, and risks positing discrete, internally homogenous literary and ethnic norms. That said, African-American literature is too often subsumed under the aegis of 'American literature' without bringing pressure to bear on the designation itself or the terms of evaluation underwriting it. To date, neither of the two volumes on late nineteenth-century American writers in the *MLA Approaches to Teaching* series treat a writer of color. Nor, within those volumes, on Kate Chopin and Walt Whitman, respectively, do the collected essays link race studies to the pedagogical transformation of literary studies. Typically, if African-American writers or constructions of race are mentioned at all, it is in the service of historical background rather than as a tool for sustained inquiry, through teaching, into traditional assessments of American literary realism.

Informing this essay's argument – that teaching fiction broadly defined as 'racial uplift' enables a reappraisal of American literary realism – is the assumption that teaching is not simply the effluvia of research. In fact, we must consider the classroom as the source rather than aftermath of critical practice – particularly if we consider that syllabuses, in a sense, enact what is otherwise merely the speculative desegregation of American literary history. My emphasis here on a critique of the way traditional syllabuses perform literary history, therefore, is absolutely imperative to truly understanding the way Anglo- and African-American literatures might better work together in any course in what goes by 'American literary realism and naturalism' is at stake. I would like also to emphasize another point I hope this essay will make clear: *fin-de-siècle* African-American literature itself invites and enables this broader reassessment of realism, naturalism, literary criticism and literary history, but does not offer any simple textual roadmap. Thus, my discussion here does not seek to pre- or proscribe texts towards an ideal course, but rather addresses the pedagogical *pre*conditions for course construction that will, in turn, I hope, lead faculty to redesign their syllabuses. Drawing largely on African-American aesthetic paradigms which foreground the provisional and improvisational, therefore, this is a proposal not prescription; and so, as I will explain, what follows is not a blueprint but, rather, what might be called a 'blues heuristic.'

Many have reconceived American literary development in recognition of what Ralph Ellison saw as the theatrical racial 'set' for nation expression in which 'the whole of American life as drama [is] acted out upon the body of a Negro giant, who, lying trussed up like Gulliver, forms the stage and the scene upon which and within the action unfolds' (137). Ann Douglas, Shelley Fisher Fishkin, George Hutchinson, Eric Lott, Dana Nelson, Michael North, Toni Morrison, and many others have explored how Ellison's prone giant rises and haunts the white imagination. Further, some excellent works, including Kenneth Warren's *Black and White Strangers: Race and American Literary Realism* (1993), Nancy Bentley's *Ethnography of Manners* (1998), and the fine collection of essays, edited by Tom Quirk and Gary Scharnhorst, in *American Realism and the Canon* (1994) all offer cogent assessments of the representation of race and the contribution of writers of color to the understanding of American literary realism. Yet there seems to be no complementary Kuhnian shift in national discussions about *teaching* American literary history, at least not about the way the material particulars of courses – including syllabi, assignments, discussion questions – engage definitions of the relationship between Anglo- and African-American literary traditions and, more generally, between the ever-shifting lines between canonical and non-canonical works. Paul Lauter echoes the interests of many, and the goals of the publications of MELUS (*Multi-Ethnic Literature of the United States*), when he points out that 'a full literary history of this country requires both parallel and integrated accounts of differing literary traditions'('Literatures of America,' 12). Yet the ongoing reconstruction of American literary history in critical debates – from *Toward a New American Literary History* (1980) to *Reconstructing American Literary History* (1986) to *Criticism on the Color Line: Desegregating American Literary Studies* (1996) – inconsistently extends to its application in the classroom and to classroom agenda.

Jim Crowing literary history

Yet collections attempting to put in practice this comparative approach, beginning with one of the earliest, *Reconstructing American Literature: Courses, Syllabi, Issues* (1983), tend to cluster African-American writers under separate headings (such as 'The Question of Race' or 'Reconstruction and Reaction'). Faculty in this way can often unwittingly separate or even pre-empt discussions of 'race' through subject headings within course syllabuses and schedules. Anthologies struggle with precisely such issues, of course, and responses vary from the confusing array of headings in the *Heath* – which categorizes some texts by topic, some by genre, some by gender, and some by period – to the absence of headings offered by the *Norton*, which has largely retreated to similarly unrevealing periodization: 1865–1914; 1914–1945; 1945–present. Arguably, doing away with headings simply substitutes chronology for interpretation. On the other hand, placing Chopin, for instance, under a title like 'Self and Society' or Chesnutt under 'Race and Politics' can overdetermine the *kinds* of conversations students have about the literature as well as *when* conversations might occur: for instance, does one discuss issues concerning autonomy and social constraints under one, and racial identity and the politics of art under another? What terms of inquiry are excluded or implied by such questions? And are those terms mutually exclusive?: in order to discuss Chopin in terms of feminine selfhood, for instance, we must examine her work in terms of race as well (Birnbaum, 323); that holds true, in turn, for Chesnutt, who needs to be taught not only in terms of race but of gender. Of course one can and many do, but in practical terms, if faculty who have just spent two or more weeks on a text ask students to return again to it from another perspective, the implied 'progression' of the class may seem disrupted to both faculty and students. And if the reading schedule appears paused or redundant, so too can the sense of historical progression.

The Tuskegee machine and the production line of literary history

Yet these disruptions and pauses forced by a serious rethinking of what it means to introduce 'race fiction' to a syllabus are precisely the salubrious challenges to American literary realism we must examine more closely. My critique of chronology here is intimately tied to my advocacy for teaching racial uplift fiction as a challenge to American literary realism. Georgio Agamben argues that

> every concept of history is invariably accompanied by a certain experience of time which is implicit in it, conditions it, and thereby has to be elucidated. Similarly, every culture is first and foremost a particular experience of time ... the original task of a genuine revolution, therefore, is never merely to 'change the world,' but also – and above all – to 'change time' (*Infancy and History*, 91)

I would like to consider here more specifically how time, race, and teaching are connected. The tacit assumption that, over the course of the semester, we are also moving on a miniature scale through historical time incurs a kind of mimetic fallacy; it also, more subtly, mimics certain racial prerogatives. This particular realist investment in plotting time and in periodization is, arguably, historically 'white.' Martha Banta, in examining Frederick Winslow Taylor, termed the so-called Father of Scientific Management as early as 1898, characterizes the corporate and narrative drives towards systematization and chronological order at the turn of the century as the 'obsession of white men [and women] with white time and motion' (7). Certainly this sense of any 'real' order is disrupted in American literature by the post-World War I era, but the negotiation and breech of such temporal narrative and historical structures is also a strategy common to African-American letters during Taylor's age as well. For example, Booker T. Washington – in perhaps the ur-'uplift' text, *Up From Slavery* (1900) – self-consciously appropriates 'white time' in implementing the educational programme at his Tuskegee Institute, carefully clocking and regulating every moment of his and his students' days. *Up From Slavery* includes elaborate timetables, 'testaments' Washington calls them, which compartmentalize his students' daily movements into discrete units, and then orchestrates activity to the minute so that the student 'force is so organized and subdivided that the machinery of the school goes on day by day like clockwork' (258). Washington's scrupulousness in documenting his own and other Tuskegeens' activities served both his ambitions and the ends of his white business patrons, who included such industrialists as Andrew Carnegie and John D. Rockefeller. His control over black bodies through the manipulation of 'white time' allows him to transform ex-slaves suspected of working on 'colored people's time' into 'new era' employees, aligning corporeal training with corporate interests, and conflating 'racial uplift' with US fiscal advancement. As such, Washington manipulates time, recognizes and exploits the racialization of time, in what Houston Baker might read as another example of Washington's 'mastery of form' (15). Such moments in African-American literary history should remind us that challenges, including this challenge to a 'realist' mode of work or narrative, can operate in subtle ways. Washington's challenge with realism here is not necessarily to counter the reign of chronology of 'white time' and order, but to work with and through the cultural narratives of 'progress.' These putatively neutral narratives of temporality and advancement, as I have suggested, have racial and national implications – just as, I would argue, they do in the mundane plotting of a survey or seminar.

Thus, teaching Washington in this way may let us begin to both complicate a-racial and a-historical notions of the 'real' during this era as well as question the larger literary historical project into which fit the very notion of literary 'realism' or 'naturalism' as steps in the inexorable 'development' of a tradition. Teaching *Up From Slavery* (1900) with Horatio Alger's *Struggling Upward* (1898) – or for that matter W.E.B. Du Bois' multi-genre *Souls of Black Folk* (1903) with Henry Adams' *Education of Henry Adams* (1907), or Sutton E. Grigg's futuristic *Imperium in Imperio* (1899) with Charlotte Perkins Gilman's utopian *Herland* (1915), or, as I suggest earlier, Howells' preface with Dunbar's *Lyrics of the Lowly* (1896) or Howells' review of Charles Chesnutt's *The Wife of His Youth* (1899) with the novel – can teach us that what constitutes the cultural 'real' is specific to a particular time and place and sometimes even to a particular race. We can use that awareness, in turn, to examine the tacit and seemingly unimpeachable reality represented by surveys and seminars on realism or naturalism. Such syllabuses irresistibly appear to *advance*, like literary history, toward some teleological end. (I do not simply refer to surveys here, which explicitly lay claim to 'breadth,' but also to any course which uncritically characterizes literary production in terms of 'realism,' since such terms implicitly invoke a move from 'romance' on one side to 'modernism' on the other, or some similar sense of progression.) These expectations are often anticipated and codified by the structure and outline of syllabuses, and may make it difficult to approach literary texts from different perspectives.

My point is that *syllabuses script literary history for students – a script that is already and always racialized in some way*. That they function as a working shorthand, especially in survey courses, is not the problem; the problem is that they pose, sometimes by default, as the master text of Literary History. Certainly most critical and theoretical work resists the simplifications of literary history, and attempts to incorporate more nuanced and complex cultural dynamics suggested through the often-rich sources and secondary material faculty might use in classrooms, including the increasing wealth of documentary footage and educational websites about the period. Yet I would suggest that the materials of the course still often fall short, despite the best-laid theories. That which students most reference in keeping track of the day-to-day classwork – syllabuses, paper assignments, proposed essay topics and the like – still often amount to a de facto endorsement of the 'same ole same ole'. I would like here to go *beyond* the usual strategies we all devise to compensate for this tendency, which include questioning the status of syllabuses as 'representative' by foregrounding their contingent nature – either by explicitly addressing the issue in course descriptions or by juxtaposing excerpts from contrasting anthology introductions that narrate and justify distinct principles of text selection. To this end, we may also circulate early drafts of students' current syllabuses to emphasize the more local omissions and choices faculty must make, or teach surveys or period courses thematically rather than exclusively chronologically to disrupt any tidy sense of inexorable progression. All of these strategies are excellent; yet none, as useful as they are, quite get at the unspoken and unseen racialization of literary history.

The racial iconography of syllabuses

So how to jog students from this naïve sense that, if not the texts, then surely the literary history into which texts are placed, rises above time, place, race? Syllabuses unintentionally encourage what historians term 'presentism' – the privileging, and retroactive imposition, of contemporary value systems in interpretation of the 'past.' They graphically stage literary and cultural relationships across time and between texts, and frequently Anglo- and African-American texts are visually held at bay as surely as antiquated laws against miscegenation. What we might call the specular function of syllabuses extends also to the way the expanse of paper upon which the literary past – and the semester's future – is writ represents for students a compelling way to assess not simply literary history but their own achievement in the class: the last page of the syllabus and course schedule becomes the end-goal, the apotheosis of literary development *and* of student performance. Spatially, and almost irresistibly, it both projects the trajectory of literary history and represents the projected completion and fulfillment of the course. This conflation no doubt misrepresents many teachers' perception of both literary history and of a pedagogy based on process (in which the course distributes grading across the semester or quarter and across types of activities rather than simply build to a 'final' exam), and should remind us that course materials are not simply a transparent translation of faculty intent. Indeed, they function not just as texts but as tableaux, read and understood in iconographic terms perhaps not fully appreciated either by the students that experience them or the faculty that compose them.

In a sense, then, syllabuses are a material palimpsest of student expectations and faculty assumptions. By bringing into visual relief the possibilities and limitations of our critical assumptions, they offer an opportunity to re-examine the apparent discontinuity between research and teaching praxis. How, for example, can so many who wish to 'teach to transgress' (hooks, 1) find themselves simply teaching the status quo despite their best efforts? In particular, we must explore the way many of our critical enterprises permit us to reconsider canonical writers without necessarily examining the racial politics of genre or period. The disjuncture between scholarship and teaching is a function of renegotiating a body of institutionalized approaches to teaching embedded in pre-existing heuristic materials. We must anticipate the risk that one might either 'reinscribe a familiar canon, now seen from the perspective of the racial trope' (Showalter, 358) or else simply annex African-American literature without actually reconceiving the critical assumptions embodied in the very title of a survey or topics course which includes the term 'realism.' Thus the answer may lie not in simply teaching realism and naturalism with a racial thematic. More provocatively, I hope, I am suggesting rethinking realism through the alternate lens, through a model of memory, history, and imperative of representation – what Richard J. Powell terms a 'jazz paradigm (or 'blues aesthetic')' (24).

The Real Thing: a blues heuristic

In Henry James' story, 'The Real Thing' (1892), the narrator, an artist for commercial magazines, concludes that he has an 'innate preference for the represented subject over the real one: the defect of the real one was apt to be a lack of representation.' He likes things, he says, 'that appeared; then one was sure. Whether they *were* or not was a subordinate and almost always profitless question.' If literary realism, too, is a function of managing and marketing the 'represented subject' – or as Amy Kaplan, in another context, puts it, claiming 'one's own cultural authority both to possess and to dispense access to the real' (13) – then there is no point in bickering over what formal or cultural features constitute 'realism.' Thus, rather than view 'New Negro' authors as simply petitioning aspirants to 'Howell's America,' or 'uplift' work as merely a gloss on a realist canon, writing assignments and discussion suggestions need to help students understand African-American writers' narrative strategies as an arbitration with competing representations of reality. To do so means resituating American literary realism as a literary engagement with the post-Reconstruction crisis in race relations. It means not only examining the trope of race in the development of a realist aesthetic in the works of 'canonical' white writers such as Kate Chopin, Henry James, William Dean Howells, Stephen Crane, George Washington Cable, Mark Twain and others. It means not only offering text selection and juxtaposition illuminating the system of patronage and influence between black and white writers – between Howells and Dunbar, Chesnutt and Richard Gilder, between Du Bois and Joel Spingarn, and so on. We can craft syllabuses that enable the discussion of racial influence in both the white and black imaginations, and the influence of race in terms of literary production, following the recent work of George Hutchinson. Of course, teaching black and white writers in terms of one another implies an interest not only in the racial 'ghosts in the machine' (13) as Toni Morrison puts it, but in the flesh-and-blood writers who embodied and (out)lived those racial constructions. We need to apply the instructional guidance offered by the many recent reevaluations of the era suggested by critics like Kevin Gaines, who argues that racial uplift writers were not apologists but rather engaged in a vigorous 'cultural politics' (3), or by Claudia Tate, who reconsidered black women Reconstruction writers as producing 'domestic allegories of political desire.' These reconsiderations suggest that simply coupling the contemporaneous literary production of Anglo- and African-American writers makes sense only when we reshape our understanding of both literary corpora. For if, in the 1880s and 1890s, writers attempted to create a 'social whole' which makes visible, even as it controls, the 'explosive qualities' of 'alternative realities' (Kaplan, 11), then certainly Jim Crow is pivotal to American literary realism across the color line – and in the classroom.

To change the relationship between racial uplift and realist texts on a syllabus – that is, to be aware of how syllabuses can function iconographically to reinscribe or disrupt teaching and critical practices – is also to potentially change the way students and faculty *experience* syllabuses, how they live it out in 'real time,' as it were. As I have suggested, offering proscriptive or prescriptive syllabuses here would only map student response and faculty participation with the deceptively compelling clarity of all two-dimensional instruction, and I wish to resist that. Teaching racial uplift and realist literatures should not be simply a matter of adding, repositioning, or recombining texts; teaching the two should, to borrow from Amiri Baraka, 'force change; it should be change' ('Revolutionary Theatre,' 1899). Truly revolutionizing the commonplace survey involves putting in practice Michel Foucault's distinction between 'geneaology' and 'history.' Genealogy, he argues

> must record the singularity of events outside of any monotonous finality; it must seek them out in the most unpromising places, in what we tend to feel is without history – in sentiments, love, conscience, instincts; it must be sensitive to their recurrence, not in order to trace the gradual curve of their evolution, but to isolate the different scenes where they engaged in different roles...Genealogy does not oppose itself to history as the lofty and profound gaze of the philosopher might compare to the molelike perspective of the scholar; on the contrary, it rejects the metahistorical deployment of ideal significations and indefinite teleologies. It opposes itself to the search for 'origins' (139–49).

Certainly, many literary 'events' dramatize precisely those values and experiences putatively transcendent of history – such as sentiment, instinct and so on – and yet, unless our surveys are nothing more than a 'great minds' series, our courses need to understand culture and text as functions of one another. In that sense, we seek to recommit texts to history: but how to historicize without giving into the 'search for 'origins' or, conversely, to avoid being 'transported by a voiceless obstinacy toward a millenial ending' (Foucault, 154). How to disrupt the sense that literary history is cumulative, for even if we teach a survey 'backwards' – present to past, one risks simply looking for 'causes' and direct lines of influence; and at any rate, it does little to correct the sense of linear time upon which the days and weeks of the class unfold like Dorothy's yellow-brick road. And certainly there are many extraliterary imperatives – such as grades – driving students to mistakenly equate the course's end with the *denouement* of literary history. Both institutional constraints and daily momentum, then, make it difficult for learning to spring the traps of both literary history and semester's close.

Yet history, argues Harry J. Elam, Jr., 'functions not as a static source of objective truth but as a constructed and constructive agent that must be mediated, negotiated, interrogated' (3). As Foucault notes, what he calls Nietzsche's 'effective history' marks genealogical moments and resists grand evolutionary trends, monumental ends, static truths. Teaching *Up From Slavery*, or almost any

'New Negro' literature from the era, can function as such a 'moment,' as I have suggested, which amidst other such moments can enable mediations, negotiations, interrogations of what constitutes an objective 'real' or 'natural.' And they simultaneously challenge, as well, traditional classroom representations of 'realism' and 'naturalism' in literary history. Washington's riff on 'c.p. time,' Charles Chesnutt's incorporation of 'conjuring' in 'The Goophered Grapevine,' DuBois' use of antebellum spirituals as epigraphs in *Souls of Black Folk*, Frances E.W. Harper's reconstruction of the past to reconstitute the present in *Iola Leroy* all expand notions of the real to include otherworldly 'ha'ants,' black oral culture, and a reflexive cultural memory. All these texts testify to a sense of literary genealogy in which time does not advance but at times offers recurrent refrains, a rhythmic structure that nevertheless does not provide easy thematic or formal resolution. In such moments, the present is resonant with sounds from the past rather than simply one more step towards a mute future. Rather than select preordained 'major' texts and authors – which reproduce traditional history's 'contemplation of distances and heights: the noblest periods, the highest forms, the most abstract ideas, the purest individualities' (Foucault, 155) – surveys therefore resist their usual claims to representative coverage *across time*. They might instead try to vertically deepen, multiply, and specify the ways in which texts, both contemporaneous and contemporary, multiply engage each other *in time* and *through time*. The self-conscious attempt to disrupt linearity and its implied tempo represents a historically African-American critique of History as 'not merely a chronicle of shifts but a series of sites in which one historical narrative has silenced others,' and so literary history and its 'realist' or 'naturalist' movements might better be represented through a 'collagist' approach, through a 'conscious anachronism' based on the improvisational styles of blues and jazz (Nadel, 4). To do so allows for historical specificity and attention to literary change; yet, folding time back on itself as a kind of Mobius strip also makes it possible for students to see the ways texts are complexly connected both forward and backward in time to each other.

Such clustering also affords a *practical* application of a pedagogical strategy whose theoretical counterpart has long been most forcefully and persuasively advanced by black feminist critics. As Hortense Spillers argues, we must not 'accede to the simplifications and mystifications of a strictly historiographical time line.' Abandoning linearity offers 'the greatest freedom of discourse to black people, to black women as critics, teachers, writers, and thinkers' (295). This discursive freedom is illuminating for students, as well. For example, Deborah McDowell points out that Joann Braxton, in a critique of traditional scholarship's 'linear logic, its dependence on binary oppositions, and its preoccupation with primacy, authorship, textual unity, completion and length,' calls for 'alternatives and supplements to the reflexive questions: "Is it first?" "Is it major?" "Is it central?" "Does it conform to established criteria?"' (55).

I would not say that clustering in this way is simply a version of Gerald Graff's 'teaching the conflicts' – which still presumes faculty stage those conflicts like puppeteers from on high – because such clustering can change the terms of the conflicts altogether. In lieu of the linear, syllabuses which present this alternative continuum of texts and time holds much greater potential for students, as Ira Shor puts it in *Critical Teaching and Everyday Life*, to 'intervene in the making of history' (48). Shor draws on Paulo Freire's statement that a liberatory pedagogy is that in which 'the learner assumes the role of knowing subject with the educator' (Friere, 29). I should say that I am not embracing Shor's Marxist commitment to stripping 'false consciousness,' beneath which lie 'resources... waiting for a reconstructed life' (87), since reconstruction of Truth represents the kind of traditional literary historical project that I suggest requires reassessment. My point is that 'liberation' is not simply a matter of faculty disingenuously juxtaposing texts for students as though syllabi were not a function of the professor's choices, as if she or he were not a critical matrix governing students' interpretations through the text selection, assignment cues, and so on. Neither the so-called 'teacherless' environment, in which faculty attempt to disavow their institutional role in the classroom as evaluator, nor even 'discussion-based' models of teaching necessarily ensure that students are participants in, rather than simply recipients of, 'knowledge' and thus become Friere's knowing subjects. Disrupting the survey's compulsive linearity will not raze all interpretive paradigms, assuming that were possible; nor does it guarantee that teachers will instead generate literary genealogies or integrate the pedagogies of African-American scholars which challenge the segregation of literary study. Yet a 'blues heuristic' might require faculty and students alike to collaboratively create more complex and emerging narratives to make better sense of the challenges different literary traditions pose to each other, and *to make good* on that sense in the classroom. I would argue that with this heuristic we have a better chance of 'making good' in practical and substantive ways because it would force change in our concrete teaching practices – the usual, orderly timetables, daily routines, and climactic exams corresponding to a trajectory of literary development that pattern complacent educational experiences for us. In this way, pragmatically changing the racialized 'space–time' of courses may move us towards desegregating racial uplift from realist and naturalist works.

Works cited

Agamben, Giorgio. *Infancy and History: Essays on the Destruction of Experience*, trans. Liz Heron (London: Verso, 1993).

Awkward, Michael. 'Negotiations of Power: White Critics, Black Texts, and the Self-Referential Impulse,' *American Literary History* 2 (1989): 121–34.

Banta, Martha. *Taylored Lives: Narrative Productions in the Age of Taylor, Veblen, and Ford* (Chicago: University of Chicago Press, 1993).

Baker, Houston A., Jr. *Modernism and the Harlem Renaissance* (Chicago: University of Chicago Press, 1987).

Baraka, Amiri. 'Revolutionary Theatre' (1969) in *Norton Anthology of African American Literature*, general editors Henry Louis Gates, Jr. and Nellie Y. McKay (New York: W.W. Norton & Co., 1997), pp. 1899–901.

Baym, Nina. (ed.). *The Norton Anthology of American Literature, Vol. Two*, 5th edn (New York: W.W. Norton & Co., 1998).

Bentley, Nancy. *The Ethnography of Manners: Hawthorne, James, Wharton* (Cambridge: Cambridge University Press, 1995).

Bercovitch, Sacran (ed.). *Reconstructing American Literary History*, Harvard English Studies 13 (Cambridge, MA: Harvard University Press, 1986).

Birnbaum, Michele. 'Alien Hands: Chopin and the Colonization of Race,' *American Literature* 66 (June 1994): 301–23.

Budd, Louis J. *Toward a New American Literary History: Essays in Honor of* Arlin Turner (Durham, NC: Duke University Press, 1980).

Clifford, James. *The Predicament of Culture: Twentieth-Century Ethnography, Literature, and Art* (Cambridge: Cambridge University Press, 1998).

Elam, Harry J., Jr. 'The Dialectics of August Wilson's *Piano Lesson,' Theatre Journal* 52 (October 2000): 361–79.

Ellison, Ralph. 'Twentieth-Century Fiction and the Black Mask of Humanity,' in *Within the Circle: an Anthology of African American Criticism from the Harlem Renaissance to the Present*, edited by Angelyn Mitchell (Durham: Duke University Press, 1994) (originally published in 1953).

Foucault, Michel. 'Nietzsche, Geneaology, History,' in *Language, Counter-Memory, Practice: Selected Essays and Interviews*. edited by Donald F. Bouchard. (Ithaca: Cornell University Press, 1980), pp. 139–40.

Friere, Paulo. *Cultural Action for Freedom* (Baltimore: Penguin, 1975).

Gaines, Kevin K. *Uplifting the Race: Black Leadership, Politics, and Culture in the Twentieth Century* (Chapel Hill: University of North Carolina Press, 1996).

hooks, bell. *Teaching to Transgress: Education as the Practice of Freedom* (New York: Routledge, 1994).

Howells, William Dean. Review of Paul Laurence Dunbar's *Majors and Minors,* 'Life and Letters,' *Harper's Weekly* (27 June 1896); W.D. Howells, 'Introduction,' Paul Laurence Dunbar, *Lyrics of the Lowly* (December 1896); W.D. Howells, Review of Charles Chesnutt's fiction, 'A Psychological Counter-Current in Fiction,' *North American Review* 173 (December 1901): 882.

Hutchinson, George. *The Harlem Renaissance in Black and White* (Cambridge, MA: Harvard University Press, 1995).

James, Henry. 'The Real Thing,' *Black and White* (April 16, 1892); reprinted in *The Real Thing and Other Tales* (1893); reprinted in vol. 18 (1901) of the New York Edition.

Kaplan, Amy. *The Social Construction of American Realism* (Chicago: University of Chicago Press, 1989).

Lauter, Paul (ed.). *The Heath Anthology of American Literature, Vol. Two*, 2nd edn (Lexington: D.C. Heath and Co., 1994).

Lauter, Paul 'The Literatures of America: a Comparative Discipline' in A. La Vonne Brown and Jerry W. Ward (eds), *Redefining American Literary History* (New York: MLA, 1990), pp. 12–26.

Lauter, Paul (ed.). *Reconstructing American Literature: Courses, Syllabi, History*, (New York: Feminist Press, 1983).

McDowell, Deborah E. 'Boundaries: Or Distant Relations and Close Kin', in Houston A. Bakes Jr. and Patricia Redmond (eds), *Afro-American Literary Study in the 1990s*. (Chicago: University of Chicago Press, 1989), pp. 55–9.

Michaels, Walter Benn. *Our America: Nativism, Modernism, and Pluralism* (Durham: Duke University Press, 1995).

Morrison, Toni. 'Unspeakable Things Unspoken: the Afro-American Presence in American Literature,' *Michigan Quarterly Review* 28 (1989): 13–26.

Nadel, Alan. 'Introduction,' in *May All Your Fences Have Gates: Essays on the Drama of August Wilson* (Iowa City: University of Iowa Press, 1994).

Powell, Richard J. 'Re/Birth of a Nation,' in Richard J. Powell et al. (eds), *Rhapsodies in Black: Art of The Harlem Renaissance* (Berkeley: University of California Press, 1997), pp. 16–33.

Quirk, Tom and Gary Scharnhorst. *American Realism and the Canon* (New York: University of Delaware Press, 1994).

Shor, Ira. 'Interferences to Critical Thought: Consciousness in School and Daily Life,' in *Critical Teaching and Everyday Life* (Boston: South End Press, 1980), pp. 48–56.

Spillers, Hortense. 'A Hateful Passion, A Lost Love,' *Feminist Studies* 9 (1983): 295.

Showalter, Elaine. 'A Criticism of Our Own' in Ralph Cohen (ed.), *The Future of Literary Theory* (New York: Routledge, 1989).

Tate, Claudia. *Domestic Allegories of Political Desire: the Black Heroine's Text at the Turn of the Century* (New York: Oxford University Press, 1992).

Warren, Kenneth W. *Black and White Strangers: Race and American Literary Realism* (Chicago: University of Chicago Press, 1993).

Washington, Booker T. *Up From Slavery* (serialized in 'The Outlook' in 1900; first published in book form in 1900) (New York: Carol Publishing, 1989).

Wonham, Henry B. (ed.). *Criticism on the Color Line: Desegregating American Literary Studies* (New York: Routledge, 1996).

6
Teaching Literature and Ethics: the Particular and the General

Suzy Anger

In any interdisciplinary course, conceptualizing the materials offers a number of challenges to both teacher and students. This chapter describes a seminar in literature and ethics, which brings together the methods of literary study with those of what to most students is a wholly new discipline – philosophy – with its own approaches and vocabulary. As it turns out, the chief difficulty as well as the chief benefit of the course is that it asks students to find a way to move between the general and the particular, between idea and narrative.

The seminar is taught at a mid-sized state university with a varied student population, which ranges from unprepared students to very strong students at the top. Seminar enrollment is limited to 15 students, all of whom are senior English undergraduates or early graduate students. The seminar is intended to be a capstone course for seniors, one that we hope will push them to new levels of complexity in their approaches to literary interpretation. It is discussion-centered, and each student is responsible for running class once in the semester. We read novels, short narratives, and essays and talk about the ways in which literature might be seen to be ethical, considering both how literary works in the past approached those issues and how we might take them up in different ways today.

Recently, as we've seen, ethical approaches to the study of literature have made a comeback (seen, for instance, in the work of Martha Nussbaum, Wayne Booth and Geoffrey Harpham) after having been dismissed as outmoded by many literary critics for decades. In the mid-nineteenth century, both writers and readers tended to regard literature as ethical. Given that many Victorians took the moral nature of a literary work as a given, their literature is a good place for a class to begin discussions of the relationship between narrative and ethics, and of the resurgence of ethical criticism. The texts for the course are for the most part Victorian, though the final readings – short Holocaust narratives written primarily by survivors – move out of the period. I end the course with this abrupt move into the twentieth century for a couple of reasons. First, the general development we trace in the nineteenth century is from a widespread agreement about the ethical force of literature in the earlier Victorian texts to a skepticism about long-standing moral views and challenges to the idea that there is any connection between ethics and aesthetics in the late Victorians. The Holocaust narratives at once continue this development and give us a point of view from which to question the whole Victorian project. Second, in recent critical discussion the Holocaust has presented what seem to be intransigent problems about the nature of ethics and narrative representation. Do the narratives, I want to ask (among other things), simply demonstrate the bankruptcy of the high Victorian ethical project, or is there a way to continue to regard them as doing valuable ethical work?

In describing what happened in the seminar, rather than focusing on one central issue, I will comment on both a number of problems that arise in bringing together these two disciplines and on those aspects of the course that are most valuable for students. Many of these remarks should be relevant to any interdisciplinary course, or, for that matter, any course that attempts to move between ideas and literary texts.

Because the course brought together two disciplines, we had multiple subjects to attend to, which can be broken into the following six rough divisions:

1. What is ethics? Here we discussed questions such as, how should one live one's life? What makes an action right or wrong? How does one balance self-interest with concern for others? Under what conditions are we morally responsible and why? How is ethical understanding influenced by cultural assumptions? by gender? Are moral claims universal, absolute, pluralistic, or relative? How can one mediate between competing ethical positions?
2. In what ways does literature represent ethical issues or pose moral questions? Does it do this through content: for instance, through the events a narrative recounts or through a narrator's commentary? Through transmission of values? Do the moral possibilities reside in literature's ability to give a reader access to other minds, cultures, or viewpoints?
3. What is ethical criticism? Can it direct us to read literature in new ways? Does it involve making moral judgments about the characters and events in a story? Is it concerned with the ethical effects of reading a book? (Can reading a literary text change a reader?) Is ethical criticism the same as or closely related to cultural, ideological, or political criticism? Do contemporary theoretical approaches to literature attend sufficiently to ethical questions? Is *all* criticism necessarily ethical in some way? Our attempts to define ethical criticism also led to the discussion of related topics, such as the relationship between moral criticism and problems of censorship.

4. What is the cultural and historical context of the Victorian texts? In this aspect, the course is like any period-based class in which students need to gain a general knowledge of the period in which the works were written.
5. What more specific background is needed to understand the particular ethical debates of the Victorian period?
6. How do we read and interpret narrative? Students had more experience with this aspect of the course than with any of the above subjects, but, as other chapters in this book demonstrate, further attention to strategies of literary interpretation is always needed.

Although many of these ideas and questions were touched upon in our discussions early in the semester, others emerged as we worked through the texts over the course of the semester; most we returned to repeatedly.

In designing the course, I intentionally chose novels that themselves foreground moral issues (although it would be possible to ask many of the same questions of texts that were not so explicitly conscious of ethical debate). Accordingly, we considered the moral views the Victorian narratives explicitly set forth (though we also asked if the novels sometimes complicated those professed views). We needed, then, to learn a bit about Jeremy Bentham's Utilitarianism and read some of John Stuart Mill's and Thomas Carlyle's work to understand Dickens's critique of Utilitarianism (as well as his simplification of the issues) in *Hard Times*. Similarly, we discussed evolutionary theory as it was applied to social and ethical issues in the period and read Thomas Huxley's 'Evolution and Ethics' as background to the ethical debates in H.G. Wells's *Island of Doctor Moreau*. We moved in the early part of the course from the less troubled ethical views of Dickens in his anti-Utilitarian novel to George Eliot's still optimistic, if more complex ethics of sympathy in *Middlemarch*, also expressed in this well-known excerpt from one of her letters:

> If art does not enlarge men's sympathies, it does nothing morally. I have had heart-cutting experience that *opinions* are a poor cement between human souls; and the only effect I ardently long to produce by my writings is that those who read them should be better able to *imagine* and to *feel* the pains and joys of those who differ from themselves in everything but the broad fact of being struggling, erring, human creatures. (*George Eliot Letters*, July 5, 1859)

Later in the semester, we looked at Thomas Hardy's challenges to conventional ethics in *Tess of the d'Urbervilles* and then turned to Wilde's claim, representative of one pole of the Victorian trajectory, that 'there is no such thing as a moral or immoral book. Books are well written or badly written. That is all' (Oscar Wilde, 'Preface' to *The Picture of Dorian Gray*).

One of the main problems that an interdisciplinary course poses when taught by a single instructor is that of expertise. I'm not a philosopher and it is important that students be made aware that the course can give them no more than a rudimentary overview of moral philosophy (I encourage them to take a class in ethics at some later stage in their studies). They would gain, I emphasized, only a general and fairly unnuanced introduction to philosophical approaches to moral issues in the seminar. Early in the semester we discussed metaethical questions: Can there be universal moral values? Is morality objective or subjective, relative or absolute? We also talked about major theories of ethics (Utilitarianism, deontology, egoism). My aim in introducing these philosophical topics is to give students a conceptual framework and a vocabulary to use as they think about moral questions in relation to narrative. This introduction will also help students make their own, usually not fully articulated ethical views more explicit. (A very useful text for these purposes is Peter Singer's *Companion to Ethics*, listed in the Appendix.) Additionally, the critical work in literature and philosophy we read (such as the works by Nussbaum and Booth listed at the end of the chapter) along with some of the novels assume that knowledge in their readers.

Most students find the philosophy very hard to read. This inevitably leads to questions about its value, questions that move out to broader questions about the value of such an interdisciplinary course: why is it useful to bring together two disciplines? Are the methods and assumptions of one discipline preferable to those of the other? Because of the long-standing argument between philosophy and literature, and the frequent recent antagonism between the two fields, these questions required a good deal of attention – of course, some consideration of recent theoretical challenges to disciplinary boundaries would be called for, in any case. At the start of the semester, I put a couple of hypotheses on the table for the class to think about as we began to read. The first was a broad rationale for such a course. I suggested that the analytical nature of ethical inquiry in philosophy, its emphasis on abstractions, generalities, and categories, can be useful for interpreting narrative. The course asks if philosophical approaches can give us conceptual schemes and vocabulary that allow us to make more nuanced claims and useful discriminations about ethics as they are represented in the literary narrative than would our vague intuitions.

The other starting point for the class was a view in some ways complementary to, in others in tension with, the above claim. This second hypothesis is presented in the form of a couple of related questions, which are essentially paraphrases of philosopher Martha Nussbaum's assertions in *Love's Knowledge*: are there some ethical truths that can only be expressed in the form of narrative? Does literature provide us with a unique and special means of investigating ethical questions because it can present complex and precise moral dilemmas, such as one faces in real life, as opposed to the abstract thought experiments that philosophy offers?

Together, the starting assumptions ask whether in some way moving between literature and philosophy enriches ethical inquiry, if the two disciplines can in fact complement one another. For if narratives suggest that morality is not always expressible in the generalities and abstract theories of philosophy, they may also have a tendency to stop at the representation of the contingencies of particular events and situations. On the other hand, the abstractions of philosophy may not do justice to the complexity of moral experience. The claims are, then, two sides of one coin and, as it happened, the relationship between the general and the particular, the abstract and the concrete, idea and narrative, ethics and aesthetics, became a central focus of the seminar on a number of levels.

Since the students were mostly English majors and had little or no experience with the discipline of philosophy, they tended immediately to accept the idea that philosophical analysis is too abstract, too black and white, too narrow, too concerned with picayune distinctions and does not allow for an understanding of the complexities of lived experience, as does a literary work. Students often express this as a preference for what they refer to as 'showing' over 'telling.' Yet despite the putative commitment to this view, it became apparent early on that most of the students let the theory, the general, take over in their analysis of the literary texts. Their early response writing and essays made clear that once exposed to the philosophy, most allowed it dominate their analysis. The ideas began to drive the interpretation (a common problem in any idea- or theory-based course).

Early in the semester, students asked what they should be reading for, pointing out that they were noticing and marking different things in the novels than they would have if they had been reading outside of the parameters of this class. While, on the one hand, I was happy that they recognized that the questions we ask always shape our reading of a text, on the other hand, I also wanted them to avoid becoming schematic, narrowing their reading to the underlining of any mention of the word 'ethics' or 'moral' in the text. I hoped that they would see that the philosophical questions we posed could illuminate the texts in multiple ways and that it was not just a matter of seeking out key terms or trying to abstract an author's philosophical position. The challenge, then, was to bring students back to their commitment to narrative and the particular, to see if they could balance the philosophy with a real attention to the specifics and particularities of the narratives. What is the relationship between the general and the specific both in ethical inquiry and in analyzing literary texts, we then started to ask, and is it possible to do justice to the methods of both disciplines?

From my point of view, it took about half the semester for the course to come together fully. For the first half of the course, students struggled to form a new context as they were exposed to the methods and claims of an unfamiliar discipline, to new questions, strategies, and materials. By mid-semester, however, the juxtaposition of various texts – novels, Victorian philosophy, introductory works in contemporary moral philosophy, and essays on ethics and literature – provided that new context, and the students began to address the issues with which the course was concerned. After that point, the quality of student observations was excellent, and – something that happens too rarely in classes – they began to talk to each other and to argue among themselves.

One reason that the class worked, I discovered, is that students felt there was a lot at stake in reading texts with ethical questions in mind. Early discussions revealed that all of the students assumed that narrative – or at least 'great' literature – had something to do with ethics, in any case. That literature teaches one how to live was a widespread (usually unexamined) assumption and often a central justification for becoming an English major. The questions that the course asked, then, tapped into ideas that most of the students were working with in not fully articulated ways, and our investigation thus helped them make those assumptions more explicit, while also complicating them in useful ways.

Another valuable aspect of the course was connected to an issue that I initially imagined might pose a problem. We were frequently asking very large and difficult questions – questions about the nature of morality or about how one ought to live one's life – philosophical questions that have been the subject of much debate and about which people hold very different views. I emphasized that we could hope to become somewhat clearer on our own views, but would have to give up the idea that we could come to know the one right answer. Interestingly, this was the first time that I have been able to fully convince a class of the impossibility of ultimate answers, which students, as we know, often want. They imagine that we can tell them what the true meaning of, say, 'Sailing to Byzantium,' is, even when we say we can't. But their own experience had already shown them that these big questions weren't going to receive conclusive answers, and thus they quickly accepted the idea that it was a matter of deciding where they would position themselves in the debates. Further, the course provided enough factual material, in the Victorian background and the philosophical terminology, both to provide a common ground for our discussion and to satisfy those students who desired to learn a body of information.

Many of the central questions in literary theory were also opened up by our reflection about moral philosophy and literature. As we asked ethical questions about texts, crucial problems of reading and interpretation emerged. Is ethical criticism, for instance, a matter of a reader's attitude toward the text? Ought we to treat a text with a certain attitude of respect? (Or, more generally, where is the locus of meaning?) Does aesthetical value matter to ethical value? Are great literary works more important for ethical interrogation than popular ones, as one student strongly believed? (Or, in more general terms, what is the canon, how do we evaluate literary works, and what constitutes literary value?) Having also taught courses in literary theory, I found it useful to discuss these sorts of abstract issues in a narrower setting and one that seemed more relevant to students than a general course in literary theory often does (many undergraduate students are not yet ready to see why theory should matter).

Similarly, the student-led discussions were productive in part because students approached the texts in markedly different ways, which allowed the class to begin to identify the theoretical and interpretive assumptions driving particular readings. One student, for example, began a discussion with an examination of some contemporary documents on the state of the lower classes in Victorian England. She wanted to ask whether these non-fiction accounts had a greater ethical impact on a reader than did a novel. But at the same time, she hoped to provide a historical context that she argued was crucial for reading a Victorian novel. Another student instead took a reader-response approach, asking the class to talk about its previous experience with the particular author, with Victorian novels in general, and with philosophical discourse. Still another student-led discussion involved the presentation of some of Eliot's non-fiction statements from letters and notebooks, thus setting the framework for a biographical and intentionalist interpretation of the novel.

Of course, saying that the interdisciplinary context of the course worked well does not mean that students always do what you hope they will do. As any teacher knows, they don't. To take one example, I focused in class discussions on Eliot's ethics of sympathy and her views on the impossibility of a general moral law. Most students, however, were more interested in talking about whether Will was a good choice for Dorothea. Yet starting with the students' ways of categorizing characters turned out to be useful. After all, the impulse of less advanced students is to talk about character and to make judgments that are in some sense ethical: 'I like him.' 'She isn't nice.' 'I wouldn't want to know her.' One way to get at the more complex questions is to start where the students are and push them on those assumptions, asking them questions such as whether their judgments seem to be those that the novel sanctions and, if not, why.

Another significant difference between the way that I wanted to approach a text and what really happened in the class emerged when we began to read the Holocaust narratives. Many of the undergraduates knew very little about the Holocaust. Hence, when we turned to the narratives, they were not interested in asking questions about the relationship between the text and ethical questions or even about the stories as narrative. Instead they wanted to talk about what had happened, and they brought up large questions about motive and action: why wasn't there more resistance by the Jews? Why hadn't more non-Jews helped? How could people act so immorally? Initially, I was unhappy with this approach; I wanted to keep our sights on the narratives as literary texts and on the ethical issues we could ask about those texts. Student papers and response writing convinced me, however, that I was wrong about this. First, it was very valuable that students learn about the Holocaust. Second, it was the students with the least knowledge of the Holocaust that returned with the greatest engagement to write about the ethical issues related to the narratives in their final papers, precisely because discussions of the events of the Holocaust had had such a strong impact on them.

The sudden shift from the Victorian period to Holocaust narratives also brought us back to the conflict between the general and the particular in useful ways. When confronted with the narratives, students found it much more difficult to be schematic, to resort to the sorts of flattening ethical interpretation that, say, Dickens' novel had led some to. They acknowledged that they did not know what to say in the face of the stories. While students were aware that the narratives both addressed and gave rise to moral questions, they also argued that the texts could not be treated as concrete answers to philosophical questions, or made into fodder for any theory. Whatever the ethical content might be, it was outstripped by the details of the narratives. Returning to the ethical questions that had concerned us throughout our discussion of the Victorians, we found that we could not confidently answer them or say anything simple about the narratives. We ended the course, then, with problems rather than solutions, with a fuller recognition of the difficulties of these questions about ethics, narrative and representation.

Bibliography

Selected readings in ethics and literature

Adamson, Jane, Richard Freadman, and David Parker (eds). *Renegotiating Ethics in Literature, Philosophy, and Theory* (Cambridge: Cambridge University Press, 1988).
Booth, Wayne. *The Company We Keep: An Ethics of Fiction* (Berkeley: University of California Press, 1988).
Bruns, Gerald L. *Tragic Thoughts at the End of Philosophy: Language, Literature, and Ethical Theory* (Evanston: Northwestern University Press, 1999).
Gibson, Andrew. *Postmodernity, Ethics, and the Novel* (New York: Routledge, 1999).
Goldberg, S.L. *Agents and Lives: Moral Thinking in Literature* (New York: Cambridge University Press, 1993).
Harpham, Geoffrey Galt. *Getting it Right: Language, Literature, and Ethics* (Chicago: University of Chicago Press, 1992).
McGinn, Colin. *Ethics, Evil, and Fiction* (Oxford: Oxford University Press, 1997).

Miller, J. Hillis. *The Ethics of Reading: Kant, de Man, Eliot, Trollope, James, and Benjamin* (New York: Columbia University Press, 1987).

Newton, Adam Zachary. *Narrative Ethics* (Cambridge: Cambridge University Press, 1995).

Nussbaum, Martha Craven. *Love's Knowledge: Essays on Philosophy and Literature* (New York: Oxford University Press, 1995).

Parker, David. *Ethics, Theory and the Novel* (New York: Cambridge University Press, 1994).

Phillips, D.Z. *Philosophy's Cool Place* (Ithaca, Cornell University Press, 1999).

Siebers, Tobin. *The Ethics of Criticism* (Ithaca: Cornell University Press, 1988).

Siebers, Tobin. *Morals and Stories* (New York: Columbia University Press, 1992).

General reading

Haight, Gordon (ed.). *The George Eliot Letters*, 7 vols (New Haven: Yale University Press, 1954–55).

Singer, Peter (ed.). *A Companion to Ethics* (Oxford: Blackwell, 1991).

Wilde, Oscar. *The Picture of Dorian Gray* (New York: Penguin, 1999).

7

Taking Lyrics Literally: Teaching Poetry in a Prose Culture

Charles Altieri

Having spent two fruitless weeks attempting to write an essay offering practical advice on how to teach lyric poetry, I had to face the perhaps bizarre truth that I feel much less hollow elaborating theoretical projections about how to direct one's teaching than I do pretending to offer practical wisdom. In this case my hollowness may in fact have been as close as I could come to wisdom. For it suggests that I have yet to find a current theoretical approach to values capable of providing an adequate framework for the practical tasks involved in teaching lyric poetry. But in my view it will not suffice to rely on sharing moderately successful teaching strategies without formulating the ends they serve or the visions of poetry that define the qualities they foreground. So here I will try to elaborate a way of thinking about the lyric that can cogently draw connections between how we might best structure conversation about particular poems and how we might describe the basic values lyrics make available or reinforce for cultural life.

For me all the ladders start with the New Criticism. That movement, in its various manifestations, had the cumulative effect of showing how a wide range of desires might be satisfied by focusing on how poems work before making claims about what they might be saying, or how they might be evading uncomfortable realities. But at the same time the actual theories proposed to defend those practices and to make claims for the overall importance of close reading to cultural life were manifestly problematic. The most obvious reason for the eventual failure of New Critical theory was that it had come to prefer text to act (or Brooks to Burke) so that it could not adequately open itself to the range of human interests that generate efforts at lyric expression. In order to develop a language of values appropriate for this hypostasizing of texts as the locus of value claims, the theorists were forced to a language of 'organic form' that simply did not have the power to mediate sufficiently between what writers can produce and what cultures need. Instead the academic culture shaped by New Criticism bought into what Denis Donoghue calls an 'antithetical' model of values in which they based the importance of literary experience on its ability to carry 'non-discursive truths' that opposed science's 'mere' ability to develop and test discursive hypotheses.[1] This commitment led critics to make claims about special 'knowledge' from literary experience that had much more shrillness than they did substance. Seeking knowledge led to thematic criticism, however eloquent the rhetoric of poetry as experience, and it proved impossible to correlate the allegory necessary for a knowledge claim with the performative energies within the text that made it seem worth heeding in the first place. Ironically, readers got so frustrated with thematic readings providing nothing workable as knowledge that they gravitated toward an idealized social criticism, where one actually could make knowledge claims about texts, if only in terms of their relationships to contexts.

This historicist inversion of New Critical projections about literary knowledge establishes the basic challenge faced by contemporary defenses of poetry. We still have to claim that extended experience of the lyric develops powers and modes of attention that are sharply at odds with many of the epistemic priorities driving Enlightenment modernity. Yet we cannot return to the old dichotomy between scientific truth and non-discursive truth. Therefore, I propose that we treat the lyric as resisting the very idea that 'truth' is a workable ideal for literary productions. This is not to say that we do not learn many things from lyric texts. It is to say that we are likely to run into trouble if we treat this learning in terms of any discourse about 'truth' or knowledge that we inherit from the Enlightenment.[2] Far better to begin at the opposite pole. Perhaps lyric is important for our culture because it invites us to explore values that are opposed to the entire psychological apparatus set in place by Enlightenment idealizations about knowledge and judgment in accord with stateable criteria.

The most succinct way to define what I mean by psychologies put in place by Enlightenment epistemic ideals is to turn to a piece of wisdom passed on to me by a humanist dean at UC Berkeley. She told me that being a dean meant constantly hearing the sentence 'studies have shown,' then bracing oneself for the disguised ideological content that follows. I will call the culture that culminates in the clause 'studies have shown' the pure product of epistemically oriented Enlightenment values.[3] An adequate theory of the lyric will have to challenge the specific general psychological tendencies reinforced by this cultural orientation. This orientation has us envision a teleology in which humans' basic goal is to know themselves. The phrase is ancient, but its force for modernity is to lead us to envision maturity as the ability to represent our own interests to ourselves, to understand the psychology involved in much the same way that we understand the interrelations of molecules, and to be able to take responsibility for ourselves because we submit these interests to public criteria for assessment. Humanists are likely to shift the criteria, to talk about 'human well-being' rather than about 'utility.' But how we represent our pursuit of well-being will be fundamentally similar to how we pursue experiments.[4]

I don't think it is an accident that phrases like 'human well-being' make me cover my pocket. If literary experience does nothing else, it makes us suspicious of generalized teleologies for the psyche, especially those which profess such a projected compatibility with calm reasoning. But I don't want to reject claims about values simply because I can't share the criterial model by which epistemic culture organizes the discussion of values. So now I need another, non-epistemic stance for theorizing about poetry, so that we then can see how poetry ultimately provides an alternative way of addressing philosophical discourse about value. In order to pursue these goals I will have to engage four basic concerns not sufficiently foregrounded when we either turn to the languages of politicized criticism or turn defensively back to academic versions of the New Critics' academicizing of Modernism. First, theory has to show why responding to these particular words in this particular order makes present for the imagination certain qualities of experience that have the power to modify how psyches are disposed toward a world beyond the text. Second, it is important to appreciate how the articulateness of these words in this order becomes a value because of the second-order identification it allows with that way of speaking. Then I have to turn to how other aspects of identification build on the articulateness to establish imaginative projections about who we become as we participate in certain dispositions of energies. These projections allow us to reconfigure what counts as significant affect and to reflect on what these reconfigurings suggest about the values involved in such dispositions. And finally I will try to clarify three basic values and modes of valuing that I think become available in our undertaking these imaginative projections. Emphasizing participation in speaking specific words in a specific order aligns us with a psychological economy based less on making judgments about knowledge claims than on processes involved in testing the range of conative powers we have available for engaging as fully as we can in what allows us to appreciate our capacities as individual agents.[5]

In my courses I set the stage for these questions by chanting the mantra that lyrics should always be taken literally – the challenge is deciding what kind of imaginative space one has to occupy in order to appreciate the qualities provided by these words in this order. Theory's task is to clarify how this literalness can be established and why that establishing matters. To do this we first must call attention to what poems manage to do with the letters that are their building blocks. This concern will obviously lead to how pages work as material objects. But most of the time poetry in the West envisions its literal dimension taking place in how readers give voice to the words. Readers have to sound the sounds, in both senses of 'sound.' Physically sounding the sounds gets us in contact with poetry's material presence in our bodies. And imaginatively sounding our making of those sounds begins the self-reflexive processes through which poetry alters our sense of what may be entailed by various provisional identifications.

The physical capacities of sound can do for poetry what color and line do for paintings, or tones and intervals for music: they can give pleasure in themselves and they offer abstract means of exploring elemental physical and psychological associations. To teach this physicality it does not suffice to point to various patterns. Students have to be led to feel the expressive capacities that their mouthing establishes, perhaps by having to project something close to chant. How many times can one say, 'Season of mists and mellow fruitfulness / Close bosom-friend of the maturing sun' without beginning to feel that one's own mouth can work as a musical instrument? The mouth simultaneously plays the tune and registers its sensuous force.

But soon sounding has to take on its second dimension. Students have to experience the reading of poetry as sensuous indulgence that overflows into the luscious delights of being able to stage ourselves as different identities or at least as having rich experiences not readily available for us without the texts. Sounding has to include voicing. (And New Critical talk about the speaker must become talk about the speaking.) For there is no better access to other identities, or to who we become because we can take on other identities, than giving ourselves over to a range of speaking voices. Then we are not watching characters on a screen or a stage; we are actually becoming the voices through which they live. One class exercise in such imaginative sensuality can be learning to hear character (and not just interpret it) by having students try to make speaking voices come alive, like the sneer of the duke in 'My Last Duchess' or the whine in 'Andrea del Sarto.' But we also have to remember that many of our most profound lyrics do not involve character at all. For example, Keats' 'To Autumn' presents a speaking that has nothing to do with character, and everything to do with inhabiting a shareable imaginative situation on levels that accommodate almost any character. Analogously, poets have been fascinated by the capacity within voice to extend these transpersonal features so that they take on a transcendental cast. How we speak the verse is crucial to the self-surrender central to the mode of prayer in Herbert, and Eliot's *Four Quartets* can be considered a desperate quest to find speakable utterances for Christian faith in the modern world.

This stress on voicing allows us to make a useful distinction between language used primarily as representation – of self or of world – and language used primarily for realization, for composing energies as aspects of a particular relation the psyche can maintain toward the world and toward other people. Even this distinction will not allow us a definition of poetry as a unique linguistic genre,[6] since several linguistic modes can make transitions from inviting the 'seeing in' basic to representation to pursuing the 'dwelling in' proposed by projects of realization. But poetry may be distinctive as a genre because it has little use-value for us apart from its capacities to invite and to reward investments in voicing the signs in particular ways.

The first important set of self-reflexive values cultivated by the lyric involves the genre's commitment to articulation as something close to a value for its own sake. Even before we quite know what we feel, we respond to the effort to make all the elements work against standard ways of formulating thoughts and emotions. To characterize how such efforts can be experienced as values I have to turn to the social psychologist Sylvan Tomkins. For he made it clear that second-order feelings and second-order satisfactions about how things get staged for self-reflection are as important for our sense of well-being as first-order satisfactions in achieving specific desired objects and states.[7] Appreciating articulateness consists in recognizing how the ways a medium is used make possible the range and intensity of first-order states that the work realizes. Lyrics invite distinctive (but not exclusive) use of this self-awareness because the articulations they offer usually invoke mental and affective resources quite different from those we experience when arguments seem to get the case just right. Poetic articulation tends to succeed best when it also keeps the difficulties alive so that we have to feel the adjustments and balances necessary for trusting any language at all in the dramatic or perceptual situation. Lyric treats articulateness as a condition of constantly flirting with the inchoate factors making us dissatisfied with what we can say about what we feel. Achieving articulateness then manages to sharpen our sense of what experience involves while keeping in focus the work of taking responsibility for intensifying and extending passionate investments in those experiences. In effect we find ourselves participating in a shared version of the all-important transition from the hidden to the manifest. Poetry offers the experience of civilizing processes literally in action.

My second topic forces me to attempt being more articulate about being articulate. What kind of actual real world powers can we attribute to this dwelling at points where the inchoate merges into what can take on expressive realization to produce formulations within which we can dwell self-reflexively? For many lyrics, articulate realization is connected directly to enabling provisional identifications with certain affective complexes or attitudes. As we identify, we also explore how the writing can reconfigure our received grammars for what constitutes various affective states. The process involves highlighting certain aspects, reducing others, defamiliarizing some while risking the melodramatizing of others. When this reconfiguration is done well, we begin to see lyric emotions as almost having lives of their own, while also recognizing the texts as establishing bare and powerful definitions of what is at stake in the investments we make in how we feel.

As an example of both what self-reflection on articulateness can offer and of how the realization of affective states can reconfigure emotional grammars

I will now turn to Elizabeth Bishop's 'Sonnet' (*Complete Poems*, 192). Let us begin with a standard New Critical strategy of first paraphrasing the poem, then asking what the paraphrase cannot capture. Here though I am less interested in the complexity of meaning per se than in how these words in this order invite us to appreciate how the intricacies of the psyche can take on elaborate metaphoric resonances:

> Caught–the bubble
> in the spirit level,
> a creature divided;
> and the compass needle
> wobbling and wavering,
> undecided.
> Freed–the broken thermometer's mercury
> running away;
> and the rainbow-bird
> from the narrow bevel
> of the empty mirror,
> flying wherever
> it feels like, gay!

Taken as statement, the poem consists of two contrasting descriptions made with a series of conceits. First, the poem develops a sense of entrapment inseparable from seeking some kind of mirror for projected identities. Both the carpenter's level and the compass needle register states of a subject left divided and undecided because it can only see itself as caught within some containing structure. The second half of the poem then presents an opposite state of mind. Here the conceit compares the effort at self-definition to dealing with a thermometer that is broken so that the mercury runs out. Metaphorically the spirit as bird can be gay because it feels it can fly away from the mirror (another instrument for self-measuring) with a sense that it is free to go wherever it feels like.

These are not uninteresting ideas. But cast in this paraphrase, the poem's rendering of freedom seems to depend on entirely negative categories. We encounter a clear instance of 'freedom from,' not 'freedom to.' And so it is no wonder that all the poem can do at the end is name the feeling. Poetry transforms nothing. At best it celebrates a fleeting and casual state that can be summarized by the adjective 'gay.' However, this picture changes considerably if we treat the poem as making certain properties of gaiety articulate by reconfiguring the elements that our cultural grammar offers as constituting gaiety. Notice how the more we attend to the structuring material forces within the poem, like the parallels between participles, the more complexly we come to understand the transience that we typically associate with gaiety. Bishop does not deny this transience. But she complements it by reminding us that this mode of transience is not incompatible with a sense of structural solidity created by complex syntactic and aural patterns. Perhaps the poem seeks to establish for fluid feelings characterizing gaiety also a sense of duration and scope usually attributed to emotions and the narratives they elicit. Gaiety becomes comparable to a condition like 'joy', even though it is traditionally seen as sharply opposed to that more substantial and enduring state. Indeed when we dwell on the tight internal relations, we are tempted to treat the concluding 'gay' as adverb as well as adjective. For gaiety pertains not just to the bird but also to an underlying persistent activity or condition of spirit expressed by the structural forces. Gaiety so composed becomes the substance of the missing fourteenth line of this sonnet.

Let me indicate how the poem's concrete forces establish this substance for gaiety and establish it as desirable state with which to identify – as an emblem for freedom and perhaps as a term for sexual preference. We have already remarked on how tightly structured the parallels are between the two basic units of the poem. Each of the two main sections of the poem is inaugurated by a past participle. But the apparent rigidity also sets the stage for complex and resonant deviations. When we turn to the complementary present participles we find 'wobbling and wavering' balancing the 'running' and 'flying' in the second part of the poem. Yet there is an important difference between the parts that realizes an active presence not predictable by the structure. The two present participles in the first stanza and the initial one in the second simply modify the preceding noun so that they function entirely as adjectives. But 'flying' also has the power of a verb to open into an indeterminate future, 'wherever it feels like.' While the other participles are limited to the role of clarifying what is already determinate, 'flying' seems capable of setting its own determinations.

This syntactic mobility set off by pattern builds to its climax in the concluding assertion. In one sense 'gay' is just another piece of description, paralleling 'undecided' and modifying 'rainbow-bird.' Yet 'gay' clearly is not confined to that specific modification. 'Gay' both names the specific condition of release and serves as an expression for an overall awareness of where the movement of the entire poem leaves us. So there is a sense in which 'gay' is not a modifier but a very general condition, even a mode of activity that might take on modifiers if it could be located in any one space. The poem returns to the opening issue of self-definition, but now it offers as substantial and weighty what is also a free space in which the person can adapt to any experience. For the agency within the poem seems no longer to need the kind of identifications that are constantly threatened by 'wobbling and wavering.' Indeed by this conclusion the poem can be said not just to refer to gaiety but to embody its central qualities. The poem's self-consciousness about its own making seems to wander free to ride its own inventiveness, even to the point of using elaborate structures without being dictated to by any logic that they set up.

No wonder then that this poem concludes with what might be the most profound exclamation mark in American poetry. The exclamation reaches beyond the stance of observation to a stance of affirmation. An effort at precise emotional description so gravitates toward its object that the language cannot be content with description but must make visible its own capacity for attaching itself to the force of certain values. Moreover this foregrounded syntactic marker takes on considerable metaphoric resonance. Now that we see how the exclamation point completes the state of gaiety, we might well wonder whether there can be gaiety or freedom without such exclamation marks. Perhaps the exclamation point simply constitutes will – most of the melodrama associated with willing as an act of judgment may be little more than humanist rhetoric. Exclamation just is the work of judgment, without problematic dependency on abstractions linking the particular to some value-conferring general criteria. Poetry's strange conjunction of restraint and excess may have something to teach philosophy.

This last claim is not without its own excessiveness. But look at all that Bishop has done to make us experience self-reflexively a force in and value for gaiety without ever losing its mobile contingency. Here there emerges a weightiness for the feeling of weightlessness because the poem produces a structural definition of a freedom that nonetheless remains so light it has nothing to do with duty or morality. There is no need to reach beyond the poem's intelligence in order to establish ponderous justifications of freedom or to invoke ideological mirrors that only destabilize identity. The exclamation mark proves sufficient affirmation because it is more attuned to self-conscious investments in these dimensions of gaiety than any more general abstract reasoning might be. Indeed part of the gaiety, and another reason for the exclamation mark, is the poem's presentation of just this chaste yet speculative intelligence sufficient for its task. At the risk of imposing a ponderous period, I want to add the moral that our most important task as teachers of poetry may be to keep that potential exclamation mark emerging from within the disposition of lyric energies.

'Sonnet' exemplifies poetry's semantic power – its way of producing a concrete experience has the capacity of modifying our understanding of the affects typically involved in this kind of experience. Now I want to shift to how we might talk about the values made available for those who participate self-reflexively in such experience. I have nothing interesting to say about the kinds of values that might be considered internal to the specific verbal act – values of craft and articulatory power. Instead I will concentrate on the question of how our reading can influence what we take to be values extending beyond the poem. Three values in particular seem to me especially important because they depend on how emotions are configured and because they illustrate the impact poetry can have on our overall conative sense of the capacities and commitments making our own lives worth living. These values are a self-reflexive feeling of one's own capacity for intensity, a sense of involvedness in which we feel our personal boundaries expanding through processes of voicing other lives and of participating in concrete efforts to engage those lives on the most intimate possible levels, and a sense of the psyche's plasticity as it adapts itself to various competing imaginative demands.

Once we see how such values become present, we have the basis for making two claims about the force poetry can have within cultural life. On the most direct level poems provide structures we can point to as the grounds for our taking certain dispositions as valuable without our having to derive the value by a chain of arguments. We can simply point to the organization of energies and characterize the psychological dispositions that become available if we attempt provisional identifications with those energies. One may not be able to argue that plasticity as an abstraction identifies an especially important state for the psyche. But if one can show it in action one has a prima facie example of the difference its various manifestations can make in people's lives. And then a second, more general possibility takes form. One can show that the reason we value the value need not be derived from any epistemic process in which we first represent the self and then test hypotheses about what might and might not satisfy it. We value the value not because we believe some argument but because we trust in or revel in some state or find ourselves able to relate differently to our surroundings and other persons. There will often be conflict between values arrived at this way and values determined by epistemic processes and social negotiations. Obviously there cannot be a strong rational case for why poetry's way of mediating values ought to prevail in these conflicts.[8] But recognizing that there are alternative routes to grounding values might help resist reason's insistence on prevailing in all these cases. Perhaps what studies show need not determine who we want to be or even what we want to do.

In discussing the first two values I will content myself with a series of allusions to representative texts. But discussing plasticity requires more elaboration, so I will spend considerable time on Wallace Stevens' 'Sunday Morning.' Intensity is very difficult to discuss because it takes so many forms and because even the most powerful instances of it need not be approached self-reflexively. I do not have to tell myself that certain sporting events or human encounters are intense in order to respond intensely. Yet because poetry's intensities also depend in large part on formal properties like concision and dense patterning, this medium usually does involve our realizing how the intensity is connected to authorial purposiveness.

No poet thought harder about intensity as a value and an access to psychological power than did William Butler Yeats.[9] So I will concentrate here on three traits basic to his treatment of this value. First, intensity tends to involve a focusing of concern so that we devote our attention to a specific 'here' and 'now,' and we feel that 'here' and 'now' as being sharply distinct from the 'there' and 'then' constituting its boundaries. One might even adapt Eliot to make the assertion that only those whose 'here's keep wandering into 'there's and whose 'now's are undone by nagging 'then's are likely to appreciate fully what this concentrative centering can involve. Yeats renders one mode of this centering as pure absorption in the self's willfulness: 'I am I, am I / And all creation shivers with that sweet cry' (285). His other basic mode occupies the opposite pole. Poetry establishes a possibility for complete identification with specific energies that consciousness comes to see give the scene its distinctive definition. When Yeats uses the refrain, 'Like a long-legged fly upon the stream / His mind moves upon silence' (328) to render the fundamental state of creative consciousness, he wants us to take the 'upon silence' absolutely literally. The mind does not move within silence but upon it, as if it had reached some fundamental material base by which consciousness could know itself utterly connected with what moves it.[10]

The second feature of Yeatsian thinking on intensity opens the dialectical possibility of reconciling the absorbing ego with the radical sense of concentration breaking through to what underlies all subjectivity. It would be foolish to say that all intensity is dialectical, or even that all lyric intensity is dialectical, especially since the insistence on the 'here' precludes any of the lack necessary to structure a dialectic. But in many of Yeats' richest visions the moment of synthesis constituting the 'here' seems always capable of unfolding into its constituents. The 'here' and 'now' are not simply events; they appear as culminations grasped in an instant but inviting elaborate explication. So I think we can make the generalization that intensity won in words or visions (rather than in pure activity like sport) provides a distinctive kind of present. It offers a present that seems complete in itself, but only because we feel the divisions and range of contexts brought together in the moment, for the moment. Then this awareness of context makes it possible to characterize various dimensions possessed by the intensity. There are at least dimensions of magnitude established by the kind of elements brought together, dimensions of compression established by the forces of resistance engaged by the act, and dimensions of sharpness established by how the intensity comes to appear as distinctive in its particularity.

Yeats is more melodramatic and problematic in proposing a third trait of intensity. But I think we have to honor the spirit of his vision, if not its particular details. This trait consists in a tendency to experience intensity as drawing consciousness toward and often beyond basic boundaries of civility. Just as 'hatred of God may bring the soul to God' (284), intense involvement in our own heightening energies positions us at boundaries where we are not sure whether we are god or beast or god demanding its own beastliness as a sacrifice so as to confirm the possibility that there is something beyond us compelling our service. 'Hound Voice' is Yeats' effort to speak for everything in the psyche and in a person's relation to the land that resists 'boredom of the desk or of the spade.' To hear those voices is ultimately to face hours of terror that 'test the soul' and waken images in the blood:

> Some day we shall get up before the dawn
> And find our ancient hounds before the door,
> And wide awake know the hunt is on;
> Stumbling upon the blood-dark track once more,
> Then stumbling to the kill beside the shore;
> Then cleaning out and bandaging of wounds,
> And chants of victory among the encircling hounds. (331)

Here even the syntax functions to make demands that normal civility cannot handle. The subject-predicate structure of the first lines of this last stanza modulates beautifully through adjective modification ('wide awake') to a series of participles, and finally to a world where only noun phrases define the action. The participles compel consciousness to a pure present within the fantasmatic. And the last line then celebrates a world in which even images are almost erased by the chants so triumphant that it is they, not the agents, who have control. The event reaches completeness only when the chants themselves come to establish the only agency possible in this perversely transcendental domain. At its most absorbed, consciousness puts itself in the proximity of absolute conditions in relation to which the fiction of selfhood seems a mere mask to be torn aside by even greater powers.

My second value has its genesis in just the opposite mode of self-consciousness, and it involves just the opposite challenge to the ego's boundaries. It is also possible to have the self's concentrative powers become a means of appreciating how we are modified by our connections with other people and with the natural world. So I locate this second value in the lyric's capacity to sharpen our awareness of the intricate ways we feel our attention and care becoming contoured to other existences. Voicing offers a clear paradigm. We feel intensely what it means to enact the situations of others within our own beings. Analogously, we can appreciate in dynamic form how our investments are solicited by the conditions calling forth these voices.

I have to be careful here to keep my focus on versions of these powers distinctive to lyric. For clearly the capacity to feel our involvedness with others and for otherness is valued in almost all contemporary ethical and political stances. Even Republicans now cloak their economic positions in a psychology of compassionate conservativism. But poetry calls our attention to the psychological mechanics of such care. It does this in part by not letting involvedness become an abstract moral principle. Instead lyrics take on imaginative force by keeping involvedness a predicate inseparable from self-reflection: our satisfaction in ourselves in such situations depends on our registering what unfolds before us as distinctively different from us and as capable of bearing values because of its articulation of that difference and that distance. Equally important, poetry can move back and forth between these particulars and some more general ontological awareness inseparable from this opening toward the other. Poetry like Gary Snyder's can reach toward something cold and pervasive paradoxically central to our being able to keep ourselves open toward what we cannot control.

Had I the space I would develop three kinds of examples of such involvedness that I can only allude to here. First, there is what we might call acts of existential sympathy like the one we find in C.K. Williams' 'Reading: The Cop,' where a full knowledge of the cop's life depends on our first understanding our reaction to him, then projecting his having to face such reactions all the time. A second form of involvedness takes Cézannian form. In much of W.C. Williams' poetry, for example, the central affective force of the texts consists in their ability to connect our appreciation of what we see to an intense awareness of the constructive energies at work in how the work organizes our seeing. And finally one could use Wordsworth's grand rhetorical passages like the crescendo in 'Tintern Abbey' to 'a motion and a spirit that impels/All thinking things... to illustrate the challenge of having poetic rhetoric build its sympathies on its awareness of its participation in general forces that it cannot control. Wordsworth's totalizing expansiveness would seem outlandish wishful thinking if he could not also work out a logic of syntactic connection distinctive to feeling, so that the totalizing uses its capacity to bypass rational judgments as its means of making inescapable claims upon us. 'Elevated *thoughts*' modulate into '*sense* sublime.' And this sense of significance so bound to immediate awareness perhaps must be considered the work of spirit. For what else but spirit could make the final transition here from the poem at its most general to the assertion 'Therefore am I still'? That 'still' is in personal time what the 'all' is in reflective space. The poem sustains a claim to identity in the present that does not involve qualifying ironies and need not fight for its imaginary sustenance by opposing itself to other people's identifications. Poetry's access to otherness enables it to come to terms with the intensity of the personal needs driving it to speech.

Plasticity is the third value that can be isolated as an aspect of our engagement in the affective forces made available to us by the work poets do. I mean by plasticity the capacity of a work or situation to become compelling for us because of the structuring of internal tensions and lines of force that compose a dynamic means of holding together in their distinctness diverse aspects of experience that all have substantial claims upon us. Consider the range of sexual tensions and threats held in a single structure by the shallow space of Picasso's *Les Demoiselles d'Avignon,* or the capacity of still lives like Braque's *Violin and Candlestick* (1911) to hold together the pull of gravity and the decentering forces released by the now foregrounded contours of shadow and *passage* moving out towards the perimeters of the canvas. There are also many powerful sculptural examples ranging from Michelangelo's late *Pietà* to the play of void and angle against the sexual intensities of Gaudier-Brzska's *Red Stone Dancer.* In all these cases the distinguishing plasticity arises because containment is treated as a relation generated from within the work rather than from without. Containment is a matter of how tensions achieve balance and of how oppositions interpenetrate and strengthen each other, often in ways that allow the interacting forces to seem open to attracting further aspects of experience.

In order to stress the cultural work that this value can perform I am going to concentrate on how it emerges within the unfolding of lyric time in Wallace Stevens' 'Sunday Morning' (66–70). The basic problem of 'Sunday Morning' is as simple as it once seemed intractable. How can this woman torn between two worlds satisfy the demands of both? One world demands honoring Sunday as a memorial to religion, which in turn offers the only feasible alternative to despair at human mortality. The other world seems capable of forgetting mortality, if not of overcoming it, simply by focusing on the plenitude of immanent sensual satisfactions. Dialectical reconciliation seems impossible because there is no mediating principle. Yet Stevens tries another kind of reconciliation – not by resolving the tension into some third term, but rather by letting the tension itself expand sufficiently to hold the opposites as dynamic interrelationships which come to include one another's basic concerns. Resolution must be a matter not of producing a new answer to the questions, but of establishing powerful instruments for dwelling within what the oppositions help unfold.

Here I have to focus on the last stanza. The stage for it is set by a process in which each time the speaker proposes eloquent arguments insisting that the second world of sensual satisfactions should suffice, the woman manages to invoke considerations that his schema cannot encompass. So the poem's final moment takes up the task of composing an elastic space where both positions become part of our dwelling in this Sunday afternoon's presence for the imagination:

> She hears upon that water without sound,
> A voice that cries, 'The tomb in Palestine
> Is not the porch of spirits lingering.
> It is the grave of Jesus where he lay.'

We live in an old chaos of the sun,
Or old dependency of day and night,
Or island solitude, unsponsored, free,
Of that wide water inescapable.
Deer walk upon our mountains, and the quail
Whistle about us their spontaneous cries;
Sweet berries ripen in the wilderness;
And in the isolation of the sky,
At evening, casual flocks of pigeons make
Ambiguous undulations as they sink
Downward to darkness, on extended wings.

Eloquence now is something realized, a composition by which the imagination reaches out to include in its purview competing aspects of a projected scene. When the poem turns to the deer, it also begins to revel in a range of sensual registers, all intricately balancing one another. The quail's spontaneous cries complement the much more enduring temporal aspect of the ripening berries. And all of these particulars spread out against the isolation of the sky – each framing the other while linking echoes of the death motif with powerful figures of fertility. No wonder that now the stanza can move from being the property of one perspective or the other to the collective presence of an encompassing 'we' given substance by what it can see in the scene composed for it.

Then there is the amazing last figure of the pigeons sinking 'downward to darkness, on extended wings.' Note first the physical plasticity. The pigeons stretch out this isolated sky (like a photograph by Felix Gonzalez-Torres), and their 'ambiguous undulations' also slow down the time framed by that sky. The darkness is everywhere, but the living creatures refuse quite to submit to it without drawing it out and extending themselves into it. This is all the bliss we can know. Second, there is the work of sound and syntax to slow down the sentence by suspending clauses and by playing long vowels and lush *n* and *d* sounds against the temporal flow of the sentence. Syntax and sound here function as the poet's extended wings allowing the psyche to dwell fully in what nonetheless he knows must pass. And finally there is the thematic work plasticity accomplishes. At first the poem could not reconcile in one space the idea of religious value and the fact of mortality. But what could not be accomplished by argument can at least be approximated by adapting consciousness to this figure of the extended wings. Religion fails when it has to be grounded in vertical relations to an order superimposed on the secular one. But perhaps poetry can restore the spiritual core of religion to the degree that it can compose horizontal space so that its folds come to contain the flow of time. Such space affords self-consciousness a vehicle for appreciating how imagination can stretch the world to accommodate and revalue the failure of our efforts to transcend it.

My fascination with the genre of the defense of poetry has more affinities than I would like with the almost hopeless quest of 'Sunday Morning' to reconcile received religion with a secular perspective. But it remains possible to argue that a good deal of the difficulty stems from accepting epistemic values, and then seeking for some way to fit poetry into the overall schema. So I want now to turn to the possibility that the specific resistances to epistemic values that we have been exploring provide a plausible ground for elaborating that resistance in theoretical terms. Suppose we were to begin with an orientation concentrating on how affective intensities get articulated. Then we might try the experiment of asking how philosophy might be adapted to that perspective. How might we talk about values if we bracketed epistemic concerns and focused on how affective lives find their richest possible satisfactions? Then the very idea of defending poetry might seem ridiculous from a quite new perspective: who would need to defend what proves foundational to the new way of understanding values?

Baruch Spinoza convinces me that such questions can be fruitful, and need not lead directly to Nietzsche, Spinoza's most powerful misreader.[11] For Spinoza is less concerned with how we know than he is with why knowing matters for us as agents. Thus it cannot suffice to seek truths. Philosophy has to appreciate how what we take as truth modifies the basic qualities of our conative relations to ourselves. And then qualities like intensity, involvedness and plasticity are not mere secondary features of experience but the very conditions that make for an enhanced sense of what is worth pursuing in our reflective lives.

Spinoza's thinking depends on the concept of the conative as that which 'as far as it can, and as far as it is in itself, . . . endeavors to persist in its own being' (109). Conative force seeks to resist all those factors 'that can annul' the sense of individual existence for itself. Then, because this emphasis so tightly weaves feeling a being's distinctive existence into an imperative for activity, the *conatus* provides the basis for a teleological account of the affects. The affects constitute the body's basic awareness of how its conative forces are deployed. For they are constantly registering the degree to which 'the body's power of activity is increased or diminished, assisted or checked, together with the ideas of these affections' (104). This last clause 'together with the ideas' is no casual add-on. Spinoza's dynamic sense of the subject enables him to treat ideas as concrete instruments continuous with affects. Ideas help individuals persist in their own being because they extend and define spaces the body can negotiate as it seeks to extend its sense of its own powers.

Even this very brief summary should indicate the possibility of using Spinoza for the arts in two different ways: (i) His work can provide the basis for a theory of why expressive activity matters for individuals as means of making visible what it is in a being that seeks to persist. And (ii) it can help construct a phenomenological account of why specific affects constitute basic values as manifestations of the body's conative investments, especially those investments involving our feeling for the concrete workings of various media. Demonstrating this seems to me so important that even at this late moment in my essay I have to ask you to consider the relevance of four specific assertions by Spinoza to the case about value that I am proposing:

1. Spinoza argues that 'the most basic and important element of our mind is the conatus to affirm the existence of our body' (111). Mind is powerless without embodiment because mind has to feel ideas as having a direct relationship to how the being is situated. Mind is body aware of its capacity to generate differences in how it negotiates its spaces. Correspondingly, embodiment is not the fact of having a body but the sense of the power to act as a body. The best metaphor for embodiment may be the mouthing that gives rhythms their purposive concreteness.

2. The ethical correlate to the mind-seeking embodiment is the fact that we do not 'endeavor, will, seek after, or desire because we judge a thing to be good. On the contrary, we judge a thing to be good because we endeavor, will, seek after, and desire it' (111). Spinoza will eventually develop a model of desire that brings judgment back into his story – this is not Nietzsche's will to power.[12] But the important point is that for much of psychic life what counts as good is governed by the orientation of the being before questions about truth and judgment enter the picture at all. For the feeling that we can determine a good is ultimately what makes for the fullest conative sense of our own powers in the spaces we inhabit. Argument is less a process of seeking authority beyond the self than of affording conative energies a comparative understanding of possible satisfactions.

3. We can make the same observation in more psychological terms by arguing that the fullest expression of conativity takes place not in our judgments but in our acts of will. For will is the 'faculty whereby the mind affirms or denies what is true and what is false' (96). Will, then, is how the conatus expresses its own sense of itself in relation to the ideas defining its embodiment. Just as the body orients itself in time and in space, will orients the spiritual being, the being with reflexive desires, in relation to a world of ideas and of values. This does not mean that intellectual judgments are not important. It means only that we have to understand what shapes our affirmation of those judgments. The intellect matters to us less because it can acknowledge the power of arguments than because it enables us to align ourselves to the world in various complex ways. Existence is passive when it is driven by factors of which we are ignorant; it is active when the intellect grasps what moves it and hence clarifies the being's sense of how its particularity connects it to universals. We honor the intellectual because of the scope it gives to our being, not because of the knowledge it can establish or the powers of reasoning with which it can identify.

4. Spinoza on imagination makes clear how closely linked that faculty can be
    to the working of will and hence to the establishment of values felt as
    demands on our immediate powers for occupying our world. Imagining is
    the developing of an idea by which the mind regards something as present,
    with emphasis on the present state of the body as it organizes its attention
    (220). Imagination dwells on something outside itself, but with a primary
    focus on the condition of the subject as it yields or withholds certain qual-
    ities of participation and investment in the images it brings before itself. So
    when I imagine a landscape I don't just see its details; rather, I see its details
    as if I were present and engaged in it. It is then not a huge stretch of
    Spinoza to treat imagination as our way of appreciating what various kinds
    of willing might do to our sense of who we are as active agents.

I am not unaware that now, in order to help teach students the values
available from close reading poetry, I am suggesting we also teach them Spinoza.
I propose two operations to save one imaginative organ that may not even be
in danger, or may not be worth saving as part of academic practice. Why make
the defense of poetry so recondite? Let me say first that it need not be recondite. The students need not read Spinoza and the instructors need only appreciate his perspective. They need not become expert in the intricate structure of
his arguments. However, then I have immediately to add that I do not think
we can substantially improve the general levels of poetry instruction or
increase the audience for what is good in our poetry instruction unless we as
professionals do the work to establish a better theory than we now possess of
the affects and their uses in our lives. I hope I have shown that basing poetry
on either its power to disclose certain truths or its power to refuse the imperatives of disclosure severely narrows the values we can bring to bear on our
reading experience. And the situation is actually worse in relation to those
current theoretical accounts that do emphasize the affective dimension of our
experiences with poetry. Most response theory collapses the text into the free
working of the responding psyche, as if there were no particular value in
having ourselves contour to the specific structural and affective demands that
the text makes upon us. And most hermeneutic theory treats affects either as
reactions to what we come to know about the text as a disclosure of being in
some form or as what we enter into dialog with in order to get to know how an
author stands toward being. Neither approach sufficiently honors the specific
affective forces organized by the poem's labors. And neither seems comfortable
with the many ways in which lyric poetry revels in what would be sheer excess
for any theory of communication or of knowledge.

If we are to clarify what poetry makes possible for cultural life, the teaching
of poetry will first have to attune students to the work that poems do in binding the forms of syntax to the possibilities of feeling. Then this teaching needs

to be able to characterize those possibilities of feeling so that we understand the imaginary as a mode of realization. Theory must provide terms for appreciating the dynamic forces given focus by the lyric as values in themselves – in part because of their power to make us see what had been inchoate taking articulate form, and in part because of the specific disposition of energies elicited by that mode of articulation. Finally, theory must facilitate the crucial transition between learning to adapt ourselves to particular affective configurations and coming to the self-reflexive appreciation of those powers. As with almost any other bodily activity, the more fully we understand the powers that it confers, the better prepared we are to put those powers to work.

The moral here almost goes without saying because it so bears repeating. Lyrics do not simply illustrate the importance of adapting an intellectual framework like Spinoza's that can account for the conative dimension of our passions; lyrics also provide dramatic proof that such frameworks are necessary if we are to understand some of our deepest human satisfactions. Teaching poetry then has to refuse to be embarrassed about leading students to pursue what can easily seem self-indulgent intellectual sensuality. At the least, these prove indulgences from which one awakens without hangovers or shame (although in place of aspirins one may have to spend some time reading Spinoza). And at its richest, this education will not be embarrassed to see itself as part of the enterprise of making our culture sufficiently plastic that it can incorporate within a secular world the modes of self-reflection once afforded by religion. It is now fashionable to criticize the lyric precisely because of this link to religion. But can the idealizing of our critical capacities really provide an adequate alternative, since that seems all the debunkers of poetry can put in its place? Far better I think to devote our teaching to leading students to know what is involved in feeling one's body so intensely and so complexly that one has to reach out beyond it to imaginary extensions of those states, for the sake simply of who they make us become during the moments that we can make them last. We can still tell our social critic friends that these states do not last long enough to pre-empt our meeting our ethical and social obligations, but what we then manage to feel should remind us that only meeting those obligations is not much of a salvation.

Notes

Details of works referred to in this Notes section are given in full in the Works Cited section.

1. Donoghue, 'Teaching Literature: the Force of Form,' p. 9. This entire collection, edited by Tucker, is important as an illustration of contemporary efforts to turn the critical tide away from historicism to languages that can afford access to values essential for the close reading of lyric poems.

2. Paul Fry's recent A *Defense of Poetry* provides an almost perfect contrast to the case I will make here. Fry begins with an impressive argument for basing a defense of poetry on a critique of Enlightenment conjunctions between the quest for 'truth' and the need for interpretation: 'To interpret, we have gradually come to realize, is to play out the game of reading within the boundaries that Plato devised in order to make sure that poetry would always lose' (2). But the crucial issue is how one casts the opposition to what I will call the epistemic emphases of Enlightenment thinking. Fry insists on the value of poetry as an art that manages to serve freedom 'through the undetermination of meaning . . . revealed in the release from the compulsion to signify' (4). He goes on to give brilliant readings of specific ways in which this refusal is sustained by 'ostensive moments' rendering an 'a-theologic astonishment' (7). And he connects the entire enterprise to 'an anthropological need to recover or at least to remember the ground of consciousness from which enlightenment, here understood as the devotion to objectivity, perforce estranges thought' (201). Postulating this ground then allows him to reconnect poetry to ethics, albeit an ethics whose only value is a sense of freedom to participate within that very Enlightenment quest while no longer feeling 'that we are chained to the assembly line' (204).

    I see two basic problems with his view. First, some important authors (not just religiously oriented ones, but certainly including those) simply do want to mean and to be understood as taking stances or exploring certain ways of engaging experience. Fry comes dangerously close to deconstruction's saving the text by turning all texts into the same basic enterprise. And, second, his critique of Enlightenment accompanied by grudging admissions of its continuing power seems to me to betray the fact that he remains too much within the very discourse of interpretation and of objectivity that he wants to resist. Fry gives us poetry as the negative of Enlightenment epistemic priorities. But a full defense of the lyric needs to locate actual positive alternatives to Enlightenment priorities so that one need not talk of finding grounds of any kinds or of having either truth or undetermination by suspending propositional force. I try in my account to develop modes of desire attached to lyric. These provide positive roles in cultural life that are treated quite reductively within epistemic Enlightenment thinking. And, indeed, these roles help make clear what is limited in the entire epistemic framework. So poetry does make actual assertions, but they are concerned with the feelings performed and extended rather than with truths realized and tested.

3. For a more precise, yet brief account of the limitations of the epistemic orientation basic to Enlightenment thinking see Richard Eldridge's introduction to *Beyond Representation: Philosophy and the Poetic Imagination*.

4. There are two basic arenas in which I think we most intensely experience the psychological consequences of epistemic culture. The first emerges in the efforts of philosophers like Martha Nussbaum to honor non-epistemic orientations in literary texts while still reclaiming the work for philosophy and hence turning affinities with philosophy into ultimate subordination to rationality. On this I have written at length on other occasions, most recently in 'Lyrical Ethics and Literary Experience.' So I will spend most of this note on the second arena.

    Here the problems arise with the 'cognitivist' perspective that until the past few years had reigned as the dominant academic theoretical stance toward the emotions. Cognitivism is best understood as a reaction against Jamesian psychology that located affects entirely in modifications of physiology. That perspective had no stable way to identify emotions, since it claimed they were determined by bodily states and hence had no reliance on intentional categories. Given that shortcoming, it has become preferable to stress identity conditions over vague claims about bodily states. And the clearest way to get identity conditions is to tie emotions closely to the beliefs and related desires giving them shape. Anger need not be some specific feeling we point to. Rather, it could be a way of orienting ourselves toward actions that follow from beliefs about what others have done or may do to us. Then our account of emotions will also have the considerable advantage of also showing how we can evaluate emotions or give directions for therapy. In principle, we can understand why we pursue specific values or feel specific emotions if we understand the beliefs driving them, and we can modify values and emotions if we modify beliefs. Values and emotions are ultimately subject to rational assessments of belief: if the emotion does not help realize what the belief projects, we have good reason to work on changing its role in our lives.

Suggestive as this stance is for therapeutic purposes, it seems to me severely limited for speculative ones. Cognitivism risks turning our emotions into responses to merchandizing catalogues because it atomizes subjectivity into discrete quests and it assumes that the only psychological concerns that matter are concerns for finding satisfactions for particular belief-driven desires. Such emphases ignore values and emotions that arise for us simply as qualities of how we experience events, whatever the consequences. And, more important, they treat emotions as means to ends and hence ignore the range of powerful satisfactions we take in emotions as ends in themselves. I desire not only to win a game or to persuade a friend, I desire also to experience all the pleasures of playing well or all the senses of pursuing intricate turns of thought, largely for the sake simply of feeling that my mind is alive and that my engagement with the other person is dynamic and fluid. There are even deep satisfactions in anger, since then at least one need not be passive before one's fate. On a more speculative level, cognitive theory buys the authority it gives truth by refusing even to allow a framework within which one might take seriously questions like Nietzsche's about how we might explain a will to truth that is difficult to characterize simply in terms of truth's capacities to afford objectivity. By evading Nietzsche in order to equate desire with belief, these philosophers can provide a powerful position from which to make judgments about ourselves and about others. But that position also blinds us to those aspects of ourselves not content with judgment or not easily aligned with its frameworks. And they simply have to ignore all those personal investments that lead us to care about our judgments.

For useful criticisms of cognitivitism, see the book I list by Sue Campbell as well as the essays by John Deigh and Richard Moran. When these philosophers challenge the cognitivist theory of emotions, they point to how the theory confines itself to atomistic emotional narratives, ignoring complex relations among feeling that are much more difficult to connect to beliefs. And they insist on forms of satisfaction projected by the affects which involve fantasy and hence cannot be treated simply as beliefs to be judged in terms of their rationality. On the most general level, these philosophers also are beginning to challenge the entire picture of desire that binds it so tightly to belief. Moran points to decisions that take place without reference to belief because they have to determine which beliefs might be appropriate. And Campbell stresses the importance of coming to know our feelings through expressing them, whether or not they connect to specific desires.

5. Anthony J. Cascardi's *Consequences of Enlightenment* provides a brilliant analysis of problems created by Kantian efforts simultaneously to save 'judgment' and to modify it so that it has powers different from those he attributes to rationality. Cascardi's closing chapter is an eloquent appeal for developing overall models of agency responsive to the roles affects play in our values and in our ways of valuing.

6. In speaking of the uniqueness of poetry I am not relying on any one set of essential properties. I think a family relations argument would do the job. Generalizing about a phenomenon like poetry is possible if one is willing to rely on what seem stable expectations within certain communities – in my case, expectations within academic communities that worry about teaching and about valuing lyric poetry. And at the center of this discourse about expectations I think one can put a share-able sense of what work poets do. Their concern for sound qualities, for example, separates them from expectations we have about philosophers and lawyers who also pay careful attention to language.

7. See Tomkins' discussion of what he calls the 'interest – excitement complex' in his *Shame and its Sisters: a Sylvan Tomkins Reader*, edited by Eve Kosofsky Sedgwick and Adam Frank (Durham: Duke University Press, 1995), pp. 92–7.

8. Martha Nussbaum's work on literature has become increasingly aware of tensions between values compatible with reason and values reason simply cannot handle. But in my view she tends to reassert the authority of reason in most cases. So she provides a telling example of how the persistence of epistemic commitments makes it very difficult to honor the full roles that affects and affect-based values play in the arts.

9. Gilles Deleuze is the contemporary philosopher who in that field seems to me most concerned with this topic. See especially his *Difference and Repetition*, pp. 222–46.

10. If I had the space, I would try to show how yeats's poem 'He and She' moves beyond the 'I am I' to an impersonal site where a plastic consciousness can put into one composition both the passive moon terrified of losing itself and this assertive sexual self-absorption.

11. Actually Hegel is as important an heir of Spinoza as is Nietzsche. But I prefer Spinoza to Hegel because one has to carry considerably less baggage in order to adapt his central claims. We need only accept the idea that concerns for something like 'identity' are not entirely symbolic but have a strong material basis in the being's need to set forces in motion that will enable it to satisfy its urges to experience its own purposiveness.

12. Spinoza brings the judgmental powers of intellect within this desire story by what I consider a brilliant transformation of Hobbes on pleasure and pain as the ultimate arbiters of value. For Spinoza, pleasure is a 'transition to a state of greater perfection' (117) while pain is the feeling of the diminishment of the power of the body (114). If we cross this with Spinoza's sense that active being is an alignment with true ideas, passive being with false ideas (because passivity is being governed by what is foreign to us), we can see that pleasure is alignment with what makes us active. And the ultimate pleasure becomes the intellectual love of God, since that love activates our most capacious relation to being.

Works cited

Altieri, Charles. 'Lyrical Ethics and Literary Experience,' *Style* 32 (1998): 272–97.

Bishop, Elizabeth. *The Complete Poems, 1927–1979* (New York: Noonday Press, 1983).

Campbell, Sue. *Interpreting the Personal: Expression and the Formation of Feelings* (Ithaca: Cornell University Press, 1997).

Cascardi, Anthony J. *Consequences of Enlightenment* (Cambridge: Cambridge University Press, 1999).

Deigh, John. 'Cognitivism in the Theory of the Emotions,' *Ethics* 104 (July 1994): 824–54.

Deleuze, Gilles. *Difference and Repetition*, trans. Paul Patton (New York: Columbia University Press, 1994).

Donoghue, Denis. 'Teaching Literature: the Force of Form,' *New Literary History* 30 (Winter 1999): 5–24.

Eldridge, Richard. 'Introduction: From Representation to *Poesis*,' in Eldridge (ed.), *Beyond Representation: Philosophy and Poetic Imagination* (Cambridge: Cambridge University Press, 1996), pp. 1–33.

Fry, Paul. *A Defense of Poetry: Reflections on the Occasion of Writing* (Palo Alto, CA: Stanford University Press, 1995).

Moran, Richard. 'The Expression of Feeling in Imagination,' *The Philosophical Review* 103 (January 1994): 75–106.

Spinoza, Baruch. *The Ethics and Selected Letters*, translated by Samuel Shirley (Indianapolis: Hachett Publishing Company, 1982).

Stevens, Wallace. *The Collected Poems of Wallace Stevens* (New York: Random House, 1955).

Tomkins, Sylvan. *Shame and its Sisters: a Sylvan Tomkins Reader*, edited by Eve Kosofsky Sedgwick and Adam Frank (Durham: Duke University Press, 1995), pp. 92–7.

Tucker, Herbert (ed.). *Poetry and Poetics. New Literary History* 30 (Winter 1999).

Williams, C.K. *Flesh and Blood* (New York: Farrar Strauss Giroux, 1987).

Yeats, William Butler. *The Collected Poems of W.B. Yeats* (New York: Macmillan, 1956).

Classroom Rituals, Old and New

8

Re-writing Texts, Re-constructing the Subject: Work as Play on the Critical–Creative Interface

Rob Pope

The highest Criticism, then, is more creative [...] and the primary aim of the critic is to see the object as in itself it really is not.

Oscar Wilde, *The Critic as Artist* (1891)

Criticism begins with the recognition of textual power and ends in the attempt to exercise it. This attempt may take the form of an essay, but it may just as easily be textualised as parody or counter-text in the same mode as its critical object. As teachers we should encourage the full range of critical practices in our students.

Robert Scholes, *Textual Power* (1985)

It is a commonwealth in which work is play and play is life.

George Bernard Shaw, *John Bull's Other Island* (1904)
cit. A.N. Whitehead, *The Aims of Education* (2nd edn, 1950)

This chapter offers a practical guide to the creative and critical use of *re-writing*. By 're-writing' is here chiefly understood such strategies as parody, imitation, adaptation and, especially, intervention. This last is the activity of re-writing a text from a deliberately off-center position, in some way 'against' or 'across' the grain. It corresponds in part to what Umberto Eco calls 'semiotic guerrilla warfare,' Alan Sinfield calls 'dissident reading' along 'faultlines,' and Robert Scholes and others call 'ghosting.' It may also be aligned with a variety of poetic, political and pedagogic projects associated with Adrienne Rich, Alice Walker and Gayatri Spivak amongst others, namely 're-visioning,' 're-membering' and 'making/listening to the subaltern speak.'[1] Intervention introduces a considered, but also experimental change into the text in hand. In principle, this can be any text (a change of slogan or logo in an advert, a change of headline or photo-caption in a news story); but here the emphasis is on re-writing specifically literary, more or less 'classic' or 'canonical' texts (such as poems, novels and plays). At the same time, 're-writing' also embraces the familiar and relatively routine activity of 're-drafting' – in the sense of revising and refining – one's own text. For to change another's words is inevitably to become aware of the provisional status of one's own. Either way, in ethical as well as aesthetic terms, the reader as re-writer is constantly involved in the process of making differences and weighing preferences.

In order to make these processes explicit, every re-write must be accompanied by a *commentary*. The commentary is the space set aside for critical analysis and comparison of the text as you found it with the text as you re-made it. It is also an opportunity for the explicit marshaling of research, and for reflection on the problems and possibilities encountered in the process of re-writing as such. Its particular function here is cultural and historical: to focus upon what this, the most recent moment of re-production, helps show about the nature of the text in its initial moment of production. More generally, if the re-write is at the implicitly 'creative,' performance-based end of the interpretative spectrum, the commentary is at the explicitly 'critical' end. In fact, the whole enterprise of 're-write + commentary' results in a clearly differentiated yet distinctly hybrid discourse: critical–creative, theoretical–practical and academic–pedagogic. To which may be added the terms featured in this chapter's subtitle and the second epigraph: work–play. In yet other words, it's about a complex of serious–fun – with equal emphasis upon both terms.

The first part of the present account comes at re-writing through larger-scale, macro-textual aspects such as genre, narrative, drama, discourse and medium; it also entails engagement with considerable historical distance and cultural difference. The text featured is an instance of long verse narrative from the late Middle Ages, Chaucer's *The Clerk's Tale*. This is used to illustrate what may be done when re-writing in such modes as collage, letters, drama, prayer, soap opera, and 'through' another text (in this case *The Color Purple*). But the same principles apply when grappling with many kinds of large-scale tale or play, in verse or prose, and sections have been organized so as to foreground what is common and transferable rather than those aspects specific to this text or period alone. The second part of this account comes at re-writing from the smaller-scale, micro-textual end of things. It concentrates on detailed aspects of word choice and combination and the finer implications of relatively local-ized changes in form and function. The text featured for this purpose is a very short lyric from the late nineteenth century, Emily Dickinson's 'I'm Nobody.' This is here reproduced in two different printed versions and set up so as to be re-written in two very different modes, in and out of biographical context. But again the insights and issues relate to the intensive re-writing of just about any short text, and the present activity can be readily adapted for many. The third part of the essay draws attention to the theoretical implications (and advantages) of an approach to textuality through re-writing + commentary. It also gestures to the kind of radically transformed subject entailed by the central incorporation – rather than occasional use – of such strategies. They can constitute the core of a comprehensively radical rhetoric – not just a bolt-on to existing practices. Finally, there is an Appendix, in which the main kinds of re-writing strategy (including some not covered by the present examples) are briefly reviewed and illustrated, and there are also some parting tips on teaching and assessing such things as assignments.

Just two more things will be added by way of preamble: one as an assurance, the other as a challenge. Firstly, it should be pointed out that all the strategies featured here have been working for over a decade – and with conspicuous success – at levels ranging from first-year undergraduate through to MA. This has been in a wide variety of institutional and national contexts. For instance, the present writer and collaborating colleagues have used them extensively at Oxford Brookes University in the UK; the University of South Australia; the University of Otago in New Zealand; and Humboldt State University and Missouri Western State College in the US. At the same time versions have been widely adapted for use in programs where English is a second or third language and where the emphasis may be upon 'language through literature' rather than literary studies alone. This has been mainly in Central Europe and South East Asia, chiefly under the aegis of the British Council and the European Society for the Study of English. There are therefore many more 'voices' than one in what follows, and some of these are distinctly cross-cultural in emphasis and orientation. Meanwhile, as already mentioned, comparable strategies of a more or less concerted kind can be traced in the work of, for example, Scholes and Sinfield, and the list can be variously extended to, say, Doyle, Corcoran, Nash, Stacey and others. And the programs involved range from (not so) 'straight Eng Lit,' through Rhetoric and Composition and Professional Writing, to (not just) Creative Writing. In short, there is already a wealth of experience and expertise informing such 'experiments.'

That said, however, there is still widespread resistance – and sometimes downright opposition – to the kinds of hybrid, critical–creative activity described here. What's more, this can come from faculty at both ends of the institutional spectrum: in 'Creative Writing' no less than 'Eng Lit' (though it should be added that the students themselves tend to be much more open to free traffic across the borders and much less obsessed by territorial disputes). With this in mind, and with a view to putting down some clear – and clearly contentious – markers, there follows a kind of *Manifesto for Re-writing*. Necessarily, this is something of a manifesto for interactive pedagogy, too. In general terms, this will serve to establish the theoretical premises upon which the present practice is based. More pointedly, it invites you, the present reader, to refine or replace any and all of these propositions as you see fit. They have a cumulative logic which people find variously liberating or inhibiting. For inevitably you will be operating in cultural conditions and with institutional agendas and personal aims slightly or very different from those assumed or asserted here. So, make a difference; express a preference. But whatever you do, don't do nothing! Reading then re-writing is what this whole thing is about. And, as usual, the most important part of the page is the space *between* the lines:

1. In reading texts we re-write them.
2. Interpretation *of* texts always entails interaction *with* texts.
3. Interaction *with* texts always entails intervention *in* texts.
4. One text leads to another and another and another – so we had better grasp texts *intertextually*, through comparison and contrast.
5. One's own words and worlds are necessarily implicated in those of others – so we had better grasp our selves *interpersonally*, through dialogue, voicing conflict as well as consensus.
6. *De*-construction is best realized through *re*-construction – taking apart to put back together differently. Just as *critique* is always, in a radical sense, about *re-creation*.
7. For *interpretation* can be done through acts of creative performance no less than of critical commentary. And we are all in various ways both performers *and* commentators, critics *and* creators.
8. In sum, *textual changes* always involve *social exchanges*. You can't have the one without . . . the other . . . and one another . . .

Re-writing narrative – the bigger picture

Chaucer's *The Clerk's Tale* is a particularly challenging case of old text meets new readers. Its story of 'patient Griselde,' the poor and long-suffering peasant girl who is married to and severely tested by an aristocratic husband, rings all sorts of alarm bells for contemporary readers tuned for democracy and sexual politics. Its emphatically Biblical underpinning – Griselde's patience recalls that of Job and her motherly suffering that of Mary, mother of Christ – poses problems for a student body that is increasingly secular and multicultural and, if religious, perhaps has other myths and beliefs in play (ranging from fundamentalist Islamic to fundamentalist Christian).

Moreover, *The Clerk's Tale* is further complicated by the complexities of its narration. The fictional narrator, the Clerk, seems to have trouble assenting to the dominant message and overall framing of the tale he tells: he twice interrupts the story to criticize Marquis Walter for being unnecessarily 'cruel.' Meanwhile, Chaucer himself, as overall narrator, seems to have had complex and perhaps divided aims, for there are in effect two morals to this tale: a thoroughly orthodox one in which Walter's God-like authority is solemnly endorsed; the other (the 'Envoy') in which, with a carnivalesque allusion to the Wife of Bath, it is freely admitted that no woman could or should possibly be that submissive.

The following readers/re-writers have much to say about all these things and more. For pedagogic convenience, their work is signalled by the genre(s) of re-writing each represents (usually there is more than one in play), followed by the title of their piece and their name. The genres of re-writing featured are: (1) LETTERS, IMITATION & HYBRID; (2) COLLAGE & PRAYER; and (3) DRAMA-TIZATION & UPDATING. Please bear in mind that these are relatively short extracts from projects ranging from 2,500 to 5,000 words, and that the balance of re-write to commentary cannot be equally represented in each case.

1. LETTERS, IMITATION and HYBRID – *'The Clerk's Tale' read through 'The Color Purple'* by Kate Wood

> dear God,
> i am fourteen year old. i han always been a good girl. may be you can send me sum sign to tell me what is happening to me. i han alway looked after my Fader best i can. i tend to sheep. do spynnynge. eek cooke and fecche his ale. thanne i lerne my lettres that i can reade the bokes my mama gaf me fore she dye. Fader do not have to beat me moche, only if i do not mak ready his herbes water for the peyne in his heed in the morwenynge...

So begins this project, which started as an IMITATION of a novel in an epistolary (LETTER) mode and developed into a hybridized text in its own right. Obviously, much of the general effect of the above passage depends upon an acquaintance with the two texts involved: Chaucer's *The Clerk's Tale* and Alice Walker's *The Color Purple* (1983). More particularly, it depends upon a recognition of the precise way in which two passages from these texts have been spliced and blended so as to produce an intertextual HYBRID which is both and yet neither, and also something new. This is how the student responsible saw it in her commentary:

> There is both a match and a mismatch. [...] We first meet Chaucer's Griselda as a kind of pious, clean-living and hard-working peasant lass, devotedly looking after 'hire olde povre fader' (ll. 204ff). Walker's Celie is a poor black girl from the Southern States in the 1920s–30s who is writing to God because her father is raping her regularly (Walker 1983, p. 3).

And this is how she described the genesis of the project overall:

> I had just finished reading *The Color Purple* and had loved it. The use of letters to make a novel was new to me, though I later learnt that they form

the basis of lots of novels. This was also around the time we were doing *The Clerk's Tale*, which I was enraged but also intrigued by. Then it clicked. Putting them all together seemed too good an opportunity to miss! I drafted and re-drafted the first letter several times, trying to get a 'style' right. I tried it out on a few people – and then it all just took off...

Another detail from the re-write will give a feel for its texture and a sense of how not just the manner but the very matter of both texts can be compounded and transformed. Griselda is here communing with – and complaining to – God about her husband's attempt to justify the removal and apparent slaughter of their daughter. The passage is replete with echoes of Celie's confusion at the hands of her rapacious father:

> His mynde is amyss. yesterday he cam to my chaumbre a-nyght and sayde the peple speke up and doune of the shame of been somtyme in servage to child born of small village – tho it bee hir owne village! He also sayde he moste tak myn doghter – 'I moot doon with thy doghter for the beste' he sayde – tho she bee *oure* doghter and *his* doghter also. He sayde what he do wil be al for the beste. I not so sure. Be this thy wil too o god?!

Once more the effect is complex. And a full appreciation of it depends, as the student's title suggests, on a 'read through' of Chaucer's text in terms of Walker's, and vice versa. There is no space here to follow this through in the detail supplied in her commentary. But the more general issue is worth pointing out. The status of the above text is primarily *inter*textual. Moving in the spaces *between* the texts, we can then see that Wood's Griselda, in contrast to Chaucer's, stops being an icon of patience and suffering (like the Virgin Mary) and begins to argue with God (as does Walker's Celie). The student reflects on the process thus: 'Celie starts off believing in the God she writes letters to, but then gradually stops believing in him and starts writing to other people instead. I got my Griselda to do the same in the end.' That last remark identifies one of the fundamental properties of *letters* as a mode of writing (as distinct from, say, essentially private and monologist modes such as the *diary*): letters can involve more than one addresser and more than one addressee *and* they can elicit replies (that is, they are potentially 'multi-vocal' *and* dialogic). In fact, the student picks up these distinctly epistolary possibilities by having Griselda's children initiate a secret correspondence and finally a conspiracy with their mother (in Chaucer's version they say and do nothing in their own right). As a consequence, the whole ending of Chaucer's version is transformed. Whereas Chaucer's denouement, like that of his sources Petrarch and Boccaccio, shows the omnipotent Walter magnanimously unveiling his – and by strong implication God's – plan ('This is ynogh,' he says in 1.1051, echoing l.365 and signaling that the grand design is complete), Wood's denouement is twisted to quite different ends. *Her* Griselda and *her* children will have none of this. They so order things that, instead of a family reunion orchestrated by Walter, he is exposed to public ridicule for his cruel obsession and effectively shamed into leaving his own house. ('"That is ynogh of yow!" I shouted . . . ', as Wood's Griselda recalls with relish in a later letter).

The kind of *language* to be used for the re-write is a particularly pressing and revealing problem. This is especially so when it comes to re-writing a text from a markedly earlier stage of the language. The issue arises with Shakespeare, of course. But a similar challenge is posed when tackling contemporary texts in relatively remote varieties: when deciding how far to imitate, adapt or in some way 'translate' the English/Englishes of Caribbean or South East Asian texts, for instance. In any event, what is at stake is the matter of linguistic and cultural *differences* and *similarities*, and also issues to do with historical and aesthetic *distance* and critical and ethical *preference*. Samples of what this particular student did with the language are available above. Here is how she broached the matter in her commentary:

> Finally, there was the language problem. Should I write the letters in modern English? But that would take away the constant reminder that this is a different culture and a different time. The writing needed to be defamiliarised in some way. I considered using the same language that Celie does in *The Color Purple* but rejected that idea too. Griselda would get lost against too strong an impression of Walker's book. Therefore I decided to write as close an approximation of Middle English as I could. But I couldn't manage 'Middle English' *and* letters *and* poetry! Something had to go, and it was the poetry. This is a real loss. It makes everything more immediate and conversational, but also in every way more 'prosaic' and less formal and musical.

2.   COLLAGE and PRAYER – *The Love Song of Griselda* by Jane Jordan

a condition of complete simplicity
(costing not less than everything) (1)*
The Angel said to Mary, 'and a sword shall pierce your heart' (2). In her image a sword has pierced mine too. Mary, blessed are you among women. Blessed was the fruit of your womb (3). You raised me as the mother of God, I am the mother of heirs to a kingdom.
I am the Lord's servant, may it be to me as you have said (4).
I came naked into this world and naked I shall return (5).
My husband is my Lord, my life, my keeper, my head and my sovereign (6). [. . .]

Love, honour and obey my earthly Lord (8)[...]
One last kiss ere I leave thee.(10) Thou mastering-me God! (11). So hard –
and a sword has pierced my heart. And in the quietness my silent voice can
scream and scream:
'Absalom, O Absalom my son!' (12)

numbers refer to notes below

So begins this instance of another mode of re-writing neither more nor less
legitimate than the traditional essay or analysis. COLLAGE – the sticking
together of potentially relevant bits of text, image, music – is a widely
favoured strategy. Done casually and in a slapdash manner (like any other
strategy) the results can be banal, trivial, superficial and incoherent. Done
carefully and after concerted research – as well as with a dash of 'devil-may-
care' – collage can be one of the most striking and suggestive ways of interpreting a text. And which is which, even if not immediately evident from the
work itself, is always made clear by the quality of critical thought and range of
reference in the commentary. This present example was given further point
and coherence by being framed as a PRAYER. (Collage is often most successful
when informed and shaped by some enabling format or agenda.) Here, to be
precise, this takes the form of an incantatory prayer or, in the words of the
writer, a 'love song.' Generically, therefore, the present text has something in
common with both the monologic form of the DIARY and the restrictedly dialogic form of the LETTER already referred to. This should not surprise us. Most
re-writes – like most originals – turn out to be HYBRIDS. So, what is the author
of this particular collage up to? And what can it show us about the possibilities of this specific mode of textuality? We can start by considering the various texts which are 'stuck together' in the above extract. Each is signalled by a
bracketed number after it in the main text and was identified in the footnotes
as follows:

(1) T.S. Eliot, *Four Quartets* (opening).
(2) *Luke* 2.35.
(3) Based on the Roman Catholic 'Hail Mary!'
(4) *Luke* 1.38.
(5) *Book of Job* 1.21; compare *The Clerk's Tale*, ll. 931–8.
(6) Shakespeare, *The Taming of the Shrew*, Act V. [...]
(8) Based on the medieval marriage service, Sarum usage. [...]
(10) Shakespeare, *Othello*, Act V – Othello to Desdemona just before he
    strangles her.
(11) Gerard Manley Hopkins, *The Wreck of the Deutschland*.
(12) King David on being told of the death of his son, *Psalms*.

According to its author, the initial genesis of and subsequent rationale for *The Love Song of Griselda* were as follows:

> I called this monologue a 'love song' with some specific types of love song in mind. Partly it's a term borrowed from T.S. Eliot's *The Love Song of J. Alfred Prufrock*, as this was the style of revelation I was hoping to achieve. And partly the title came from the love songs of Solomon in the Biblical *Song of Songs*. Unlike Solomon's love songs, however, Griselda's is significantly absent of any form of physical love or affection. The monologue is Griselda's love song to God, her children and her husband. The fact that it is to all of them creates problems and tensions. That is why I chose to put pieces of different texts together, as a way of suggesting the possible frag-mentation of her love and her faith through their inner contradictions.

Meanwhile, what prompted this particular re-write is revealed to be both deeply personal and urgently relevant. For the author intimated that she had herself been through a period of intense religious belief, doubt and then loss of faith, and that it was this extreme 'testing' aspect of *The Clerk's Tale* she wished to explore. Here it is important to observe that the opportunity to express such things *indirectly*, through the re-writing of another's text, rather than directly, through an unmediated confession 'in one's own voice,' proved particularly enabling. And this is generally true of such an approach. The personal can be made public without being paraded, and acute issues can be broached with relative impunity. Thus the present (re-)writer is able to declare that 'I wanted to present Griselda as a woman whose faith was so ingrained as to be part of her very being; who would obey her husband because she has vowed to before God but whose faith was tested almost to breaking point by the murder of her children.' And there is another lesson to be learnt here. For it is often an acute need to push a text's contradictions to the limit ('almost to breaking point' is how Jordan puts it) that is the real driving force behind collage. It is a mode of verbal composition (or for that matter visual and musical composition) dedicated to the exposure and exploration of the processes of fragmentation – *de*-construction on the cusp of *re*-construction, a complex moment and movement of *dis/integration*. And charac-teristically, because of the sheer implicitness and dispersedness of this strategy, we are left with more questions than answers and a heightened awareness of problems being posed rather than solved. The peculiar appropriateness of collage when attempting to express a continuing and ultimately insoluble problematic can be illustrated by the way in which the above example ends:

> . . . For he is my husband as I vowed myself before God on my wedding day.
> I shall submit, I shall submit, I shall submit.
> Amen.

> Lord, I do not doubt. I cannot face this world with doubt. With faith I can survive, rise
> up and pray. But why my little children, Lord. In sickness and in health! Is this sickness, Lord?
> He's not so kind as on our wedding day. Inner is the pain and inner is the grief.
> Comforter, where, where is your comforting? (31)
> Why my little children? Say!

It is not necessary to recognize all the allusions here (particularly those to Hopkins's 'Terrible Sonnets,' note 31) in order to register the general effect of this passage. The flurry of questions and injunctions, the tension between faith and doubt – persistent control and imminent disintegration – virtually speak for themselves. However, the last word on this particular collage will be left with the person who put it together. As in the most successful collages, it concerns the artful framing of questions rather than a plethora of arbitrary answers, an openness to ongoing process along with an acknowledgement of responsibility for the final product – however notionally provisional the latter may be: 'I began by wanting to present a woman ruled by her faith and grieving the loss of her children. I wanted to combine the saint and the mother, the parable and the realism. [...] But eventually I realised I had shown how Griselda's intense suffering leads to the crisis of asking or commanding God to speak back.'

3.   DRAMATIZATION & UPDATING – *Trinasty* by Mark Bradley

The last example will be presented in skeletal form for reasons of space. It features the kind of re-write – 'Chaucer as soap opera' – that can (like any other writing activity) be the assignment from hell or a blessed refreshment. As always, it depends what expectations are raised and how these are met (see the close of the Appendix at the end of this chapter for tips on discouraging the former and encouraging the latter). Here I will simply leave readers to weigh this example for themselves and perhaps to flesh out the problems and the possibilities with their own experience of work in this line.

From the preface...

> Walter Maquisa is the idle son of an oil-baron, a member of the international jet-set – handsome, carefree and popular with everyone. He's a philanderer, unwilling to sustain a meaningful relationship with any of the women he meets. His father, who has recently had a stroke, tells him that he must marry in order to have children so that the family fortune will remain intact. Among the employees of their vast business empire there is a man called Janicula, an illegal Italian immigrant worker. He is beholden to the Maquisas who have

provided him with a job and a place to live near one of the oil pumping stations. His wife is dead and he lives with his devoted, beautiful daughter Grisella. They are devout Catholics. One day Walter visits the site where Janicula works and sees Grisella bringing her father some lunch. Walter is struck by her humble grace and lack of affectation. He asks her father to see him:

From the re-write...

WALTER: Your daughter out there – she looks after you O.K.?

JANICULA: Grisella? Why yes. She's a good girl – she studies hard at school, keeps the house fine. Since my wife died...

WALTER: (*cuts in*) Is she dating any guys?

JANICULA: No. No. She's a good girl – she never no trouble. Her mother – God rest her soul – never...

WALTER: (*cuts in again*) Janicula. This is gonna surprise you. I wanna marry your daughter.

JANICULA: Marry her?! Mr Maquisa – you joke with me? A poor girl – a rich man like you?

WALTER: (*curtly*) I have no time for jokes, Janicula. Look. You have a good job with my company, a nice place to live – and no one knows you're not supposed to be here. You value all this?

JANICULA: Why, yes sir. You're very good to us...

WALTER: Fetch Grisella inside then. I want to talk to you both.

JANICULA: But Mr Maquisa – sir. She's just a simple girl – she wouldn't know how to... all your friends... your family...

WALTER: She'll be fine. That'll all be taken care of. Fetch her!

From the commentary...

By updating *The Clerk's Tale* into a modern American 'soap' it has become necessary to qualify some of the relationships and reinvest the setting with similar but different cultural terms of reference. The old 'feudal' system of villagers beholden to the rich landlords is re-interpreted as the family business empire and the 'oil-rig' workers living in company-owned accommodation. [...] The dependent relationship of poverty on wealth is retained, indeed strengthened by the fact of the modern Janicula's questionable citizenship rights in the United States. It gives an extra card in the hand of Walter, whose cynical ruthlessness could be developed in the manner of a 'J.R.' type of character. The exaggerated caricatures of *The Clerk's Tale* should, I hope, transfer quite well to the fairy tale world of modern 'soaps'and whilst we can acknowledge the existence of 'powerful' women such as Alexis, they operate in a male-dominated world of business. And for our 'virtuous and decorous' archetype we need look no further than the 'Crystal' character in *Dynasty* – hence, of course, my title *Trinasty*.

Re-writing lyric – the smaller picture

As a writer I know that I must select studiously the nouns, pronouns, verbs, adverbs, etcetera, and by a careful syntactical arrangement make readers laugh, reflect or riot.

Maya Angelou, from Conversations with Maya Angelou (1985)

The journey is one of choices, judgements, of logic – if . . . then . . . and also . . . if not . . . and therefore; the small words that have little use become instruments of power.

Janet Frame, The Carpathians (1988)

The second part of this essay concentrates on the detailed re-writing of a short text. It is an example of a 'split group' exercise in which two halves of the class (disposed in suitable size subgroups of three or four) tackle different aspects of the same task. In this case they are presented with two different printed versions of Emily Dickinson's short lyric 'I'm Nobody' and asked to do different things with them. The exercise should be pretty self-explanatory from the hand-out materials that follow. But a few words on how the teacher may frame and approach the session as a whole will be useful:

(1) to begin with, the two halves of the class work independently, without much idea of what the other is doing;
(2) in the middle of the session pairs of subgroups – one from each half – present their findings and makings to one another;
(3) everyone in open forum finally discusses the pros and cons of the various kinds of reading and re-writing they have been engaged in.

Meanwhile, what the teacher knows throughout, in theory at least, is that the group is split and the tasks are set so as to explore two major aspects of textuality and interpretation. On the one hand, Text/Task A invites a relatively Formalist, text-in-itself, poem-on-the-page response. On the other hand, Text/Task B invites a relatively Historicist, text-in-context, auto/biographical response. An extra formal *and* historical dimension is added to the exercise because there are two versions of 'the same text' in play. This gives a twist to the tales of intra- and intertextuality that each text tells on its own and in relation to the other. As a result, the editorial process itself is put firmly in the foreground as a crucially constitutive form of reading and re-writing, rather than being treated as incidental or ignored completely. Also bared to view is the whole pedagogic business of framing tasks with specific constraints and requirements. The strong implication is that there is no 'innocent' lesson plan any more than there is an 'innocent' choice of text. However, whether all this is what the students themselves see, in practice, may be another matter. But that's all part of the interest, too. Teaching is all about 'best-laid plans' – and then seeing what happens. So, if you can come up with better or simply different ways of doing what follows (with these or other texts), then plan it carefully – and see what happens. Either way, the present reader-teacher is asked to weigh how you, as a writer-learner, might respond to each of the following activities, sketching a response to each text and task in turn. After that, compare what you have in mind or on paper with what other students and teachers have come up with in the past (some samples follow immediately after the boxed instructions). Finally, as usual, go on to adopt or adapt these activities and substitute other texts as you see fit.

Text/Task A

Retaining the overall form of the following text, re-write it so as to produce an alternative which is different yet recognizably related. (Restrict your changes to relatively localized matters of word choice and combination: inversion, substitution, deletion, addition, re-sequencing, etc.).

> I'm nobody! Who are you?
> Are you nobody, too?
> Then there's a pair of us – don't tell!
> They'd banish us, you know.
>
> How dreary to be somebody!
> How public, like a frog
> To tell your name the livelong day
> To an admiring bog!

Text/Task B

Combine and adapt these two texts so as to produce a single text suitable as a script for use in Tv, film, stage or other performance, or print (e.g. as part of a novel, educational textbook, and so on).

(i)
> I'm Nobody! Who are you?
> Are you – Nobody – Too?
> Then there's a pair of us?
> Don't tell! they'd advertise – you know!

Text/Task B   (*Continued*)

How dreary to be Somebody!
How public – like a Frog –
To tell one's name – the livelong June
To an admiring Bog!
Emily Dickinson, c. 1861

(ii) Emily Dickinson (1830–1886) lived all her life in Amherst, Massachusetts. By the age of 30 she had become an almost total recluse, never leaving her father's house and garden, dressing completely in white, receiving very few visitors, and carrying on most of her many friendships almost solely by means of correspondence. She wrote well over a thousand poems; but only seven were published during her lifetime. The above poem was not one of them. It was found after her death, with the rest, carefully parceled up in a chest. Since their first publication in the 1890s (when many of Dickinson's distinctive features of punctuation, meter and idiom were 'standardized' or simply changed by the editors), her poems have steadily increased in readership and reputation. Indeed, since the 1970s 'Emily Dickinson' (as both poet and personality) has become something of an enigmatic cult figure – especially amongst feminists. The above text (ed. Thomas Johnson *The Complete Poems of Emily Dickinson*, (London: Faber, 1970), no. 288, p. 133) restores Dickinson's word choice, punctuation and meter to that in what appears to be the (a?) final draft. It is generally agreed to be a preferable text to that produced by Todd and Higginson in 1890. Text (ii) – the current text – is itself a conflation of the entry in Ian Ousby (1990) *The Cambridge Companion to Literature in English* with information in the introductions to the editions by Johnson (1970) and Ted Hughes (1969) as well as the article by Nancy Walker 'Wider than the Sky: Public Presence and Private Self in Dickinson, James and Woolf', in Shari Benstock (ed.), *The Private Self: Theory and Practice of Women's Autobiogaphical Writings* (London: Routledge, 1988), pp. 272–303.

Responses to Text/Task A (with main points from commentaries)

a1

I was some body! But who were you?
Couldn't you have been some body too?
Then there were two of us. Oh well . . .!
We should've welcomed her – no?

How dreary to be a nobody
How private like a toad
Croaking her name the dark night through
Under a stone by a road.

a2

He's nobody! Who's she?
Is she nobody, too?
Then they are a pair, aren't they?
We'd banish them, wouldn't we?

How dreary to be nobody!
How private, like a fish
Never telling its name the livelong day
To the scorning pond!

a3

I've no body! What you too!
Or have you a body – two?

How lucky to be doubled
How fortunate for you
To have yourself in stereo
No monotones for you

How splendid to be nobody
And keep your name a secret
How weary to be everybody
And only half completed

Commentaries drew attention to such things as: the consequences of inverting and permutating pronouns with respect to point of view, agency and gender; change of objects/animals referred to as these affect metaphorical resonance; the more or less im/personal mode of address relative to self and other; a frequent tendency to conventionalize punctuation, make meaning more overtly coherent and smooth out syntax – or, conversely, to introduce arbitrary changes and increase the sense of *dis*continuity and *in*coherence. Most students found their re-writes interesting and illuminating but decidedly quirky and inferior when compared with the initial text. Some complained of feeling constrained by the instruction, and some felt anxious about committing a kind of sacrilege.

Responses to Text/Task B (with main points from commentaries)

b1

[This was read out loud by two voices: a woman for the text of the letter; a man for the narrative commentary in brackets.]

Amherst Mass
April 1, c. 1861

Dear Nobody

> I'm Emily – Who are you?
> I know you are – not Emily – too
> (She said, putting on her white dress)
> There's only one of me. You as well.
> (She said, not answering the door)
> Don't tell – or pull the bell.
> (She said, in a letter to a friend
> which was not posted
> till much later
> then advertised and published and read
> by EVERYBODY!)

yours

E.D.

b2

> I am Emily Dickinson
> All my life clothed in nebulous white
> I see nobody
>
> Are you nobody too?
> For I deny you exist
> And yet I write for you.
>
> How dreary to be dragged
> standardised from distinctive features
> of punctuation for publication
> for my modern readership and growing reputation.

b3

> from: e.d. @FROG
> to: x.h.@BOG

> Who are you, dear Mr Higginson?
> I'm NOBODY!
> Are you – Nobody – too?

But do not advertise there's a pair of us. You know how dreary it is to be Somebody! During your life time and become something of an enigma, a cult figure – especially amongst feminists. To become public and to tell my name and use my word choice punctuation and metre. It is generally agreed to be a preferable text to an admiring bog.

Commentaries drew attention to such things as: tensions between text and context, words and the rest of the world, people and paper; dialogues between 'there and then', 'here and now'; transformations of genre and/or medium; reorientation of poem to other ends; meta-textuality and open awareness about the editorial process; playful and yet serious. All students found the task challenging and most confessed to quite liking their re-writes. They recognized that the latter were related to yet different from the initial text – not damaging or competing with it.

Theorizing – and transforming – the subject

> English Studies should be reconstituted as the study of how verbal and written fictions have been produced and used, socially channelled and evaluated,... institutionalised, transformed... The Study of English will then provide a creative base for active experiments with cultural production (verbal, visual and aural) which enhance, improve and diversify rather than narrow and homogenise our cultural life.
>
> Brian Doyle, English and Englishness (1989: 142)

This last epigraph, like all the others, can be challenged and changed. Perhaps it might run:

> *English Literature, to be precise – not some vague 'Studies' – should continue to be the respectful and informed study of great literature. It should cultivate scholarly rigor and critical discrimination, and it should support a capacious yet coherent view of culture. More to the point, it should not dabble in creative writing but leave that to acknowledged authors or another department.*

There is some truth in that. Just as there may be some over-statement – and over-extension – in the conception of English Studies offered by Doyle. The present reader is by now probably aware where, on balance, my own sympathies lie. But that in itself is not particularly important. The real issue is that we have the power, capacity and perhaps opportunity to get ourselves and our students actively engaged in precisely such acts of critique and counter-critique – in creative as well as scholarly ways, taking risks even while exercising rigor. Researching *and* re-searching re-visioning . . . re-membering . . .

After all, let's face it, there are much worse ways of getting students to grapple with and get excited about such issues as, say: the 'death' of the author/artist; the rebirth of the reader/viewer; the nature of cultural re/production and inter/ textuality; the play of 'difference' and the exercise of 'preference;' de- and re-construction; textual change as a function of social exchange; the nature of 'value'; genre and gender; and so on. One of those 'worse ways,' I would argue, is to make students read lots of theory and ask them to 'apply' it to a text. Another, only slightly less stifling, is to get them to study lots of different 'readings' of a text and to choose the one(s) they favor. (The usual result, with some star exceptions, is a dull and dutiful rehearsal of orthodoxies, old or new.) Other ways – much better, I *do* argue (in the opening *Manifesto* for a start) – include some such strategies as are explored and illustrated here. And I further maintain that the 'subjects' that get 're-written' must be many and various. 'English' as a subject gets re-constructed as a critical *and* creative activity, drawing together advanced skills in rhetoric and composition with knowledge of literary history and precision in textual analysis. Students – 'the subjects who study' – get to re-create themselves as agents in their own rights/writes, even as they allow themselves to be subject to the demands and delights of writing by others. The texts and authors featured, meanwhile, remain both completely untouched and profoundly transformed by the whole experience. They are still there 'in their original forms' to be read and re-written over and over again. But in other respects, also as always, they can never be the same. In genuinely imaginative education, you *can* have it both ways. You *can* have your cake and eat it. You *can*, in fact as well as fiction, have 'a commonwealth in which work is play and play is life.' And if you can't, then it's not education at all. It's simply training for the death-in-life business of mere existence.

Appendix: types of re-writing and tips on teaching and assessment

Types of re-writing

- *Alternative summaries and the arts of paraphrase.* Summarize the text in different ways so as to draw attention to its various aspects and emphases – and also to the premises of the paraphraser.
- *Changed titles and openings.* Cue the reader for a slightly or very different reading experience – one with different expectations as to genre, center of interest, discourse, outlet, market, communicative relations, and so on.

- *Alternative endings.* Alter the ending of the initial text so as to draw attention to some option not explored or in some way foreclosed.
- *Preludes, interludes and postludes.* Extend the text 'before,' 'during' or 'after' the events it represents so as to explore alternative points of departure, processes of development, and points of arrival.
- *Narrative intervention.* Change some 'turning-point' in the narrative so as to explore alternative premises or consequences; also consider ways of re-framing the narrative so that the very process of narration is bared or concealed.
- *Dramatic intervention.* Change the direction of a scripted drama or transcribed conversation by intervening in a single 'move' or 'exchange;' also consider figures that might be re-cast, removed or inserted so as to alter the emphasis or choice of topic and the course of the action.
- *Narrative into drama – drama into narrative.* Explore 'showing' through 're-telling,' and 'telling' through 're-showing,' thereby investigating the peculiar configuration of re/presentation in the initial text: the stories it may tell and the 'voices' through which it may speak.
- *Imitation.* Devise a text using another as model, or re-cast one text in the manner – and perhaps matter – of another (perhaps by a different author, director, film company, and so on).
- *Parody.* Exaggerate certain features of a text, or introduce incongruous (perhaps anachronistic) frames of reference so as to throw its characteristic style or preoccupations into relief.
- *Collage.* Gather a diverse and perhaps disparate range of materials directly or indirectly relevant to the initial text (sources, parallels, contrasts, bits of critical commentary, relatable words, images, pieces of music, etc.), then select from and arrange these materials so as implicitly to make statements or ask questions about the initial text.
- *Hybrids and 'faction'.* Re-cast two or more related texts in a new textual mould so as to produce a compound – not merely a mixture – perhaps blending conventionally 'fictional' and 'factual' texts so as to produce 'faction' – in every sense. (Alternative metaphors for this process include grafting and hybridization.)
- *Word to image, word to music, word to movement, word to . . . ?* Film, video, photography, painting and sculpture; music, dance, mime and performance; even clothes, architecture, smells, touches and tastes – all offer alternative ways of in every sense – through every sense – 'interpreting' texts.

Tips

Emphasize that it is about re-writing *an existing text rather than* creating *a new one.* This makes it sound secure and doable: it reassures students who get over-awed or turned off by the idea of 'being creative' ('But I can't . . . ', 'Not me, thanks') and reins in those who simply want to do their own thing ('I've already got this novel I'm working on . . . '). Students will in effect create a new text anyway. This simply tricks them into it.

Get them into the idea of re-writing through periodically asking the questions: 'What if . . . ?' and 'What might you change?' during class. Then get them to turn over the possibilities in groups.

If in doubt – jump right in and have a go! The biggest initial anxiety is where to start and what to do. Another, rather less common problem is over-planning. But the only sure way is to turn over a few ideas on paper or through discussion (mind-maps, brainstorming, etc.) and then actually do some re-writing. This trial piece may or may not survive into a final version, but it helps establish what the problems and possibilities are.

Be prepared to draft and re-draft, chop and change, revise and refine AND eventually to settle on a final version, however provisional. This is the two-sided golden rule in all writing, of course: recognizing cumulative process but also requiring an achieved product. It applies with redoubled force when the focus is on the act and fact of re-writing.

The re-write *is the response to the text: the* commentary *is the reflection on that response.* Where the former works implicitly through performance (narrative, drama, poetry ...), the latter works explicitly through explanation (argument, analysis, abstraction ...). Both draw on research, knowledge and insight; but they do it in different modes. The overall result is a unified yet differentiated text woven from complementary discourses: creative and critical, playful and serious, practical and theoretical, the text as (re-)made and the text as (re-)discovered. And, in the event, all and any of these functions may be performed by the re-write and/or the commentary.

The assessment is therefore for overall achievement, insight and evidence of thought and work – as for any other piece of writing. You don't grade the two parts separately. And you don't insist on a particular proportion of re-write to commentary (though the latter often tends to be longer). But you do ask that the whole thing in some way hangs together; and you do grade for qualities of insight, knowledge, organization, and expression, as for any piece of course-work. The only difference is that you may need to 're-write' (extend and enrich) some of your expectations and criteria.

Notes

1. For further discussion and fuller references with respect to *re-writing* in general and *intervention* in particular, see Rob Pope, *Textual Intervention: Critical and Creative Strategies for Literary Studies* (London and New York: Routledge, 1995); *The English Studies Book: an Introduction to Language, Literature and Culture* (London and New York: Routledge, 2nd edn, 2002), esp. Part 4; and *Creativity* (London and New York: Routledge New Critical Idiom Series, 2003), esp. Chapter 5. Other relevant books of general and recurrent usefulness are listed in the bibliography at the end of this volume.

9

Schooling Misery: the Ominous Threat and the Eminent Promise of the Popular Reader

Richard E. Miller

For those who live and work outside the academy, it is hard to know which is more amusing: the spectacle of academics decrying popular culture's power to unravel a nation's intellectual, social, and moral values, or the efforts of academics to seem hip and 'with-it' by offering courses on Madonna, MTV, and the fashion industry. In either case, the ephemeral appeal of any given product of popular culture never seems to live up to all the critical attention: for every measured denunciation of 2 Live Crew as obscene, violent, and misogynist, for instance, and for every celebration of the resistant, counter-capitalist impulse that is said to reside at the core of hip-hop, there's always a readily available clip of some blasé concert-goer proclaiming, 'Hey, man, we're just here to party.' And so, given that the products of popular culture come and go at such a dizzying pace (does anyone even know who 2 Live Crew is any more?) and that the consumers of these products don't tend to take them too seriously, why bother with them at all in the classroom? Or, more specifically, what, if anything, is to be gained by bringing popular culture into a literature course?

The question of what kind of texts should be admitted to the literature curriculum is as old as the discipline itself. But, if one attends carefully to the long history of the academic criticism of popular culture, one finds submerged within all the highly agitated rhetoric about the sanctity of the western canon a sense that the *real* threat of popular culture rests not so much with the products themselves or even with the values those products might seek to promote in the culture at large, but rather with how those products are consumed by the popular reader. For example, no one would dispute the fact that, when F.R. Leavis published *Mass Civilization and Minority Culture* in 1930, he was clearly disturbed by the rising popularity of the cinema. But close inspection of his argument reveals that he located the most ominous threat in those consumers who 'surrender, under conditions of hypnotic receptivity, to the cheapest emotional appeals, appeals the more insidious because they are associated with a compellingly vivid illusion of actual life' (9–10). This sense that there's something malevolent in the popular audience's relationship to popular culture was reiterated three decades later in Dwight MacDonald's definition of 'masscult' as the grinding out of 'a uniform product whose humble aim is not even entertainment, for this too implies life and hence effort, but merely distraction. It may be stimulating or narcotic, but it must be easy to assimilate' (5). And, of course, for further evidence of the critic's revulsion, one can always turn to Allan Bloom's jeremiad, *The Closing of the American Mind*, which reliably offers any number of examples of a critic horrified by what the consumption of popular culture might be said to signify: what makes rock and roll particularly sinister, for instance, is that it

> artificially induces the exaltation naturally attached to the completion of the greatest endeavors – victory in a just war, consummated love, artistic creation, religious devotion and discovery of the truth. Without effort, without talent, without virtue, without exercise of the faculties, anyone and everyone is accorded the equal right to the enjoyment of their fruits (80).

Hypnotized, distracted, hungry for artificial exaltation: consumers of popular culture pose a threat not so much because of what they consume, but because of the way they consume it.

It's not terribly surprising to find that critics have expressed this enduring contempt for what might be more sympathetically termed the 'literate practices of popular readers.' After all, the ways of reading practiced in the academic community – careful, comprehensive, complex, critical, disinterested – find their absolute antitheses in the ways of reading that are presumed to define the literate world of the popular reader – careless, incomplete, simplistic, effortless, prejudiced. Although it is true that in the past two decades there have been numerous, sustained counter-efforts to recuperate the objects, artifacts, and styles of popular culture as suitable for academic study, these efforts do not, in themselves, signify that the academy's relationship to the popular reader has changed. In fact, with the obvious exceptions of ethnographic and reception studies, the general inclination within these movements has been to proceed by applying academic literate practices to popular texts, without ever considering how those texts have circulated among actual popular readers. In their ground-breaking work, *Bond and Beyond*, Tony Bennett and Janet Woollacott offer a particularly astute assessment of the way most studies of popular culture have handled the problem of accounting for the way popular readers read popular texts. As they see it, in most cases, working with popular culture has meant 'doing the same old thing, analyzing texts, and then saying generously that, of course, interpretations may vary, even to the point of entertaining the prospect of unlimited semiosis' (63). That Bennett and Woollacott do not set out to answer their own call for an investigation of 'the range of meanings that have *actually* been produced in relation to' the James Bond novels and films, but attempt instead 'to open up a theoretical space within which the empirical study of reading practices might be located,' is a sign of the intransigence of the problem the popular reader poses for the academic community.

Led by my desire to do something other than 'the same old thing' with popular culture and by my interest in this conflict between the ways of reading fostered in the academy and the ways of reading engaged in outside the academy, I designed an undergraduate critical writing course entitled, 'Investigating Popular Literate Practices.' I placed Stephen King's *Misery* at the center of this course for a number of reasons, not the least of which was the fact that the novel transforms a three-word cliché – 'misery loves company' – into a 300-page meditation on the set of ambivalent relationships that exist between a popular writer, his reading public, and the literary-critical establishment. King's assault on the popular reader begins less than ten pages into the novel, when Paul Sheldon, *Misery*'s protagonist, describes himself as writing 'novels of two kinds, good ones and best-sellers' (7). Of course, the actual readers of King's *Misery* might not even pick up on the insult implied by this distinction or they might think the insult applies only to readers of another genre of fiction, since Sheldon is not, at least at the beginning of the novel, a writer of best-selling horror stories, but of romances featuring the trials and tribulations of a character named Misery Chastain. However, when Sheldon goes on to describe the women who read his novels as 'too stupid' or 'too set' in their ways to understand his more overtly literary efforts, as '*not just unwilling to change, but antagonistic to the very* idea *of change*' (27), it becomes increasingly difficult to read the novel as just a story about a romance writer both literally and figuratively imprisoned by his readers. Indeed, within the economy of the novel's own critical terminology, one could argue that those readers who can't see that King is also discussing his own situation are simply 'too stupid' or 'too set' in their ways to understand the self-reflexive quality of the story he is telling. Thus, Sheldon's assertion that 'He could write a modern *Under the Volcano, Tess of the D'Urbervilles, The Sound and the Fury*; it wouldn't matter. They would still want Misery, Misery, Misery' (28) simultaneously describes both the actual readers of King's novel, *Misery*, who, for that moment at least, are eschewing such canonical texts, and the regular readers of King's novels who have foregone reading *Misery* because it isn't like his other books. Were it not for his audience, Sheldon could become the next Faulkner; were it not for King's audience, the opening of the novel suggests, similar heights of literary achievement might be available to him as well.

If, at the level of performance, the novel thus begins by having the writer slap his reader around a bit, reversing the action in the story itself, all of these relationships get shaken up when Annie Wilkes – Sheldon's captor, nurse, and 'number one fan' – forces him to destroy his 'serious' novel, *Fast Cars*, and to start writing a sequel to *Misery's Child*. Now, at first glance, this task might seem impossibly difficult, since Misery died in childbirth at the end of *Misery's Child*. However, given Sheldon's assumptions about the kind of people who read his novels, the requirement that he resurrect his heroine seems more unpleasant than impossible: 'After all, a man who could drink from a floor-bucket should be capable of a little directed writing' (61). Thinking his reader 'too stupid' to know the difference, Sheldon easily slips back into the 'corny and melodramatic' world of his heroine (105), quickly pounding out part of a first draft that brings Misery back to life through a miraculous, experimental blood transfusion. Sheldon is 'flabbergasted' when Annie returns with the judgment that this initial effort is 'not right' (105) and that 'it's a cheat'(106). As Annie details all of the reasons why the blood transfusion could not have worked based on the conclusion to *Misery's Child*, Sheldon is forced to reassess his initial assumptions about his reader: 'She really *was* Constant Reader, but Constant Reader did not mean Constant Sap' (107). Realizing that she is right, Sheldon sees that whatever solution he comes up with wouldn't have to be 'all that *real-istic*,' but it would have to be 'fair' (109) – it would have to play by the rules he had established in his novels which meant, among other things, no miracles.

At the point Sheldon concedes to the charge of having cheated, the roles in the novel get reversed and the derogatory representations of the popular reader come to an end: Annie, without any knowledge of words like '*deus ex machina*,' becomes a teacher rather than a cultural dope; Paul, with his knowledge of latinate words and his collection of best-sellers, assumes the appearance of 'a conscientious student' (109); and King settles comfortably into the business of attacking his real enemy – not the doltish and addicted reading public he started with, but the effete literary establishment that has failed to recognize the significance of his achievements. Thus, as Sheldon listens to Annie's explanation of why his draft wasn't 'fair,' he comes to understand 'how she could like what he had written and still know it was not right – know it and say it not with an editor's sometimes untrustworthy literary sophistication but with Constant Reader's flat and uncontradictable certainty' (110–11). In one fell swoop, then, Annie goes from being a member of the mass of readers who have prevented Sheldon from realizing his highest literary aspirations to being his ideal reader – one who, through the sincerity and straightforwardness of her response, eventually gets him to produce what may be 'the best thing [he] ever wrote, mongrel or not' (315). While Annie continues to be the person who physically imprisons Sheldon, from this point on in the novel, 'literary sophistication' appears more and more insistently as the enemy responsible for misleading Sheldon about the importance of popular fiction and the validity of his occupation.

One can trace the novel's slide away from its pretensions to being a part of 'high culture' in the references that head its four sections: King begins with quotes from Nietzsche and Montaigne, but concludes with John Fowles and Paul Sheldon, who is of course King himself. And, although the novel is sprinkled with references to a wide range of canonical writers – Fitzgerald, Hemingway, Faulkner, Maugham, Twain, Dickens, and Hardy, to name a few – it draws just as insistently on the realm of popular culture for its inspiration – The Lone Ranger, Superman, the novels of H. Rider Haggard and H.G. Wells, and, in an open wink to the knowing reader, John Fowles' *The Collector*, which served as King's template for *Misery*. In contrast with the playful heterogeneity of the novel's references, King's critique of the 'untrustworthy' literary terms that preoccupy the critical establishment is consistently negative. For example, Sheldon tries to console himself with the thought that his destroyed novel, *Fast Cars*, was a book that *'Peter Prescott would [have] shit upon in his finest genteel disparaging manner when he reviewed it for that great literary oracle, Newsweek'* (44). From editors with their 'sophisticated' literary terminology to reviewers for the most pedestrian of news journals, no one in the literary-critical end of the publishing business can be trusted to accurately assess the quality of Sheldon's work.

Over the course of the novel, Sheldon develops his own apparently straightforward literary-critical vocabulary for assessing the success or failure of a work to replace this language of sophistication and fine genteel disparagement: 'Can you?' – the ability to produce narrative on the spur of the moment (116); 'Did he?' – ascertaining whether or not the narrative succeeded, that is, whether it was 'fair' or it 'cheated' (117); and, eventually, 'the gotta' – achieving enough narrative momentum so that the readers must finish the story (242). The first two terms, drawn from a story-telling game played at summer camp, allow Sheldon to foreground the particular merits of his own work, which might escape the attention of readers using a different critical apparatus:

> *There are lots of guys out there who write a better prose line than I do and who have a better understanding of what people are really like and what humanity is supposed to mean – hell, I know that. But when the counselor asks* Did he? *about those guys, sometimes only a few people raise their hands. But they raise their hands for me ... or for Misery ... and in the end I guess they're both the same. Can I? Yeah. You bet I can.* (117–18)

While Sheldon is able to assert a defiant sense of pride and accomplishment in his own writing by the use of these two terms, he comes to his most significant and lasting realization about his relationship to his occupation as popular novelist by thinking about his final term, 'the gotta.' Although Sheldon initially felt he just wrote popular novels to support his more important 'real work,' he comes to see, through writing *Misery's Return*, that telling stories of this kind both truly entertains him and keeps him alive as well. Or, as Sheldon succinctly puts it during one of his internal dialogues, *'you were – are – also Scheherazade to yourself'* (239). Reader and writer simultaneously, and unaware in both roles exactly where his own evolving story is going to go, Sheldon himself is imprisoned and liberated by 'the gotta' of his stories.

Sheldon's realization occasions one final reversal, where the popular reader, deprived of the power either to imprison or to collaborate with the popular writer, is once again demoted to the role of the entranced, addicted, passive spectator. Thus, while Annie does suggest the bee that comes to play such a central role in *Misery's Return* (148), she quickly returns to a position of subordinate importance in the production of the novel, filling in the missing n's in the manuscript by hand and saying things like, 'I *do* want to know how it comes out. That's the *only* thing left in the world that I still want, I suppose' to explain why she won't kill them both before the novel is finished (174). In Sheldon's final assessment of his position as a writer, then, the popular reader doesn't even figure in the equation: *'The reasons authors almost always put a dedication on a book, Annie, is because their selfishness even horrifies themselves in the end'* (304). Sheldon has been trapped not by his readers, but by a culture that had convinced him that he was being compelled to do something he didn't like, when in fact he enjoyed his work immensely all along. Having come to see that he has been made miserable by a critical community unable to see that they 'were dealing with a young Mailer or Cheever here,' Sheldon asks rhetorically, isn't this what drove his writing to become 'steadily more self-conscious, a sort of scream? *Look at me! Look how good this is! Hey, guys! This stuff has got a sliding perspective! This stuff has got stream-of-consciousness interludes! This is my REAL WORK, you assholes!'* (286). And, of course, as Sheldon reflects on his work in this light, King himself provides commentary on what he has been up to in *Misery* as he has toyed with sliding perspectives, stream-of-consciousness interludes, self-referentiality, layered textuality in the multiple typefaces, telling stories within stories within stories, and the blurring of genres. In the end, it seems King, like his protagonist, has come to the conclusion that, while the kind of formal play celebrated in canonical texts can be deployed to good effect in the realm of popular fiction, in the end it amounts to little more than 'a sort of scream' directed at a group of people who are, ultimately, just a bunch of assholes.

In this way, King's *Misery* concludes with what may seem a baffling gesture of contempt, since it dismisses the significance of both the popular reader and the critical community, asserting that, ultimately, it is the production of popular culture and not its reception that is of primary importance. Because the novel was so successful at suspending this set of antagonisms between high culture and popular culture, writing (as masculine) and reading (as feminine), 'authentic' writing (narratives) and 'derivative' writing (criticism), and horror and romance, it seemed the perfect object of study for a course devoted to the investigation of popular literate practices. While I was certainly interested in seeing how my students would respond to the novel's generally unflattering depiction of the popular reader, on the one hand, and its dismissive portrayal of the critical community, on the other, my overarching concern was to have the novel function as a laboratory of sorts for studying competing definitions of literacy. Thus, the students would not go about working with the novel in 'the same old way' of simply analyzing the tensions and reversals in the text as I've done here, but rather they would research how the novel itself had been received as a way of examining actual instances of popular and academic literate practices in action. In pursuing the project, they would thus be continuously working with and against the questions: What can we learn from *Misery* about how the popular reader has been represented? And what does the reception of the novel itself tell us about the differences between academic, critical, and popular literate practices?

There are limits to having students 'investigate' popular literate practices in an academic setting, of course. First of all, there's the problem of determining the status of the students' own responses to the novel in this context, since it goes without saying that the way students read a book for class differs considerably from the way they read a book on their own. Then, there is the additional problem that what I found interesting about the novel was the result of a particular academic way of reading: rather than attend to the gore in the novel, I had focused on self-referentiality, the construction and deconstruction of binary oppositions, and the reversal of power relationships among the characters, in order to make a larger argument about the problematic representation of the popular reader by literary critics and popular writers alike. There was no guarantee that my students, deploying different ways of reading, informed by different acts of attention, would end up seeing *Misery* as a novel about popular literate practices. Although the students might decide to focus on other aspects of the novel that I felt warranted attention – the complacency with which it trades on the image of Africa as the site of unbridled savagery and ignorance; the numerous instances where femininity, maternity, and castration are linked; or the physical and mental violence (*'so vivid,'* as Sheldon would say) depicted throughout – they might just as easily decide to attend to what most of King's readers find exciting and pleasurable about his work: its surprises and terrors, its suspense and violence.

That there are different ways of reading *Misery* that produce, through their various and necessarily incomplete acts of attention, conflicting senses of what the novel might be said to be about, struck me at the time less as a crippling limitation to the course than as an instance of the very problematic the course was most concerned with studying. Thus, in seeking to 'school' *Misery*, rather than to castigate or celebrate it, I assumed the course would reproduce the larger cultural tensions that exist between a definition of reading for pleasure that stands in opposition to reading critically ('We're making too much out of this. It's just for fun.') and a definition of reading that involves consciously situating oneself in relation to what is being read ('This is a misogynist text that celebrates violence against women'). The work of the course was not to determine which of the multiple readings was 'right,' per se, but rather to investigate the different literate practices that produced these multiple readings. Thus, instead of arguing about which reading was right, my students would research the ways the novel had been read and ask: what makes certain ways of reading available to some readers and not to others? Which ways of reading the novel seem to predominate? How can one distinguish between a 'popular' reading of the novel and an 'academic' reading of it?

Before my students began working with *Misery*, they had already done a good deal of thinking and writing about different ways of reading culture: they had read Mary Douglas' 'Jokes,' which considers the social context and function of humor; Robert Darnton's 'The Great Cat Massacre,' which interprets the symbolic violence done when a group of disgruntled workers killed their employer's wife's favorite cat; and Clifford Geertz's 'Deep Play: Notes on the Balinese Cockfight,' which interprets the cultural significance of Balinese cockfighting. The students had also written and revised essays describing their own efforts to apply the ideas of each of these authors to situations from the students' own experiences. Thus, by the time they reached Stephen King's novel at midterm, they were prepared to consider some of the ways that a particular artifact of culture might be read. The students began their work with *Misery* by writing up their sense of what 'the novel has to say about the writing process and the relationship between writers and readers,' as my assignment put it. They then moved on to collectively produce what we came to call 'the reception database' – an archive of sorts containing all the information we could find that related either to Stephen King, the novel or the movie version of *Misery*, or any of the other affiliated issues that students felt might be relevant to staking out a position in relation to King's text. My directive for collecting this information was fairly open-ended:

In his essay, 'Thick Description,' Clifford Geertz defines anthropological interpretation as 'tracing the curve of a social discourse; fixing it into an inspectable form.' We, as a class, are going to try to trace the curve of the social discourse (or, we may find, the curves of the social discourses) that surrounds, precedes and emanates from Stephen King's *Misery* and the film version of King's novel. Before any such tracing can begin, however, we will need to collect as much information as we can about the book and the film and the context surrounding the reception of each.

The result of this effort to collect together, in 'inspectable form,' as much material evidence of actual instances of reception was a thick, ungainly, heterogenous 'book' that included among other things: interviews with King, reviews of the novel and the film from every conceivable mass-market magazine, articles about the popular book trade and the marketing of King's work, critical essays and excerpts from longer works examining the King 'canon,' and even a self-styled miniature ethnography cataloguing the reactions of family members, friends, and colleagues to the film adaptation of *Misery*. Thus, the end product of this joint research effort was neither a comprehensive sampling nor a judiciously balanced example of the range of the ways *Misery might* have been read; it was, instead, a text that allowed us to initiate an investigation of some of the ways that the novel *had*, in fact, been read.

One of the immediate benefits of having the students communally produce a text of this kind was that it meant there was no way I could claim mastery of the material they had collected. Indeed, the virtue of the database was that it provided all the students with a unique configuration of the novel's 'receptive' world, one that offered them the possibility of making original connections, of testing real hypotheses, and of genuinely assessing the merits of their own insights. From a certain perspective, then, the students were, in a limited but nonetheless real sense, 'free' in their final project for the course to make whatever they wished of the material. They were simply instructed to 'offer a reading of the [reception database] drawing attention to whatever [they found] most striking or significant about it, and articulating what 'story' – to borrow Geertz's term – that material has to tell about the culture that produced it.'

Now if the representations of the popular reader provided by Leavis, MacDonald, Bloom, and King are to be believed, one might expect that the best one could hope for in this situation would be that some students might struggle to achieve a docile compliance with their teacher's assignment, producing a sort of well-intentioned, but imperfect act of ventriloquizing what the teacher wants to hear. Meanwhile, one could anticipate confidently that the rest of the students, drawn hypnotically to popular culture, would simply feast mindlessly on what was put before them and then stumble on to the next trough. And yet, predicting what students might do under these circumstances isn't as easy as it seems, since by virtue of their position in a critical writing course, they are in the process of learning how to structure arguments, marshal evidence, and draw conclusions and are, thereby, acquiring and refining the powers of discrimination that are of such concern to the likes of Leavis, MacDonald, and Bloom. Thus, the student papers that follow should not be read as 'pure' examples of popular reception (whatever that ideal act might be construed to involve), but rather as evidence of how two students negotiated the gap between popular ways of reading the novel and the demands of writing about those readings in an academic setting. Neither 'purely' popular nor 'purely' academic, the writing that follows oscillates between both worlds: heterogenous in its discourse and its strategies, this writing exemplifies a liminal literate practice, or rather a literate practice of liminality that has more than a little to teach those academics interested in speaking with the public rather than at or about them.

Dot Javorski, a self-described 'Stephen King fan,' concludes her essay by taking a stand against making too much out of the seeming connection between the popularity of Stephen King's novels and the violence that defines American society:

It would seem then that our reading practices do indeed say something of our culture. However, by looking at any one type of genre, (in this essay Stephen King literature) a distorted view of our society might be obtained. What is being said in this case is not pleasant. We might be led to believe that our lives in this culture have become nothing more than a struggle to survive. And, in this struggle, we have lost the ability to entertain ourselves through positive experiences. Rather our literature would seem to be filled with stories of anger, rage, and violence...Are our lives really so horrible that it is only by viewing stories of those worse off than ourselves that we are able to cope? I think not. 'The culture of a people is an ensemble of texts, themselves ensembles, which the anthropologist strains to read over the shoulders of those to whom they properly belong' (Geertz 269). This one 'text' that I have chosen to discuss is in itself made up of various other texts. Yes, a Stephen King novel or film does fulfill certain needs some of which have been discussed in this paper. However, this same reader may at another point in time read love stories, historical novels and yes, even romance novels. While discussing the Balinese cockfight, Geertz states that 'the Balinese forms and discovers his temperament and his society's temper at the same time. Or, more exactly, he forms and discovers a particular facet of them' (268). This then was the work of my essay: to portray one facet of our culture. Not to categorize it, nor to make a judgment on it, but to simply examine it for what it may reveal about one area of our society. Yes, we are a violent society as can be evidenced by the news each day. And, yes, perhaps we have become so desensitized to the inhumanity of it that we are at times entertained by it. However, there are other parts of our culture reflected in the popularity of such novels/films as *Gone with the Wind*, *Dancing with Wolves*, and even *Mary Poppins*, that in fact balance the views we might obtain of our culture.

Although Dot's own work with *Misery* has led her to argue that the novel satisfies a cultural lust for violence, she nonetheless resists the pressure to condemn the work, its readers, and the society that consumes such material. Instead of reading King's popularity as a sign of some larger cultural malignancy, Dot draws on Geertz's notion of culture as 'an ensemble of texts' to argue that King's work must be seen as one text among many at the popular reader's disposal. Far from exhibiting the characteristics of a reader uninterested and unaccustomed to 'effort,' this King fan demonstrates a striking facility at working with a number of different texts simultaneously, producing in the process writing that argues through its form and its content that blithe claims about cultural decline are not entirely warranted. Reluctant to 'categorize' or to 'make a judgment' on King's work, Dot seems content to insist on maintaining a kind of neutrality, balancing the 'views we might obtain of our culture' from *Misery* against other very different popular texts.

Eric Lieb takes a very different approach in his paper when he borrows terms from Janice Radway's study of romance readers to argue that the 'simple transmission–reception model' for reading is inferior to 'the method that involves constructing a meaning from the text.' Dissatisfied with the fact that 'a great number of people' seemed to read *Misery* according to the first model, getting only 'the cheap thrills of blood and gore' from the story, Eric goes on to argue that:

> it is necessary to look past the surface of texts. In Radway's essay, she looks past the typical image of a romance reader that we formed in class on the third of June. The readers of *Misery* must look past the blood and gore surface. From these thoughts, I conclude that it is necessary to construct your own meaning in order to get the most out of a text. For example, the way that Geertz forms many ideas about cockfighting in order to understand the Balinese. I find it very interesting that Radway and Geertz learned so much by reading a single event in culture. I find what King did in *Misery* even more interesting. The idea that King is writing about himself, through Paul, has been brought up numerously in class. In Deborah Drylie's critical essay, she quotes King, 'I thought to myself, you're talking about *The Thousand and One Nights*, and you're talking about what you do.' In doing this, King actually performed somewhat of a reading of himself. Earlier, I thought this was impossible. In my revision, 'Tense Intersections,' I point out that it was not possible for one to read themself in a social situation. Now that I see that it can be done, I wander if it is possible to go beyond constructing your own meaning of a text, that is, to construct a meaning of yourself.

Word sheriffs will no doubt feel the need to point out Eric's use of 'themself,' his substitution of 'wander' for 'wonder,' and his paratactic prose style, missing the way Eric has constructed his own, self-reflexive response to King's novel. Unlike Dot, Eric is untroubled by the fact that one can learn 'so much by reading a single event in culture.' To the contrary, it is by reading 'past the blood and gore surface' that Eric finds himself in a position to refute an argument he himself made earlier in the course, enabling him to insist now that it is possible both to produce a 'reading' of yourself and 'to construct a meaning of yourself.' If the syntax is somewhat awkward, the insight is nonetheless worthy of attention: by focusing on the fact that King writes about himself through Sheldon, Eric suddenly feels a sense of empowerment – he, too, can construct a meaning of himself through writing. This kind of discovery, Eric argues later in his essay, simply is not available to 'people who are not in touch with the academy.' Thus, while Dot works to recuperate a way of reading King that takes a certain pleasure in the 'blood and gore,' Eric is at pains to repudiate this way of reading, issuing a clarion call for 'teaching people to be active readers of social contexts and situations.'

Taken together, these two student essays dramatize the fundamental difficulties that inevitably arise in reception studies: the students took the same course, read the same assigned essays, participated in the same class discussions, and worked through the same mass of reception data, and yet they ended up arguing diametrically opposed positions. Despite their divergent conclusions about how best to account for the reception of King's novel, however, the two student responses exhibit common strategies: both students go out of their way to marshal evidence and cite sources in making their arguments, while simultaneously working to see how any of these issues might possibly affect them personally. Dot thinks about the significance of the fact that, aside from being a fan of Stephen King's, she also reads novels from a host of other popular genres; Eric, similarly, is led by a student's quotation from a King interview to wonder if it is possible to go beyond constructing meanings of texts to constructing a meaning of oneself. What drives their writing, in effect, is the effort to find out what the course's protracted discussions of reception and popular literate practices might possibly have to do with them.

As they oscillate between the demands of the academy to stake out a position, establish an argument, and present evidence of their own particular concerns, these student writers develop a relationship with the academy that has more in common with Stephen King's than with Allan Bloom's: they speak, in other words, from the outside and work to determine whether or not they want to come in, rather than speaking from the inside and demanding the right to determine whether or not others may enter. That Dot ends up arguing for the importance of reserving a place for literature like King's, while Eric is led by the same work to insist that people outside the academy need to be taught to read in more sophisticated ways does not alter the fact that both students responded to the difficult task of writing about popular culture in an academic setting by establishing an overt connection between the academic issues raised by the course and their own personal experience. This may seem a small point, but I believe it provides an important insight into one of the principal differences between popular and academic literate practices. Unlike their academic counterparts who can, for instance, discuss the significance of *Misery* in relation to more general issues about popular reception and education, these students can only commence their investigation of these same issues by simultaneously considering the ways in which the issues have an impact on them personally as readers and writers in the academy. It is only after the students have made this personal connection to the 'larger' intellectual issues that they are in a position to experience, to appropriate King's terminology, 'the gotta' of critical writing, for it is at this point that what initially appeared to be 'merely' academic to the students is seen to have the possibility of being personally revelatory, as in Eric's case, or personally threatening, as in Dot's case.

I am continually amazed at this ability in students to wrench from the university system an education that they themselves might possibly value. It serves as a reminder to me of the power of popular readers to participate in negotiated acts of reception, to question what they read, and to establish connections between texts. In empirical studies of King's work, the acts of reception discussed here would register as nothing more than two blips in a display of sales figures. In discussions of how King's novel positions its reader at the confluence of a set of irresistible ideological forces, these 'anomalous' acts of reception would appear as nothing more than overdetermined responses to the codes that necessarily govern the interactions between teachers and students. In criticizing this way of understanding the popular reader, I do not mean to imply that the critical and theoretical issues that preoccupy the academic community are without meaning or value. Indeed, it should be clear from the structure of my course and the focus of its concerns that I find these issues to be of central importance – so much so, in fact, that I am committed to producing an educational environment where the students may productively engage with these issues themselves. Thus, my goal has not been to derail the study of popular culture in the academy so much as it has been to suggest that attending to the actual responses of popular readers can serve to inform and enliven our study of this material, jarring our discussions out of their frequently predictable, paradigmatic conclusions about the consumers of popular culture as manipulated dopes or resistant heroes. And in this regard, my project in the classroom is not unlike King's project in *Misery*, for in both places the work pursued concerns troubling dominant representations of the popular reader.

I would argue, in conclusion, that opening up the classroom so that students may participate in the investigation not simply of popular culture but of how popular culture is actually consumed helps to ensure that such work is informed by an ongoing reluctance to accept the representation of the popular reader as a passive recipient of culture. Indeed, having students write about the reception of a novel that is itself concerned with the problem of reception is not to turn the classroom into a hall of mirrors, but to promote the establishment of an educational environment where students openly negotiate their relationship to popular culture and the academy. If the student essays discussed here are any indication of what can happen when students engage in this kind of work, it may turn out that the real 'threat' of the popular reader has less to do with an undiscriminating palate than with an insistence that intellectual issues be made relevant to personal experience. While there are certainly ample theoretical grounds for objecting to this way of constructing personal experience as an unproblematic category, such objections do not in any way address the fact that personal experience functions as the principal category popular readers rely on to organize their world of priorities. Thus, for those educators who hope to reconfigure the relationship between the academic and the popular communities, and for those seriously interested in reclaiming the lost role of the public intellectual, the work that lies ahead involves learning how to read and respond to the concerns of actual popular readers, rather than developing more and more sophisticated ways of saying that what is *really* happening in popular cultural texts takes place 'behind the backs' of popular readers at some, presumably deeper, ideological and/or psychological level. By reconceiving the classroom as a site where popular and academic literate practices are placed in dialogue with one another, rather than as the place where popular literate practices are cast aside, the important work of education gets redefined not as a process of eradication but as an ongoing act of negotiation between competing desires and concerns. That every classroom provides a more or less captive audience of such popular readers goes without saying...

Works cited

Bennett, Tony and Janet Woollacott. *Bond and Beyond* (New York: Methuen, 1987).

Bloom, Allan. *The Closing of the American Mind* (New York: Simon & Schuster, 1987).

Darnton, Robert. *The Great Cat Massacre and Other Episodes in French Cultural History*. New York: Basic Books, 1984.

Douglas, Mary. 'Jokes,' in Chandra Mukerji and Michael Schudson (eds), *Rethinking Popular Culture: Contemporary Perspectives in Cultural Studies* (Berkeley: University of California Press, 1991), pp. 291–310.

Geertz, Clifford. 'Deep Play: Notes on the Balinese Cockfight.' Reprinted in *Rethinking Popular Culture*, edited by Chandra Mukerji and Michael Schudson (Berkeley: University of California Press, 1991), pp. 239–77.

King, Stephen. *Misery* (New York: Penguin Books, 1988).

Leavis, F.R. *Mass Civilization and Minority Culture* (Cambridge: The Minority Press, 1930).

MacDonald, Dwight. 'Masscult and Midcult,' *Against the American Grain* (New York: Da Capo Press, 1983), pp. 3–79.

Radway, Janice. 'Interpretive Communities and Variable Literacies: the Functions of Romance Reading.' Reprinted in *Rethinking Popular Culture*, edited by Chandra Mukerji and Michael Schudson (Berkeley: University of California Press, 1991), pp. 465–86.

10
The River and the Chestnut Tree: When Students Already Know the Answers

Ann Dean

This chapter describes an encounter with students' expectations and assumptions about literary study, an encounter I found particularly mysterious because those expectations differed significantly from mine. To work with this situation I had to consider the interactions between course design, students' behavior, cheating, theories of reading, definitions of literary knowledge, and literary study in secondary schools. I present this account as an example of the difficulty of interpreting students' work and also as one model for creating a situation where students can change the way they write and think.

The events I'd like to discuss took place in a course called 'Introduction to the Novel.' The students ranged from age 18 to about 40, and had similarly various experiences with the study of literature. I had designed the course around questions of genre: What makes a novel? How do novels define themselves? What roles do novels create for their readers? In *The Origins of the English Novel*, Michael McKeon observes 'the necessary continuity of [older forms such as romance] on which the decisively different forms of modernity [such as the novel] are dependent for their dialectical negation' (19). I set up the syllabus around this relationship, asking students to look at the ways that novels referred to, borrowed from, and distanced themselves from earlier forms such as epic, folk tale, and romance. We began the semester by reading book 20 of the *Iliad* and a section of a romance, *Eric and Enide*. We then moved to *Moll Flanders*, *Pride and Prejudice*, and *Jane Eyre*.

By the time we were well into *Jane Eyre*, I was fairly satisfied with the course. I had a bright, interesting group of students; class discussions were going well. But there were one or two problems: a group of students on the left side kept up an incessant whispered conversation during class, just low enough not to be openly rude but obviously unrelated to the work of the course. And then there was the chestnut tree.

The mystery of the chestnut tree

Periodically during the course, I asked the students to write a short essay in class, using 15–20 minutes at the beginning of the period. This was a way of making sure they kept up with the reading, as well as giving them a chance to work with the ideas and concepts central to the course. Usually I would take an idea I had introduced in a previous class and ask them to use it to say something about the new reading they had just completed. When they had read chapters 20–27 of *Jane Eyre*, I began a class by putting a list on the board of all the ideas we had been discussing up to that point. Each of these ideas was related to the problem of defining the novel as a genre:

- the novel as a novelty – a form newer and more modern than epic or romance
- references to other genres – fairy tales, romance, travels, poetry, landscapes, drama
- dialogue and narration as ways of representing character
- continuous and discontinuous narrative – what elements of the book does the writer sustain, what elements are introduced and then dropped?
- interiority and socially constructed identity
- realism

I asked the students to choose one of these and use it to interpret a passage from the novel, using quotations and reading them closely.

I collected these papers and found many students doing interesting work. But four of the papers presented me with a mystery. All four of these papers discussed the symbolism of the chestnut tree in Mr Rochester's garden. It is under this tree, readers will remember, that Jane agrees to marry Mr Rochester, not realizing that he is already married. Almost immediately, the tree is 'struck by lightning in the night, and half of it split away' (244). These papers expatiated on the symbolism of the roots of the tree, the protective spreading branches, the foreshadowing of the sudden strike from above. They explained how Brontë's skill as an artist showed up in her ability to use this tree to tie the novel together.

I walked around campus for several days pondering these papers. They made no gesture at even mentioning any of the terms from my list. They treated the novel as entirely continuous and unified, without social context. They ignored the question of genre completely by discussing the symbol of the tree without reference to the book's realism, or even to narrative – they could have been discussing poetry. So, while it is certainly the case that the chestnut tree serves as a symbol of the possibilities of love, as well as of Jane's connection to and separation from nature, sexuality, and the knowledge of good and evil, such claims ignored entirely the ongoing conversation and work of this course.

What could I possibly have said, I asked myself, to make these students go off in this particular direction? And how could four different students have so similarly missed the point? They had written the essays in class, without notes, under my watchful eye, so the problem was not one of simple cheating. I have a vivid memory of standing motionless in the university parking lot, my keys in my hand, asking myself these questions over and over.

The source of the chestnut

By wondering what *I* had done to produce this effect, I assumed that my actions were central to students' experience of the course. But the framework I had set up for the course was not the only available way to treat reading or to think about the novel. Students had been asked to read and to think about reading quite differently in their earlier education. But I was so involved in my teaching project that I couldn't imagine that anyone in the class could have declined to enter the conversation.

I might never have made the imaginative leap required to notice students who weren't involved in my vision of the course, if I hadn't just by chance come across an answer to my questions. In the university bookstore, my eye fell on the rack of *Cliffs Notes*, packaged commercial study guides for students in English courses. I picked up the *Jane Eyre* guide, opened to the 'commentary' on Chapter 23, and there was the chestnut tree in all its symbolic richness:

> Nature provides the setting for Rochester's proposal. At the foot of an old, familiar horse-chestnut tree, he clasps Jane to him and fiercely professes his love. An abrupt change in the weather, however, disrupts their intimate confessions. Before they can make more definite plans for the future, thunder and lightning, wind and rain force them to hurry into the house. Symbolically, they are dampened, and they are spared the fiery clash that sends lightning through the old, enormous horse-chestnut tree, splitting half of it away. Nature's violent display preludes the coming tragedy and separation.

My students had, either their first time round with the novel in high school or this time, bought the *Cliffs Notes*, studied ahead of time, and come into my class to write their essays about symbolism.

I was so happy to have made sense of what had been an entirely mysterious phenomenon that I wasn't even very upset about the possibility that my students weren't reading the novel at all. At that point, I realized that the students who had written about the chestnut tree were the same group that kept up the incessant buzz of whispering in the class. This particular group of students, the ones using the *Cliffs Notes*, was made up of first-year students who had been 'advanced placement students' in high school. They had told me this on the first day of my class, in response to a questionnaire. They also tended to gossip with each other during class and to challenge my interpretive authority, trying to score debating points during class discussions and then losing interest.

These students were acting in these various unappealing ways, I think, because of their model of literary knowledge. They were confident that books yielded single, unified, correct readings. Thus there was nothing new to be learned about reading, and particularly about these books they had read before. They knew that literary writers assemble symbols. These symbols work like windows into literary texts, allowing students to see the deep structure. This deep structure is so fundamental and foundational, and the texts that contain it are so unified, that having once seen the structure a reader has no reason to return to the book at all.

Because the students knew these things about literature, they knew that neither they nor I could make new knowledge. They did not believe that we could all do anything other than rehearse the knowledge available to us from reading the books in the same way, again. So they had not listened very closely, and they had not heard anything to disabuse them of these ideas. They had not learned what I was trying to teach them. This failure to learn was not a sign of their stupidity – instead it was an indication of how thoroughly they had learned the kind of interpretation presented in the *Cliffs Notes*. Because they had been such successful students in high school, because they were bright and had been 'advanced,' they understood how to do a particular kind of writing even in the inhospitable conditions of the class I was teaching and the writing assignment I had given them.

Several responses to this situation presented themselves to me. I could have failed the students on their papers, accused them of cheating from each other or of plagiarizing from the study guide. But I was most interested in breaking through their certainty that there was nothing to learn. I thought they would be willing to try a new way of reading if I could convince them that such a thing was possible. I did give them Ds on their papers, explaining that they had done only part of the assignment. They had worked closely with a passage from the novel, as I had asked them to, but they had not used any of the terms from the class. And then I designed an exercise that would bring the two ways of reading into direct contact in the classroom.

What I did

By the time I had figured all this out, the class was a few chapters into *Adventures of Huckleberry Finn*, a novel I had chosen to complement and complicate the first-person realism of *Jane Eyre* and the narratives of upward mobility in all three of the novels we had read so far. In the first part of the course, we had talked about Moll Flanders' interiority as discontinuous – her ideas and feelings appear and disappear in the narrative in unpredictable ways, while her economic calculations and actions are continuous and causally related. I had intended to direct the students' attention toward the way Twain represents Jim's character in *Huckleberry Finn*, developing an interior life for him and then dropping it when it threatens narrative resolution. I wanted the class to work on the ways in which writers negotiate ideologies of class and race through the formal problems we had been attending to. Now I realized that I had to address the issues of reading I had discovered, or I would find myself reading essays about the symbolism of the river.

I asked the students to look back through their notes and describe the kinds of reading we had been doing in the class so far. What had we looked for? What kinds of questions had we asked? What aspects of each book had we noticed? Was there any kind of pattern to our work? I listed their responses on one side of the board. Then I passed out a page that I had photocopied from the *Cliffs Notes* on *Huckleberry Finn*, without any citation. I told them that this was a particular critic's reading of the novel. I asked them the same questions I had asked about our readings. What kinds of questions does this writer ask about the text? What is he looking for? What aspects of the book does he notice? I asked them not to name the book or critic if they recognized anything, but just to describe the reading.

Again, the class as a whole read this excerpt very perspicaciously. When we had done the exercise, the board looked like this:

In this class, we have looked at	The critic from the photocopy looks at
• Money and class. • Descriptions of clothes and furniture – things that make the narrative seem real. • Places where the narrative broke up or where events didn't fit together. • Interiority – the sense that characters had inward lives. • How elements from romance and epic reappear in novels. • Continuity and discontinuity – which elements does the novel sustain and which does it bring up and then drop? • Manners.	• Symbols. • Unity and integration: 'This novel is a complete work of art in its own right, is self-contained, and is not dependent on other works'(14); 'Twain presents each theme as an integral part of the narrative structure of [the] short, first chapter'(16). • Controlling themes.

When we had filled the board, I took a step back from it and asked what they saw. Did the two sides of the board fit together? Obviously they did not. I asked the students whether they thought I would like the reading on the right. They said no.

When I told them that the reading was the *Cliffs Notes*, there was a shocked silence. I do not think they were surprised to find out that I did not like *Cliffs Notes*. Everyone knows that such guides are for cheating and that, because of this, teachers don't like them. The surprise, I think, was created by having the text out in the open in the classroom to be interpreted, rather than kept at a distance as an object of moral exhortation.

We then talked about the differences between the sides of the board. In thinking about social context, about discontinuities rather than unities, and about genre, we had been asking different questions than the writer of the study guide had been asking. This writer was part of a different conversation. Beyond that problem was a more serious one. This writer treats symbols as puzzles, to be solved by finding a single meaning. In the case of the chestnut tree in *Jane Eyre*, the answer to the puzzle is the narrative itself – we know from the brief sunny moment and ensuing storm that Jane's happiness will end, and something terrible will happen to 'split in two' the happy pair.

Having made the observation that the tree and the heroine experience the same narrative events, a strong paper would then raise a question: what does this similarity suggest about language, about the way stories make implicit moral and intellectual arguments, about the ferny dell in which the happy couple resides at the end of the novel? It would be possible to pursue any of these enquiries in an interesting way. Neither the study guide nor the students who used it, however, pursued any of these questions, or any questions at all. Rather than using the symbol to frame a question about the novel, these students treated the symbol itself as an answer. Reading, in these papers, was not a method of inquiry and a spur to re-reading, but a search for an answer that would shut down inquiry and sum the whole novel up in a sentence or two. My objection to this reading, then, was twofold: it performed an entirely different kind of literary analysis from the one I had been teaching – and it performed that analysis badly.

I wanted my students to question this kind of reading, rather than performing it routinely upon *Huckleberry Finn*, because such a symbolic reading would make it difficult, if not impossible, to consider the questions of Jim's characterization, of interiority, and of discontinuity that Twain scholars since Henry Nash Smith have investigated. If students used the river as a symbol of life, freedom, and individuality in order to read the novel, in the words of the *Cliffs Notes*, as 'complete,' 'self-contained,' 'integrated,' and 'controlled,' they would quickly develop readings of the novel so final that I would have a doubled load of work in trying to raise further questions about race, about the novel's complex generic identifications, or about social mobility and middle-class subjectivity, as I had planned to do.

I did not just want to make my students stop doing one thing and begin doing another, however. At best, I think that this course was more than an exercise in behavior modification. I wanted my students to be able to see the two ways of reading in relation to each other, and to a history of the discipline of literary study. Just as the novel as a genre is indebted to older forms for its own generic self-definition, particular forms of academic inquiry refer to each other in a larger scholarly conversation. The most important thing I wanted these four students, and all my students, to learn was that there is more to be learned, that readers and writers together continue to make new knowledge. Bringing different ways of reading into explicit contact and conflict in the classroom placed the students and their own work in the context of this ongoing inquiry.

When my students could describe the *Cliffs Notes* and their own papers as examples of different types of literary analysis, they were using the ideas about how texts define themselves that I wanted to teach in the class. They had also, of course, gained a set of tools that would make them more sophisticated cheaters if they chose to use them in that manner. If those students plagiarize in the future, they will make their choices with a clearer idea about the teacher's interests and with a more sophisticated understanding of the history of the field. Thus I do not present this narrative as a 'cure-all' for plagiarism. Some students plagiarize even when they understand the goals of the class entirely. And as teachers we will always have the unpleasant task of finding evidence, confronting the students who plagiarize, and taking action. In this case, however, the problem was shared by an identifiable group of students with a similar institutional history and a similar conceptual framework. They presented me with a problem that was behavioral, interpretive, and theoretical. I needed to think and act on all three levels in order to get past the block that my students and I had created together.

This story has a happy ending. My students' writing improved, and they stopped whispering in class and making debating points that had nothing to do with reading the books. But I don't want to offer it just as a teaching tip. I want to suggest that as teachers we deal with issues like grading, plagiarism, and decorum based on our ideas about what reading is and what literary knowledge is. Your students' understanding of knowledge will shape the way that they respond to what you do. If the two understandings are in conflict, then that conflict is the central problem you and your students face. Facing that problem together, in class, forces everyone to articulate a position and to acknowledge the existence of other positions. In doing so, students take a first step toward intellectual inquiry and active interpretation.

Appendix

Exercises in bringing new ways of reading together with old

- Have the students write briefly about the day's reading. Direct them to a passage from the reading, or ask them to choose one, and ask them to explain what is important about it for students of literature. Circulate the papers and ask each student to describe the reading in the paper that lands on his or her desk. What questions does it ask? What parts of the passage are most important to this writer? Why? Ask the students to go through any criticism you have read in the class, or through the syllabus, and decide which ideas have most strongly influenced that writer.
- Photocopy a single student paper and bring it in for everyone in the class to read and analyze as described above.
- Having carried out one of the exercises above, introduce a critical article and ask the students to describe this new (and probably more complicated) sort of reading. How does it differ from the student paper? What patterns do they see in the kinds of questions the writer asks, or the aspects of the literary text that he or she notices?
- When the students read the next few chapters of a novel, or the next poem on your syllabus, ask them to try out two different ways of interpreting what they have read. They might borrow ideas from two different critics, or from one critic and one student paper. What kind of literary knowledge do they develop through each mode? Which seems most satisfying? Most complex?

Writing assignment

The purpose of this paper is to allow you to explore for yourself the relationship between the novel and other forms as we have been using those terms in this class. The assignment has two parts.

Part I (2 pages minimum)

Choose a scene from a novel we have read. REWRITE that scene in the style of a different novelist or of a different genre we have read in this class. In other words, you can rewrite Mr Collins' proposal as an epic, or Jane Eyre's time in the red room the way Austen or Defoe or de Troyes would have written it.

Part II (3 pages minimum)

Write an analysis of what can be learned about form from your rewritten scene and from the experience of writing it. What has been gained and lost from the scene by its translation to a different form? What effects are achieved by the original form? By the new form? What difference does form make? What kind of narrative was the original scene part of? What kind of narrative is the rewritten scene part of? Relate the scene, in its original form, to a view of form in the novel as a whole. Use the terms that have been introduced in class discussions.

Hints and Advice

Be sure to choose a combination of scene and new form that will give you intelligent things to say in your analysis. Parody is OK unless it keeps you from paying close attention to what is really going on in both texts.

Choose a scene that we have not talked about extensively in class. It is fine to work with one we mentioned briefly or looked at in a different context.

In the analysis, you MUST discuss quotations from both of the texts in their original forms AND from your rewritten scene. Derive general statements from careful examination of quotations, rather than starting from general statements and using quotations to support them.

Cheating, plagiarism, and the Internet

The Internet makes it easier and easier for students to find material to introduce into their papers, as well as finding entire papers to hand in as their own work. Some sites also employ writers who will produce a paper in response to a particular assignment for a price. The best response to this situation is to engage students in the work of YOUR course. Here are two specific ways to do so:

1. If it is possible, ask students to write in class. Then you will have samples of the students' work to compare with the work they hand in later. Short in-class assignments work well. Another alternative for large classes is to ask students to write just a few sentences at the end of class; they can define a term in their own words or explain one aspect of that day's class that they have a question about. These will give you a sample of the students' prose style and interests, as well as suggesting to them that you are interested in what they think. As my anecdote above suggests, this is not a 'cure-all'. Instead, it will bring problems to your attention before the end of the term, when there is still a chance of dealing with them as a teacher rather than through disciplinary action.

2. Give very structured writing assignments, and strange ones. Rather than 'write a paper about *Jane Eyre*' or even 'write a paper about interiority/realism/gender/narrative form in *Jane Eyre*,' give an assignment as structured as the one given above. Such papers are more difficult to find on the term paper sites, which tend to feature papers that take familiar approaches. Ask students to frame their papers around a particular phrase from a critical article, or a term that you and the class have developed through discussion. Ask the students to argue two different positions and then choose one, or to write a letter to F.R. Leavis about their experience of reading, or to create a correspondence between Charlotte Brontë and Geoffrey Chaucer. It is still possible to require careful reading, textual citation, and argument in such unusual assignments, and students often enjoy them.

It will never be possible to forestall all plagiarizers. Some students will always plagiarize. In these cases, the Internet can be a help to the instructor as well. Typing a few words of the student's paper, in quotation marks, into a search engine such as Yahoo! will often produce the site from which the paper came. Then it is your responsibility to inform the student, in private, that you have discovered the plagiarism, and to follow your institution's procedures on academic integrity. If you do so, this student will learn something too.

Works cited

Brontë, Charlotte. *Jane Eyre* (New York: Bantam Books, 1988).
McKeon, Michael. *The Origins of the English Novel 1600–1740* (Baltimore, MD: Johns Hopkins University Press, 1987).

Roberts, James L. *Cliffs Notes on Adventures of Huckleberry Finn* (Lincoln: Cliffs Notes, 1997), pp. 14–16. Note: in 1997, the company was still reprinting an edition originally published in 1971. The 2000 edition has a new author and has been substantially revised.

Snodgrass, Mary Ellen. *Cliffs Notes on Brontë's Jane Eyre* (Lincoln: Cliffs Notes, 1996), p. 57.

11
The Place of the Implicit in Literary Discovery: Creating New Courses

Philip Davis

I have been reading Jonathan Rose's *The Intellectual Life of the British Working Classes* which tells the story of what, for people who could not take reading for granted, it was like to discover the world of books. Suddenly, says one self-educated potter, in a luminous phrase, 'We had the freedom of the universe.'[1]

These were men and women who were short of books and of teachers, and almost literally hungry for education. For them, it seems, culture was not indoctrination in bourgeois values but a form of individual discovery. Here is the daughter of an impoverished Dundee book-keeper, born in 1880, remembering the moment when she first came across Carlyle's *Sartor Resartus*, at the age of 14:

> It seems that from our earliest years we are striving to become articulate, struggling to clothe in words our vague perceptions and questionings. Suddenly, blazing from the printed page, there are the words, the true resounding words that we couldn't find. It is an exciting moment...'Who am I? The thing that can say I. Who am I, what is this ME?' I had been groping to know that since I was three. (Rose, 46)

Of course, we cannot expect the relatively privileged, cool young people in the universities of the West to be so obviously needy these days: it is a sign of a welcome social and material progress that they are not. You will be quick to tell me, surely, that there is no point in being nostalgic.

Indeed, Rose's self-educated working people, who discovered the power of literature as if for the first time, were naïve – even to the point of hardly being able to tell, in the midst of the experience, the difference between fact and fiction. In 1815 a young artisan, Christopher Thomson, persuaded his anxious puritanical mother to let him see Shakespeare's *King John* in Hull's Theatre Royal – and found himself utterly unfamiliar with the conventions and illusions of theatre. To the ignorant spectator, between the rise and fall of the curtain, it was no cliché to think of theatre as a sort of magic:

> It might be a dream, but what if it was? It was a waking one! The only fear was, would it be as 'Baseless, as the fabric of a vision', and so throw me back again upon the every-day world?...I was every thing by turns; now ready to 'hang a calf-skin' over the recreant Austria, or rave with Constance for her 'absent child'. By the time the fourth act came on, all my fear of the play ending was gone. I thought of nothing but the story...I sat absorbed in that new mode of visiting the inner-soul by such strange realities. (Rose, 100)

Waking dreams, visitings into inner realms of reality via external shows: what was going on? Notoriously, even more unsophisticated members of the audience might shout out in the midst of performances. To take it so literally, as though it were real, was what philosophers now call a category-mistake.

I believe in all sorts of category-mistakes – confusing books with realities, thinking there is something behind the words, identifying inside with fictional characters. Category-mistakes are the places where the real power of metaphor and imagination begins, before you ever realize that this *is* metaphor, this *is* imagination. When the ignorant audience member stands up and shouts at Othello, in protest at the imminent murder of Desdemona, it may be, to put it mildly, a misplaced instinct – a misunderstanding of the nature of art and a failure of correct psychic distance. But it is the *right* thing, albeit in the wrong place. The story of evolution is that what at first was an outright physical impulse becomes a silent mental one, and individually we repeat that biological story not once but throughout our lives.[2]

Thus, when, in *Grace Abounding*, John Bunyan thought that, in reading the Bible, it was speaking to him personally, I don't think that this was schizophrenia. I think that what some may call schizophrenic in Bunyan is no more than a heightened example of what is normal in the most serious reading – the persistent sense of being on the verge of a secret personal message, some minor inner revelation. The great thing about the reading of literature is that it simply isn't like a science – incrementally progressive in its discoveries – but has to keep going back to its sources, recovering the first feelings. Each time someone genuinely re-discovers a book, it is as if that book is alive for the first time again. That is why it is good to teach first-year students – if you are lucky enough for them to be rather naïve and lacking in confidence, somewhat ignorant and inarticulate, and yet enthusiastic and (in their own ways, often secretly) in need.

Creative originality in students is not so much to do with thinking something new, but thinking something which is new to *them*, as individuals, *and*, moreover, close to the very *origins* of the work, of the thought, in question. No matter, then, how many learned articles have been written about it subsequently, until the insight has become taken for granted. For thoughts do not get superseded: the study of literature is closer to re-creative memory than to history, for it brings thoughts back to life in the present, making the reader feel what it is like to think this thing as at first, from the inside. Literature, I want to argue, is the enemy of 'taking-things-for-granted,' of education as mere explicit knowingness.

For reasons both good and bad, modern education does produce knowledge *about* things in place of the experience of the things themselves. It is not hard to think of subjects in which ideologies, methods, concepts, opinions and names replace attention to first-order reality. The study of literature should not be like that. Personally, I hate essay questions and assignments that, however well-meaningly, tell the students what to look for, or seminars that offer 'two different critical approaches' to the book instead of the book itself.

Literary studies have two advantages. We have access to rich primary sources that are constantly with us, in ways they are not for students of history, for example. That means that literary study is not merely a closed subject, sufficient to itself: in its emphatically secondary status, it must never try to establish primacy over the works and the language that are its objects of study. And, secondly, literature itself is the one form of writing that reminds us that what we have in front of our eyes is not simply literal but a form of utterance that exists suspended *between* living speech and written fixity – making silent and implicit calls to be felt, innerly performed, translated and understood, and not just passively received.

In 1986 I set up a part-time MA in Victorian Literature because on the full-time course we had begun to attract an interesting range of genuinely mature students, from the ages of 25 to 75, and wanted more of them: people who could only manage to study on a part-time basis, who hadn't read English as their first degree, or if they had, felt worn and rusty, or, alternatively, hadn't ever been to university at all. Although we talk a lot about widening access now, it would be much harder to initiate such a course these days. For in England at present there are a lot more regulations about entry requirements, and a good deal more cosmetic paperwork required, with respect to listing explicit 'aims and objectives,' 'transferable skills' and notional 'learning outcomes,' before ever you can get the show on the road.

I can see now (though I did not in advance) that I had made it a course on Victorian Literature for two connected reasons: (i) nineteenth-century realist novels are powerfully related to quite ordinary concerns of human life; (ii) Victorian literature characteristically finds those concerns on that borderline between secularization and religion where most serious questioning takes place. Without my spelling it out, the course nonetheless attracted mature students who *had* something, as it were – something about them, as adults; though often they themselves felt they were more in search or want of something than in possession of it:

> But often in the world's most crowded streets,
> But often in the din of strife,
> There arises an unspeakable desire
> After the knowledge of our buried life.
>
> [...]
>
> But hardly have we, for one little hour,
> Been on our own line, have we been ourselves
>   (Matthew Arnold, 'The Buried Life'[3])

These days we are encouraged to tell people in advance what to expect from the course, to offer them long secondary reading-lists offering critical texts and historical context, and, above all, we are told to be as explicit as possible, listing individual module titles and their predetermined rationale. What could be less like the way literature itself works? For why should the language of literary study be the very opposite of what it studies, explaining everything away? The part-time MA offered no literary criticism, no historical background, no introductions, no papers to kick off the session. What is more, we banned the use of the 'V' word: the Victorians thought this, the Victorians were like that. We told our students that they did not need reassurance (they did; but *this* was it), and that we weren't interested in substitute 'knowledge' (which they, of course, were half-expecting, half-dreading from a higher university degree).

I freely admit that as an experiment this may seem somewhat riskily extreme. But we wanted what the students *didn't* know, from those places where both the lack of confidence and the sense of need were most powerful. It is a mistake of the modern English mind, wrote Ruskin in 'The Nature of Gothic,' to prefer 'the perfectness of the lower nature' to 'the imperfection of the higher.' In search of that 'higher' education, we refused to give our people ready-made essay titles; we urged them out of the mechanical schoolchildren's essay, with a safely planned beginning, middle and end; and we asked them for their own imperfections instead. That is what Ruskin wanted from his workers, architectural, artistic or mental:

> If you will make a man of the working creature, you cannot make a tool. Let him but begin to imagine, to think, to try to do anything worth doing; and the engine-tuned precision is lost at once. Out come all his roughness, all

his dulness, all his incapability; shame upon shame, failure upon failure, pause upon pause; but out comes the whole majesty of him too.[4]

What was great was when books on the course began to shape the course itself. That was when we knew it was a genuinely Victorian degree that was coming into being.

But we started with books, not ideas, just *The Christmas Carol, David Copperfield, Middlemarch* ... I didn't have much conscious idea of how the books fitted together and emphatically did not pick them to do so, but rather for their own sake. The books were all too good, too deep to be put in labeled pigeonholes explicitly marked 'Literature and Society' or 'Literature and Gender.' Students were told that they were to find places in the books that moved them, or seemed strangely powerful, without their necessarily knowing how or why. Always we started by reading those individually chosen passages out loud, to get the primary presence of the book in the room, and then we began to bring its feeling back again within the realm of attentive thought ('Why does that word "hardly" make so much difference in "But hardly have we, for one little hour,/Been on our own line"?'). The rule as it developed was: first, no thoughts without feelings; and second, no feelings without thoughts. In that order.

There *were* rules that emerged in practice. I didn't want and wouldn't have pre-formed opinions or generalizations. Initially, people could only talk about what they liked, not what they didn't. We must try to analyze, with precision of attention, and not just paraphrase. I didn't let people go on to some other part of the book till we had looked carefully at what was in front of us now: only when people were full of the *experience* of those specific passages, could they begin to try to find more words for what was going on. The most intellectual formulations could only come last, like a conclusion to a paragraph, like the final top part of our evolutionary experience, frustrated by delay into becoming an achieved discovery. When a student said, 'It is almost as though ... ' as a launch-pad for speculative thought (rather than, 'Isn't this just Victorian class-prejudice?' – where the word 'just' is the give-away), then I knew we were getting somewhere.

What surprised me most, however, was that eventually even austere and rather intellectually formidable non-fictional prose seemed to be having powerful effects on the group, without the solid attractions of plot or character. For example, read this – as they did:

It is no proof that persons are not possessed, because they are not conscious, of an idea. Nothing is of more frequent occurrence, whether in things sensible or intellectual, than the existence of such unperceived impressions.... How common is it to be exhilarated or depressed, we do not recollect why, though we are aware that something has been told us, or has happened, good or bad, which accounts for our feeling, could we recall it! What is memory itself, but a vast magazine of such dormant, but present and excitable ideas? Or consider, when persons would trace the history of their own opinions in past years, how baffled they are in the attempt to fix the date of this or that conviction, their system of thought having been all the while in continual, gradual, tranquil expansion; so that it were as easy to follow the growth of the fruit of the earth, 'first the blade, then the ear, after that the full corn in the ear', as to chronicle changes, which involved no abrupt revolution, or reaction, or fickleness of mind, but have been the birth of an idea, the development, in explicit form, of what was already latent in it.[5]

This seemed to be about a sense of experience, at once so common and yet so subtle, that it was almost denied its right to itself. Yet the mature students on the MA were glad to find its existence confirmed: perhaps the reason they could not easily explain themselves was more to do with the depth of those selves and what they were considering – and not, as they had feared, the superficiality of their formal intellects. People are easily daunted and humiliated in educational institutions, when the assumption is that the ability to articulate is the first thing. It isn't: it is the second thing. The first thing is to have something to articulate, which inevitably at first must resist quick and easy formulation. This passage indicated that intelligence did not just arise out of consciousness; it arose out of something anterior, silent, inchoate, latent or implicit – all those words – that did not feel like intelligence at all. Yet it was a life's intelligence, coming into being: 'In other words, all men have a reason, but not all men can give a reason.'[6]

The first task of the teacher in the class was to ensure that the men and women there knew that, somewhere in themselves, they did 'have a reason' for their strongest reactions, that they were implicitly thinking; the second task was to lead them towards writing which sought to find and give the reason which they somewhere had. In real writing and thinking, what is implicit or pre-articulate comes first; the explicit is the struggle in the second place to bring to light, under the pen, all that is anterior to itself. I'd say, cheekily to the group, that even Socrates could be wrong: speaking isn't sufficient, it is writing that convinces you that you can make something of yourself on your own.

These passages about implicit and explicit reasoning from Newman's *University Sermons* were delivered to young students of theology at Oxford between 1826 and 1843. The word 'sermon,' for once, didn't put the students off. They forgot the big words, such as 'religion,' because, suddenly, apparently small details of syntax became very important; it was mentally significant, for example, that these formulations were made in *one* sentence and not two:

> In other words, all men have a reason, but not all men can give a reason.
> It is no proof that persons are not possessed, because they are not conscious, of an idea.

Try the effect of writing it out as two sentences. People may not be conscious of an idea. But they may still have it at some level. The paraphrase is informative and sensible, but the thought isn't *happening*, as if for the first time again, and consequently everything goes flat and unexcited. It is not just that such syntax as Newman's constituted an extraordinary evolutionary tool, enlarging the mind that could hold it; such complex sentences as these also form an image of the mind itself, working almost simultaneously at different levels.

Conversely, we sometimes find that we write three sentences which really are all parts of each other, though on the page they look so separate. Prose looks so literally straightforward a medium, the norm that anyone can use; for in prose, it seems you do not have to be special like a would-be poet. Yet even here the mental leaps or tacit gaps between or within sentences are filled with latent connectives of implicit and invisible thinking. Newman was insistent that words do not have a literal 1:1 relation to the thoughts they represent; that, likewise, thoughts, being immaterial, are not coterminous with the material beginnings and endings of the sentences in which they are lodged. Even in discursive prose, arguably the most direct form of written language, no sentence could ever be exhaustively explicit or flatly self-explanatory: there is always something implicitly meaningful in the space behind or around it. And that is to say what Newman's own characteristically approximative phrases, 'so to speak,' or 'as it were,' so often seek to remind us of: namely, that writing and reading are (and I have to use this word) spiritual. Quite rightly, people frequently baulk at the 'spiritual,' myself included; but all I mean by it is, neutrally, 'whatever the meaning that cannot be explained solely by the literal or physical appearance of the marks on a page.'[7] That is the area in which literary study has to work. When students do their thinking *without* their own spirits, at whatever level, that is a failure for us as teachers. We do not want to produce second-hand people.

The future for teaching, in literary studies, lies in finding strategies for the encouragement of a genuine spirit of creative thinking. That is what people need; it is why they should be readers. Readers are those of us who require other people's poems to get into those areas of thoughtful resonance which we often cannot initially summon for ourselves. 'Often in the world's most crowded streets... There arises an unspeakable desire...'. What makes literary study still a discipline, however, and not just a therapeutic act of self-expression, is that it offers a creative thinking not at the expense of the books but arising out of them. Hence the need for genuine reading with attention – an act too often dismissed as merely professionalized 'close' reading or 'old-fashioned' practical criticism. There is only one form of reading – reading with attention, without knowing where we are going: everything else is a more or less helpful version of taxonomy, putting books into the pre-established categories of 'theme and image,' as it used to be, or 'class and gender,' as it often is now. It is not that I am not interested in theme or image, or class or gender – as they arise, however, as sudden thoughts, not as institutionalized concepts. But if there is one 'transferable skill' I do like, it has to do with readers thinking much more as writers think, creatively.

If you want your students to experience, almost physically, what creative thinking is like – how thought comes dynamically into being in literature, as something quintessentially *live* in time – then you have to give them Shakespeare, above all. Watch actors carrying out workshops or master-classes, or in rehearsal. Bring them into your universities and colleges. In those contexts, you cannot dismiss attention to the individual lines as an exercise in close reading – this is reading in practice, this is intelligence implicit and incarnate.

For once, other words besides Shakespeare's are used only to get Shakespeare's words right. That is to say, witness a master-class given by the actress Janet Suzman on a monologue by Benedick in *Much Ado About Nothing*, immediately after over-hearing his friends' ruse in talking of Beatrice's supposedly secret love for him:

> This can be no trick, the confidence was sadly borne, they have the truth of this from Hero, they seem to pity the lady: it seems her affections have their full bent: love me? why it must be requited . . .
>
> (II. iii. 212ff)

The drama student in this class, quite understandably, read this headlong prose in such a way as hurriedly to skid off the surface of it. What Janet Suzman did was to interject very quietly in the implicit spaces between the phrases, turning soliloquy back into what it originally evolves out of – inner dialogue. Thus:

Student: This can be no trick
Suzman [*sotto voce*]:   *Why not?*
Student: the conference was sadly borne
Suzman: *Ye-es. But what else?*
Student: they have the truth of this from Hero
Suzman: *And is Hero trustworthy?*

Student: [nods]
Suzman: *Then what else?*
Student: they seem to pity the lady
Suzman: *Pity her? Why?*
Student: it seems her affections have their full bent
Suzman [*teasingly*]:   *Oh! interesting . . .*
                She then must . . .
Student: Love me?
Suzman: *Love you! Well, what are you going to do?*
                Tell her to shove off?
Student: Why, it *must* be requited.

And requited by you: how generous! And so, on it goes.[8] 'Other dramatic writers give us very fine paraphrases of nature,' says Hazlitt in his essay on *Hamlet*, 'but Shakespeare gives us the original text.'[9] Janet Suzman's interjections were not like the paraphrases that literary criticism too often makes of Shakespeare: they helped release that original, underlying text. Otherwise, in such situations, if the actors cannot give the lines the life they need, then the whole thing simply dies on its feet.

That is why the director Peter Brook was not exaggerating when he called Shakespeare 'a school for living': 'We are constantly betraying reality, which we don't succeed in perceiving, grasping, and living, and we're continually diminishing and reducing it. It's always a highly diminished view of the present moment as it might be.' But, he goes on, the Shakespearean vision most dramatically reminds us that:

> The human faculty for apprehension is not static, but is a second-for-second redefinition of what it sees. Now to me the total works of Shakespeare are like a very, very complete set of codes, and these codes, cipher for cipher, set off in us, stir in us, vibrations and impulses.[10]

This talk of Nature's original text or a set of neo-genetic codes is not as esoteric as it may seem, but practical. Imagine a simple enough example: a workshop on *Hamlet* for, say, 12 students, concentrating on Act III scene iv, the confrontation scene between Hamlet and Gertrude:

> H: Now, mother, what's the matter?
> G: Hamlet, thou hast thy father much offended.
> H: Mother, you have my father much offended.
> G: Come, come, you answer with an idle tongue.
> H: Go, go, you question with a wicked tongue.
>   (III. iv. 8–12)

Those who know their Shakespeare will recognize at once that this is a version of the correlative verse that structured the early comedies – the sort of rhetorical code that in *A Midsummer Night's Dream* has Hermia and Helena poignantly saying together: 'The more I hate, the more he follows me,' 'The more I love, the more he hateth me.' Thus, what the students who are taking the two main roles immediately discover is that they cannot 'act' their characters *separately* at this point. They have instead to let their symmetrical speeches play off against each other, through a mutual rhythm that creates between them a third thing: namely, and almost literally, the now-charged *space* between Hamlet and his mother in which is lodged the alienating issue between them. Some of your students, of course, will not be the actors on this occasion: let's call this audience the Thinkers or Note-Takers. They exist to think *off* what is happening: to turn the transient shift of shapes on the stage in front of them into more permanent thoughts afterwards. You will need to ask them to report back on what has suddenly happened here.

At any rate, Hamlet knows what is happening. For into that space between them, he now puts on stage the alternative protagonists – the two fathers mentioned in those early lines, Hamlet's real father, now dead, and the stepfather who murdered him:

> Look here upon this picture and on this, –
> The counterfeit presentment of two brothers.
>
> (III. iv. 53–4)

But, say we don't use pictures but instead, more literally, ask two students to stand in front of Gertrude, like physical ghost-thoughts, one extreme left, one extreme right, to make her turn of head and mind as wide as possible. Ask the (perhaps) two students you have set to be the Directors where to position Hamlet in all this. Again, it is to do with our natural evolution that the feeling of physical space will create an emotional effect which itself is implicitly cognitive. So a good decision might be to place Hamlet himself not in front of Gertrude, between the two brother-fathers who are tearing him apart, but now behind her, even physically forcing her, in the turn of the neck one way and then another, to look as though through his eyes. There are vibrations within this positioning. Something is happening to Gertrude, physically, emotionally, and finally mentally – always in that order.

The Thinkers need to be warned now: as we play the rest of this scene, can you sense the line that it has all been leading to, the mental break-through? One of the lines that grows out of the space now created by Hamlet's experiment is of course Hamlet's own 'I set you up a glass / Where you may see the inmost part of you' (19–20). For we begin to realize that it is not really the pictures of the two brothers, Hyperion to a satyr, that Gertrude is now having to look at. As her head is turned to and fro, as the words are piled into her ears from behind, as eventually she cannot bear to look at all any more but seizes her own head in her hands, it all leads to this – and, again and again in my experience, the students suddenly realize it:

> O Hamlet, speak no more:
> Thou turn'st mine eyes into my very soul.
> (III. iv. 88–9)

'And there I see such black and grained spots' (90): where seeing can stand no more, thinking in the mind's eye has to begin. It is the sheer continual re-beginning of thinking that Shakespeare relishes, as though an event. Here the very process towards explicitness makes the explicit itself, charged with all that brought it into being, almost miraculous. That's what Shakespeare does: in the shock of violent change, the audience *feels* her thinking across the atmosphere, a sense of the invisible inmost soul now made almost palpably visible in the language, on the stage. That is the sudden coming of language into being.[11] Your students should write about this, after experiencing it, in order to try to make the thing last longer and become real knowledge. But above all, writing in this way should become itself a form of re-performance, re-creation, in a different mode at a different level of being.[12] There are evolutionary laws involved here, and at Liverpool we are becoming increasingly concerned with the evolutionary-biological function of artistic creativity – in particular, the emergent powers of the brain released by the acts of reading, performing and writing.

At any rate, it is at this point in the workshop that students might be most ready to understand what Hazlitt meant in his *Essay on the Principles on Human Action* and why it is a Shakespearean philosophy that is being offered there, or what he was trying to say in his *Lectures on the English Poets* (1818):

> In Shakspeare there is a continual composition and decomposition of elements, a fermentation of every particle in the whole mass, by its alternate affinity or antipathy to other principles which are brought into contact with it. Till the experiment is tried, we do not know the result, the turn which the character will take in new circumstances.[13]

Reaching areas of the brain almost inaccessible by other means, literary study consists of experiments and experiences in mental chemistry, in the continual creation and re-creation of mental worlds without fixed determinants. It is time to show the world outside what teachers of literature stand for and can do, in that resonant holding-ground we occupy between all the other more explicit disciplines. We begin that task when we show our students how they are experimenters in schools of creative thinking.

Appendix

Specimen Exam Paper

(3rd year undergraduate course, with more informal coursework as 40% of the final assessment)

READING IN PRACTICE

2 HOURS

ANSWER QUESTION 1 AND *ONE* QUESTION FROM SECTION 2

Section 1

1. Make a *careful and thorough* critical analysis of the following poem, using, where appropriate, your knowledge of Renaissance poetics:

Chorus Sacerdotum

1	Oh wearisome Condition of Humanity!
2	Borne under one Law, to another bound:
3	Vainely begot, and yet forbidden vanity,
4	Created sick, commanded to be sound:
5	What meaneth Nature by these diverse Lawes?
6	Passion and Reason, selfe-division cause:
7	Is it the marke, or Majesty of Power
8	To make offences that it may forgive?
9	Nature herselfe, doth her own selfe deflower,
10	To hate those errors she her selfe doth give.
11	For how should man think that he may not doe,
12	If Nature did not faile, and punish too?
13	Tyrant to others, to her selfe unjust,
14	Onely commands things difficult and hard.
15	Forbids us all things, which it knowes is lust,
16	Makes easie pains, unpossible reward.
17	If Nature did not take delight in blood,
18	She would have made more easie ways to good.
19	We that are bound by vowes, and by Promotion,
20	With pompe of holy Sacrifice and rites,
21	To teach beleef in good and still devotion,
22	To preach of Heavens wonders, and delights:
23	Yet when each of us, in his owne heart lookes,
24	He findes the God there, farre unlike his Books.

Note

The title 'Chorus Sacerdotum' means Chorus of the Priests
Line 11 'that': that which
Line 15 'lust': pleasure

Section 2: When answering these general questions, you are advised to use specific literary examples to establish your argument.

2. 'Poetry exists to provide the poetic experience. It is easier to point to than to define or delimit. But it is what people read for, as much as for information, though they may be shy about saying so, in an age which distrusts "mystical" talk and prefers to hide its spiritual needs' (Les Murray).
What do *you* understand by 'the poetic experience'?

3. 'Normally a poem is *performed* when it is originally written, or when it is read silently or aloud, or chanted, or sung by the poet or by a reader. Only at those moments can it be truly a poem, an artwork alive in time; otherwise it remains just a *text*, closed up within a book or opened to critical attention, an object relations with time a critic may describe but which remain potential not actual' (Douglas Oliver).

EITHER: How helpful do you find the distinction between poem as 'performance' and poem as 'text'?
OR: What do you understand by a poem being 'alive in time'?

4.
> 'Thence may I select
> Sorrow that is not sorrow, but delight,
> And miserable love that is not pain
> To hear of, for the glory that redounds
> Therefrom to human kind and what we are.'
> Wordsworth, *The Prelude* xii

Do you think that the reading of works of sorrow is or is not a sorrowful experience? Give reasons and examples in making your case.

5. 'What we need are not critical theories or detached, impersonal critics. What we need are places, i.e. a table with some chairs around it, in which we can learn again how to read, how to read together. It is not more critics we require but reading-schools for more and better readers' (George Steiner, adapted).
EITHER: Is there a useful distinction to be made between 'critics' and 'readers'?
OR: What do you think a 'reading-school' would or should be like?

6. 'Shakespeare is not a *communicator* but a *creator*. Shakespeare does not offer us a series of explicit "messages" but a series of impulses that can produce many understandings' (Peter Brook).
Test the force of this modern director's account of Shakespeare with reference to TWO or THREE plays of Shakespeare.

7. 'In Shakespeare, the actor should start not by trying to work out the intention and motivation of his character but with the language only. It often pays off to go for each scene as it comes, rather than try to iron out the inconsistencies. The words must be found or coined or fresh-minted at the moment you utter them, as if they are spoken for the first time again' (John Barton).
In the light of specific examples, would you say that this is good advice to actors and/or to readers?

8. 'Nothing can be made *fully* explicit even by the clearest language: there is always a background of presupposition which defies analysis by reason of its infinitude' (A.N. Whitehead).
Discuss in relation to your own acts of reading and analysis.

9. Examine the issues that arise out of your consideration of either one *or* both of the following propositions:
a) 'The meaning of action is inseparable from its meaning in place' (Wendell Berry).
b) 'We do not *think* real time. But we live it' (Henri Bergson).

10. 'This is one of the features that makes us understand the role, at once essential and limited, that reading can play in our spiritual life: namely, that what for the author could be called "Conclusions" are for the reader "Incitements." Our wisdom must begin where that of the author ends' (Proust).
Debate the implications of this view – that the author's conclusions are limited to being no more and no less than our own starting-points.

Notes

1. Jonathan Rose, *The Intellectual Life of the British Working Classes* (New Haven: Yale University Press, 2001), p. 67. Hereafter cited as 'Rose'.
2. In *Vestiges of the Natural History of Creation* (1844), Robert Chambers argued that ontogeny – the history of the individual – recapitulates phylogeny – evolutionary genealogy. For a modern neuroscientist's account, in relation to neurobiology and emotion as a messenger of thought, see Antonio Damasio, *The Feeling of What Happens: Body, Emotion and the Making of Consciousness* (London: Vintage, 2000) and its demolition of the Cartesian mind/body dualism.
3. Matthew Arnold, 'The Buried Life' in *Collected Works of Matthew Arnold* (Murrieta, USA: Classic Books, 2001).
4. John Ruskin, *The Stones of Venice*, volume 2 (1853), chapter 6 ('The Nature of Gothic'), paragraph 12.
5. John Henry Newman, *University Sermons 1826–43*, ed. D.M. MacKinnon and J.D. Holmes (London: SPCK, 1970), (Sermon 15, 'The Theory of Developments in Religious Doctrine'), p. 321.
6. *University Sermons*, Sermon 13, 'Implicit and Explicit Reason,' p. 259.
7. See Douglas Oliver, 'Poetry's Subject' in *Real Voices On Reading*, edited by Philip Davis (Basingstoke and London: Macmillan and St Martin's Press, 1997), p. 100. I am also particularly indebted to the essays by George Steiner and George Craig in that volume.
8. Also see Janet Suzman's *Acting with Shakespeare* (New York and London: Applause Acting Series, 1996).
9. Hazlitt's 'Essay on Hamlet', in *Selected Writings by Hazlitt* (New York: Oxford University Press, 1999).
10. In Ralph Berry, *On Directing Shakespeare* (London: Hamish Hamilton and Penguin, 1989), pp. 137, 149–50.
11. I attempt to show this in *Sudden Shakespeare* (London and New York: Athlone and St Martin's Press, 1996).
12. See also the late Douglas Oliver's wonderful book, *Poetry and Narrative in Performance* (Basingstoke and London: Macmillan, 1989), including as it does the philosophical consequences of some impressive experiments in registering the voice-patterns of students' readings, by means of wavelengths. What Oliver does with voice, neuroscientists may be able to do with regard to brain chemistry.
13. 'Lecture 3, 'On Shakespeare and Milton,'. *Lectures on the English Poets*, edited by C.M. Maclean (London: Everyman, 1967), p. 51.

12
From Teaching in Class to Teaching Online: Preserving Community and Communication

Susan Jaye Dauer

In the early 1990s, I began working for an educational software company, The Daedalus Group, started by fellow graduate students at the University of Texas; while I was working there, I was also working as an adjunct at a local community college. I decided to try the software, the Daedalus Integrated Writing Environment (often called DIWE), for myself. The first class I was assigned in the networked computer lab, my first online class, was, of all things, American Literature I: Puritans to the Civil War. I was somewhat amused (and, confidentially, bemused) at the idea of using computers to teach William Bradford and Jonathan Edwards, but I think Benjamin Franklin would probably have approved. I spent some time reviewing my notes, trying to decide what lessons would work online, what could be made into discussion questions, and what could be used to help students to review the materials through study questions and quizzes.[1]

Almost immediately, I found myself in the middle of one of the most enthusiastic classes I had ever encountered. I was forced to set up the next day's online discussions before I left school for the day, rather than coming in a little early to do so. The students were arriving in the classroom before I could get there, up to a half an hour before class time during a summer session, to see what the day's questions were and to get started on the discussions.

The first set of actual numbers I saw on how online discussions change the classroom dynamic came from Rebecca Rickly's 1995 Ball State University dissertation: *Exploring the Dimensions of Discourse: A Multi-Modal Analysis of Electronic and Oral Discussions in Developmental English*. Her study, conducted while she was teaching for the University of Michigan's highly regarded Composition Board, showed that in oral discussions, teachers accounted for 71 per cent of the discussion, while in InterChange®, the synchronous 'chat' function of DIWE, teachers accounted for only 11 per cent of the discussion.

She also found that in oral discussion almost no interaction took place between students, while in InterChange® student-to-student discussion accounted for 53 per cent of the conversation and 24 per cent was student-to-class. If the normal sophomore literature classroom finds the teacher talking back and forth with three or four students, while twenty or more nod and try to look interested, then the online classroom can, and does, turn that around (for further discussion, see Dauer, 'Computers').

There has also been some serious research on the benefits of computer classrooms for women and minority students. *Race in Cyberspace*, edited by Beth Kolko, Lisa Nakamura, and Gilbert Rodman, and *Wired Women*, edited by Lynn Cherny and Elizabeth Weise, are collections of essays by a variety of instructors that show how technology has affected their students, both male and female, across the lines of race and gender. Additionally, the advantages to the shy student, who is likely to be female and from a minority group, are myriad, as has been documented in *Language Learning Online* by Jerome Bump, Phillip Markley, Lester Faigley, and Peggy Beauvois, among others. In the electronic classroom, shyness really doesn't matter. One semester, in a World Literature I class in the computer classroom, three female Hispanic students took advantage of the environment to correct others' misconceptions about the creation myth we were discussing. Of course, this can also work against the instructor. Once, when I left the room, one exceptionally quiet student took the opportunity to post, completely out of context, an incredibly obscene joke. Two other students posted notices indicating that her joke was out of line, and that ended that particular discussion thread.

There are many other reasons for student silence in a proscenium-style classroom. Admittedly, some students know that they will not have to participate and don't prepare, but many of their classmates have other reasons for their silence. Some students fear blurting out something 'stupid.' Other students are not interested in the points the teacher raises, but are reluctant to raise their own questions and comments in light of the teacher's authoritative position, both literal and figurative.

Using a synchronous chat, such as DIWE's InterChange®, students write their comments on one screen, editing them if they wish, and then send them to the group. The teacher is often the one who posts the first, so-called 'seed' question, but students can create additional conferences to ask their own questions or ask them in the middle of a discussion. Class participants can move with ease among various aspects of a single work, various works by a single author, or other topics. Additionally, through the use of pseudonyms, the class can discuss controversial subjects without causing students embarrassment or anger. Debate addresses statements, not the status of the commentators. I was once invited to participate in an online class taught on a MOO (Multi-Object Oriented), a kind of online chatroom. The students in that class all chose neutral pseudonyms before they logged on. At the end of the discussion, the invited guests, myself included, were invited to try to guess the gender of the various students. We got about half correct. It was enlightening, especially for the students, many of whom seemed to think we'd guess everyone correctly.

A final barrier, though a subtle one, is removed when the class goes from the LAN (Local Area Network) to the WAN (Wide Area Network) classroom; the speed of typing is no longer even a question. The asynchronous forums of software such as Blackboard or WebCT further even out the playing field by allowing students even more time to work on their responses to general questions, or to find the best ways in which to ask their own. Using these online software environments, students can have discussions, exchange papers, send emails, and have private conversations with their instructors, all in the privacy of their own homes and at the hour of their choosing.

My community college students have introduced their own questions about the characters in *Death of a Salesman* and about sexuality in the poetry of Allen Ginsburg. They have had lively and intelligent discussions about banning books from secondary schools, about how a runaway slave might make it to Canada from Texas in modern times, and about what Young Goodman Brown is really doing in the woods. They have written up to thirty pages of single-spaced commentary in fifty minutes. They have discovered that they and their classmates can comment intelligently and that they can converse with one another without the teacher's constant intervention.

Do class chats always work perfectly? Of course not. As with any class, a teacher needs to be prepared for the fact that some things won't or don't work as planned. In the computer classroom, there is the added problem of technology, which, despite our dependence and confidence, does not always perform as we would like. Parts of networked software programs can lose their paths, individual computers can suffer breakdowns or freeze, the electricity can go out, and things can inexplicably disappear or be accidentally, or even purposely, erased. Problems can affect a school's networked computer labs or an individual student's home computer.

Besides these difficulties with the technology, there is also the problem of what has come to be known widely as 'flaming.' As one teacher has claimed,

Everything went rather smoothly for a while, but toward the end of the hour, the students shifted topic, chose pseudonyms, and began making suggestive comments to each other, some involving profanity. I felt very out of control, the way a high school teacher might feel when her class is throwing spitballs, or some other quintessential act of rebellion. I realized electronic communication isn't always ideal. (Blair)

Thus, the instructor needs to be prepared. There are a variety of ways to handle LAN problems. The easiest fix, for technical or flaming problems, is for the instructor to step in with an alternate lesson plan. Preplanned study questions on grammatical or general genre issues can be placed in other modules of the DIWE program, which will solve the difficulty if the problem is with InterChange® and not the software as a whole. Individual searches of the World Wide Web can be assigned if the problem is with the DIWE software as a whole, but not the actual computers, and if the classroom has access to the Web. Finally, oral class discussions can be initiated by having students turn their chairs away from the screens, if the computers are not working or the electricity is out, or, as has happened, someone erases part or all of the program from the machines. When the problem is social, turning the chairs around also reminds students that they are writing their comments to people. It reminds them that they are not playing with the Internet, that they cannot treat class the way they treat their Usenet or Listserv discussions of rock bands or television or mountain biking. It reminds them that they are in a formal setting, but, also, more importantly, that they are dealing with classmates as well as text.

Even while recognizing the potential problems of the Internet, it is possible to take what one has learned from the traditional classroom and the LAN classroom and to use it in a WAN class. As another colleague pointed out, back in 1995,

> there's a less tangible, though perhaps more important, quality to wide area networks that writing teachers are becoming increasingly obligated to offer students: exposure to the global nature of information, and the collaboration and knowledge that is available via computers, that cannot be controlled by the confines of English classrooms and current-traditional writing curriculum. The days of quiet, tidy, correction-oriented composition pedagogy are not long with us. (Peterson)

While programs like DIWE, and the module called 'InterChange,' allow students to test the ways in which the Internet works, they don't allow for exactly the same experiences, for good or ill.

In planning WAN classes, I found, with very little trouble, a wide variety of websites that addressed the subjects I was interested in – everything from other courses on the same or similar topics to online texts to research societies. Searching for these references was difficult only because it was hard not to become distracted by particularly intriguing sites. I believe that this is an element of the online course that is potentially overwhelming, particularly in light of the variety of sites – good, bad and bizarre – available not only to me, but to my students as well.

All of this notwithstanding, I can say that the biggest challenge to most instructors moving from LAN to WAN, or from traditional classrooms to the WAN environment, is not the details of moving course materials from one environment to another (whether traditional notes or LAN texts), nor is it the problem of finding new information to add or supplement. The biggest challenge to the completely online class is the 'learning community.' How does one take a small group, one that has never met face-to-face, not even via the magic of the ITV classroom (televisions and computer technology that connect students on different campuses), and make them into a group with an interest not only in the topic, but, perhaps more importantly, a group with an interest in one another? In fact, how does the instructor convey his or her own enthusiasm for the subject?

In my DIWE literature classes, in the LAN classroom, I was able to talk to my students, to literally lean over their shoulders and point to their screens, and to provide immediate hints and answers. After teaching in that computer classroom, I gained a real appreciation for the ability of the machinery and the software to allow students to communicate so easily. The forums and the Discussion Board of BlackBoard are not lacking in their appeal, but my first experiences with forums were as a student rather than a teacher. My classmates and I were not a 'traditional' class in terms of who we are (teachers studying the online environment), nor were we working without seeing one another and talking to one another because we had both face-to-face and hands-on sessions with the instructor in a lab, ITV meetings with our peers on another campus, and, of course, face-to-face meetings with our classmates on our own campuses. Thus, this did not completely prepare me for the impersonality of a WAN class.

And, yet, like traditional and LAN classes, WAN classes do have personalities. In the world outside the classroom, and occasionally even within it, people literally put faces on their words. We have body language, the language of crossed arms, blank stares, and the back of someone's head; we have smiles, frowns, laughter and glares; we have eye contact and the avoidance of eye contact; we have raised arms and ducked heads. Furthermore, we have tone of voice. The question is thus: how can the instructor create the kind of environment online that allows for the necessary interaction?

Most computer classroom software, LAN and especially WAN, must address four areas of importance to the online instructor, as noted by Rena M. Palloff and Keith Pratt in their *Building Learning Communities in Cyberspace*: the Technical, the Managerial, the Pedagogical, and the Social. The WAN class is extremely challenging in that social interaction must be developed between students who have never met face-to-face, nor online in a synchronous chat environment. One of the great things about a WAN is that students from different time zones or different time preferences can take the same class.

Students from Zaire, Alabama, and Canada can all study Literature or Technical Writing, Algebra or Physics, in one setting, and never 'meet.'

How, then, does the instructor build community in the WAN environment?

- *Require students to construct personalized webpages.*
  It's amazing how much students are willing to reveal, when given the space to tell about themselves. Something as simple as what photo students choose to post can say a great deal about interests, personality, and willingness to share.

- *Require introductory email or forum messages.*
  Almost every instructor I know who teaches online uses some form of introductory message. This allows students to share basic information about one another in the same way as they might in a face-to-face environment. It can be helpful to community building for students to know that they are not alone in being first-time users, that others are as isolated or overworked as they are, and even that there is a person with dreams and plans at the other end of the bytes.

- *Allow the class to discuss its own norms through participation in a class discussion of goals, ethics, liabilities, communication styles and a Code of Conduct.*
  At its simplest, Netiquette (net etiquette) requires students to refrain from flaming (insulting) one another and spamming (sending extraneous and useless information to the discussion boards or via class email). Students can also be invited to enter into a discussion of additional requirements. Some classes put limits on what kinds of rebuttals are acceptable, others wish to place limits on the kinds of language or topics that can be discussed. So long as the class as a whole allows itself to be self-censored in this way, I've never objected.

- *Create a distinctive gathering place for the group, either within the confines of the software, or through the use of a chatroom or MOO elsewhere online.*
  It's helpful to have a private space where the students can talk without the teacher listening in. Closed groups can be set up by the instructor (WAN) or system administrator (LAN) that allow the students the freedom to whisper and exchange ideas outside the realm of the course. In DIWE, I called this space the 'Grafitti Wall.' Others had equally creative names for their student-only spaces.

- *Promote effective leadership from within the group by asking students to take charge of particular discussions.*
  Early in the semester, particularly with online novices, the instructor should be responsible for posting the first questions or comments to any online discussion. However, once the semester is underway, it's valuable to leave a discussion open, now and again, and invite students to ask one another (and the instructor) questions of their own devising. This can lead to sharing of the 'seed' work, as both instructor and students open new discussion forums or InterChange® sessions, under whatever name their software provides.

- *Allow for and encourage the formation of subgroups.*
  Just as traditional classes benefit from group work, so, too, can online students. Smaller groups have to contact one another more frequently. Some instructors set the groups up randomly, some wait and then make sure they have mixed groups which include some students with a knowledge of the software and some novices.

- *Expect members to solve their own disputes, whenever the dispute does not violate class conduct rules or threaten to engulf other students.*
  As my example above – where the student very inappropriately posted a dirty joke in the middle of an online conversation – demonstrates, sometimes students should be allowed to 'police' their own classmates. This will increase their sense of ownership of the class.

It is always wise to remember that there are communities 'out there,' or, if you prefer, 'in there,' on the computer. There are chat groups, listservs, MOOs, MUDs, MUSHs, Usenet groups, IRCs, and intra-office email directories. These groups exist because of a shared interest in some topic, cause, career, or fantasy. Personality and community can be found both in text and online. Keep in mind that you may encounter classes, as I have recently myself, where three or four of the students already know each other from previous online experiences. Their easy exchanges and conversations might intimidate a few students new to the environment, but only at the start. The presence of these students also shows the newbies that online courses can be both enjoyable and enlightening.

Though many instructors were taught that they were going to be in charge, that the classroom was theirs to run as they saw fit, the move to LAN and now WAN classrooms has changed the dynamic. No longer will the communities of learning be based on the ideas, demands, and expectations of one person, howsoever much he or she may flaunt the gradebook. Community building, particularly in the WAN environment, demands the participation of the entire

community. It is this challenge that those of us enamored of computer technology must remember.

Note

1. The author would like to thank the Modern Language Association for permission to
   expand upon her short article: 'Computers and Literature' which was originally
   written for *Innovations in Undergraduate Teaching*, edited by Heather Dubrow, Andrea
   A. Lunsford, and Catherine Porter, Supplement to *MLA Newsletter*, Summer 1998.

Works cited

Blair, Kristine. 'Authority, Resistance, and Empowerment: the Possibilities and Constraints of InterChange.' *Wings* 3.1 (Spring 1995). Online. Internet. 19 October 2001.

Cherny, Lynn and Elizabeth Reba Weise (eds). *Wired Women: Gender and New Realities In
Cyberspace* (Seattle: Seal Press, 1996).

Dauer, Susan Jaye. 'Computers and Literature' for *Innovations in Undergraduate Teaching*,
edited by Heather Dubrow, Andrea A. Lunsford, and Catherine Porter, Supplement to
MLA Newsletter, Summer 1998.

Dauer, Susan Jaye. 'Daedalus® Across the Disciplines: 100 Great Ideas for InterChange®
& Mail for Macintosh® and Windows™' (Austin, TX: The Daedalus® Group, Inc.,
1996).

Kolko, Beth, Lisa Nakamura, and Gilbert B. Rodman (eds). *Race in Cyberspace* (New York:
Routledge, 2000).

Palloff, Rena M. and Keith Pratt. *Building Learning Communities in Cyberspace: Effective
Strategies for the Online Classroom*, The Jossey-Bass Higher and Adult Education Series
(San Francisco: Jossey-Bass, 1999).

Peterson, Nancy. 'InterChange: Local Conversations, Global Concerns.' *Wings* 3.1
(Spring 1995). Online. Internet. 19 October 2001.

Rickly, Rebecca. *Exploring the Dimensions of Discourse: A Multi-Modal Analysis of Electronic
and Oral Discussions in Developmental English*. Diss. Ball State U, 1995.

Swaffar, Janet K. *et al.* (eds). *Language Learning Online: Theory and Practice in the L2 and ESL
Classroom*. Austin, TX: Labyrinth Press, 1998.

13
'Subject: RE: I absolutely *HATED* Achebe's *Things Fall Apart*: Teaching World Literature on the World Wide Web

Tanya Agathocleous and Jillana Enteen

In the fall of 1999, the authors of this chapter were teaching at different universities (Rutgers, the State University of New Jersey, and the University of Central Florida, respectively), but we discovered that we had both been assigned world literature classes for our spring semesters. The idea of collaboration was immediately appealing – not only could we discuss issues and concerns about the aims of the course and its syllabus, but we could also share our knowledge about particular authors and texts and pool resources about classroom strategies. Our discussion quickly turned to the question of how to extend the notion of collaboration to foster discussion and cooperation among our students.

The World Wide Web was the most obvious forum to enable this kind of distance-based interaction, and one that seemed particularly appropriate to the project of teaching 'world literature in English': a still relatively undefined field which was taking shape as prominently on the Web (which provides linkages between a wide, theoretically 'global' range of literatures and discourses) as it was through the publication of anthologies and the institution of new classes in English departments. The fact that students had clearly participated in launching many of the postcolonial and world literature sites on the Internet reinforced our sense that it could serve as an important pedagogical and scholarly resource for the contemporary world literature syllabus.

George Landow's influential work on hypertext argues for the inherently collaborative nature of web-based work: 'Hypertext has no authors in the conventional sense. Just as hypertext as an educational medium transforms the teacher from a leader into a kind of coach or companion, hypertext as a writing medium metamorphoses the author into an editor or developer. Hypermedia... is a team production' (Landow, 100).[1] Landow's influential and widely-cited website 'Contemporary Postcolonial and Postimperial Literature in English' (http://www.scholars.nus.edu.sg/landow/post/misc/postov.html), made up largely of links and essays created by students, demonstrates the particular relevance of this kind of de-centered and innovative work to the project of teaching world literature. Alongside its other strengths, the site offers a more genuinely global perspective on postcolonial studies than other similar sites, connecting writing produced in universities in Zimbabwe, India and Singapore with material originating in the US.

Inspired by Landow's work, we decided to link our classes over the Internet, allowing students to engage in dialogue through email exchanges and to write collaboratively using a shared discussion board; online conversations would also provide fodder for class discussion. Specific webpages such as Landow's 'Political Discourse: Theories of Colonialism and Postcolonialism' (http://65.107.211.206/post/poldiscourse/discourseov.html) could serve as an in-depth, yet convenient knowledge base from which our students could draw; his site would also illustrate the presence of student research in the extensive catalog of authors and theorists, thereby encouraging our students to think of themselves as participants in a widespread conversation and contributors to a nascent field of knowledge.

This essay describes the decisions we made in setting up and conducting our world literature class, both as they relate to the project of teaching world literature and as they relate to the particulars of using a web component and teaching collaboratively. Because our class was not traditional in content, theoretical aims, or class requirements, we faced a range of new pedagogical challenges, in addition to the more familiar ones of drawing students' attention to form, explicating difficult concepts and staying on schedule. For instance, we had to choose texts from an extremely large and unformed 'canon' and to build national and international historical contexts for students with little preparation in this area. World literature classes, as opposed to postcolonial literature classes, often attract non-English majors because of the general focus that their titles suggest, and because they often fulfill humanities elective requirements or 'minority culture' requirements. We were therefore preparing to introduce students both to literary studies and to a new and challenging area of study within the field.

In undertaking these tasks, we found the Internet to be an indispensable informational resource both for ourselves and our students, as well as a space that enabled – through our use of a web bulletin board that connected our two classes – avid and searching discussions of the class' texts and issues. Significantly, the practice of posting weekly on assigned texts, and in response to other students' posts, had a notable impact on the amount and quality of student writing over the course of the semester: students were more likely to be critically incisive about the texts and other students' comments on the Web than in class and in the papers (at least at first). More evidently a dialogical forum than the literature essay, and less intimidating than the class discussions, the Web enabled students to see themselves as part of a scholarly community that extended beyond the borders of the physical class. While this would be true of any literature class, it was particularly helpful for the study of world literature, since the students' new-found authority on the Web enabled them to raise complicated questions about cultural difference provoked by our texts that they were often more timid about broaching in the classroom.

Setting up

'World literature in English' raises a number of difficult structural issues, even before the question of adding on a web component is considered. How would we prevent the course from purporting to cover all space and time, as the title 'world literature' suggests? How would we be able to assemble a 'canon' out of the vast number of texts that were available to us in this emergent field, encompassing complex, yet underrepresented histories, and often with no common thread of intertextuality? What does it mean to have a world literature class, with all the diverse cultures and languages that such a class should entail, in an English department? How could we exploit the Internet's potential as a site for information, new kinds of conversations and new environments for interactive learning?

We were concerned that both the Web and world literature classes often aspire to a false conception of democratic globality, erasing the troubling persistence of western bias and privileging of western-based practices. Literature in English authored by non-western writers necessarily utilizes at the very least the means of production of the colonizers – the writing, publishing, and advertising of books, for instance, or, as electronic technologies become ever more pervasive, the use of western-derived computer applications (Microsoft Word®, for example) for writing and print layout; the Internet as a site of publishing, advertising, and disseminating information is also still largely dominated by the US, replicating and enhancing previous inequities.

Instead of ignoring or attempting to resolve these crucial but formidable problematics, we decided to use them as the founding questions of our course, making them integral to our syllabus and structure, and drawing our students' attention to them throughout the semester. We focused the course around the concept of twentieth-century Anglophone literature outside of the US and UK, thereby choosing to use a postcolonial context as an organizational and theoretical framework. Many other humanities classes, cataloged under Comparative Literature, Western Civilization, Art History and other disciplines, that use the formulation 'world literature' often focus on European-derived texts in translation; programs such as Area Studies that do read African, South Asian and Caribbean texts in the original or in translation, often read them in isolation from each other. The postcolonial classroom, then, offers the only site for Anglophone literature that highlights both formal conventions and postcolonial situations. For reasons of underrepresentation, we could also have chosen to include ethnic American literature, diasporic literature, or the literature of settler colonies, such as Canada, Australia or New Zealand. We decided, however, that one way to meet our theoretical goals and unify our texts (at least provisionally) would be to examine the remnants of colonial presence in postcolonial sites; we therefore determined to concentrate chiefly on texts from ex-British colonies in the Caribbean, Africa and South Asia.

In December 1999, very few anthologies existed that conceptualized a global Anglophone canon (by now there are a few more, such as the useful *Colonial and Postcolonial Fiction: an Anthology*). Texts like Norton's *Anthology of World Masterpieces* supplied versions of the western canon, while *The HarperCollins World Reader: Single Volume Edition* seemed to be attempting to corner the world literature market by striving to encompass world history *and* geography with an overwhelming array of disparate texts, ranging from the *Iliad* and the *Old Testament* to the writings of Columbus and Sara Suleri's *Meatless Days*. We found Arnold's *Anthology of Postcolonial Literatures in English* more useful in its focus on contemporary literature and its attention to previously overlooked populations and ended up using it for some of our poetry and short-story selections. Like many anthologies, however, it provided little historical context and often presented fragments of texts, thereby divorcing them from their literary contexts. Foregoing an anthology, we decided, would not only allow us a more active participation in the creation of a 'world literature' canon, it would exemplify for our students the provisional and adaptable nature of that canon.

For the purposes of our class, the Web was a much more pertinent ready-made teaching aid than the literary anthology; it offered a remarkable database on the class' topic and a myriad of links to information about postcolonial writers, relevant theoretical texts, and sample syllabi from other global Anglophone classes. As a form, the Web also responds uniquely well to a loosely-conceived concept such as 'world literature,' reflecting intellectual trends more quickly than academic publishers and diminishing the physical isolation of academics interested in postcolonial issues. In one of the many essays on Landow's site, Prasenjit Maiti writes, 'Transatlantic communication... has evolved from sail power to... the telephone, ... and now to the Internet. Yet states have become neither weaker nor less important during this odyssey.' The dramatic increase of Internet communication (and writing in English, in general) worldwide without a corresponding decrease in concerns about nationalism, the state, and the politics of location meant that the Internet was also the pre-eminent vehicle for contextualizing the themes we planned to cover in our classes, as well as a necessary communication medium to consider if we planned to reflect contemporary concerns.

We then thought about ways to enhance our class discussions and assignments using web-based technology. We wanted our students to be able to speak to an audience that extended beyond the boundaries of the classroom while directly addressing the texts and contexts of the class. In other words, we sought to supplement the classroom experience with a conversation that was both more and less formal than the traditional classroom: it would be more formal in the sense that students would be writing for an unknown audience and would therefore be less 'chatty,' practicing writing skills as they 'conversed': and it would be less formal in that the conversation wouldn't follow the genre restrictions and hierarchies of the traditional classroom and would thus encourage debate and, potentially, a more original and engaged discussion.

We therefore set up a threaded discussion board (using WebCT, a forum much like Black Board) on which students were required to post weekly and to start a thread at least once over the course of the semester. Our prearranged schedule ensured that there were new posts each week so that students would be responding to each other rather than posting in isolation. In order to set a high standard for students' web interaction, we told them that we would delete non-substantive posts and required that posts incorporate close reading of class texts and full citations. To ensure that each class had an ongoing sense of the other, we created a calendar indicating what each class was reading when; the calendar was also a good place to include links to websites that were relevant to each reading. (See the syllabus in the Appendix of this chapter for a full description of the web policy adopted on this course.)

As class instructors we would keep a low profile on the bulletin board, posting some opening questions at the beginning of the semester, but then restricting our participation to reading posts and addressing them in class. In this manner, we retained a panoptical presence that encouraged students to take their web work seriously, but hoped that our lack of written participation would make the discussion board a less hierarchical space than the classroom. We did, however, email students regularly about their posts, addressing questions that they had about readings, and they were able to email each other automatically using the WebCT technology. The anonymity of the Internet space we had created, then, in which students did not all know each other by face, was supplemented by the intimacy of constant private email exchanges between student and student, professors and student, as well as professor and professor.

Our class syllabus stressed that using the Web was necessary to gain credit for the class, but that no experience was required. In order to provide students with all the information they needed to be able to use the Web for class, overcome technophobia, and encourage them to get involved in the web component of the class early on, we arranged to meet our respective classes in a computer lab in the second class of the semester. For this meeting, they were required to visit Deepika Bahri's 'Introduction to Postcolonial Studies' website (http://www.emory.edu/ENGLISH/Bahri/Intro.html) and write a paragraph in response: a consideration of postcolonial studies that would help to frame our subsequent readings of literature. Students were told to bring their paragraph on a floppy disc to the computer lab, where they would be introduced to the WebCT technology and taught how to cut and paste from word-processing programs onto the discussion board in order to encourage thoughtful, edited weekly posts rather than off-the-cuff responses. They were also introduced to a number of additional online postcolonial resources, such as websites that supplied maps of the countries whose literature we would be discussing, and taught a variety of ways of assessing the relevance and quality of websites to make sure that their use of the Web would be as rigorous and informed as possible. For instance, we suggested that they use the Uniform Resource Locator (URL) as an indication of the site's affiliation and resulting perspective (for example, the CIA World Factbook offers satisfactory general information on all countries, but is compiled to serve the interests of US foreign policy). After this initial session, students received handouts that outlined the use of WebCT and listed a number of sites they could refer to so that those that might have been intimidated by the forum would be able to spend more time with it on their own.

The classroom in practice: the Achebe files

The web component of the classroom produced some unexpected results – it worked better than we could have imagined, yet also produced challenges that we hadn't anticipated. One of the most symptomatic and interesting discussions on the board, concerning Chinua Achebe's *Things Fall Apart*, was prompted by the post that gives this essay its title: 'I absolutely *HATED* Achebe's *Things Fall Apart*.' The author of the post, X, was in Enteen's class.[2] A vocal, well-prepared older student, X possessed a disproportionate amount of cultural capital in the classroom. She regularly presented extraneous information to the class to supplement her (and sometimes disrupt the teacher's) authority. For example, although Enteen had asked the class to focus on the text of Shani Mootoo's *Cereus Blooms at Night* in their interpretation of its representations of sexuality, X ignored this guideline and, at the beginning of a class, stopped the discussion in order to read from a website that disclosed the sexuality of the novel's author.

X's post, as its title indicates, was an angry response to the gender politics of *Things Fall Apart*. Interestingly, it seemed far more vitriolic than might a similar response in the traditional classroom because on the Web people can 'raise their voices' by using capitals and punctuation and 'speak' at length without interruption or teacher intervention. X disliked the novel because she found it gravely sexist and faulted it for its supposed lack of realism in portraying a society that worships women, yet also depicts their domination by men; she also criticized the author's sympathetic presentation of Okonkwo, a character she saw as misogynistic and therefore worthless. X was unable to read Achebe's critique of masculinity as a case for the novel's 'feminism,' nor was she able, at this point, to imagine that the novel had value even if it wasn't feminist, though the possibility of both these perspectives had been raised in class. She presented her views quite eloquently, and at great length, concluding with the following statement:

> I do not care how my words are received because the opinions expressed on this page are exactly that; my own. Thus, please do not think that a brief but invective filled reply will alter my opinion. My opinion is unchangeable simply because, in my eyes, it is the truth.

The unrelenting relativism in which her argument was framed – her truth is 'unchangeable' simply because it is uniquely hers – might easily have shut down discussion in a classroom, particularly a discussion that involved X, who was a forceful presence, rarely challenged by other students in the classroom. Surprisingly, however, many responses quickly followed her post; on the WebCT discussion forum, X's age and assertive classroom practices seemed to carry much less weight. One student wrote:

> Greeks had many female deities yet also treated women as second class. Although you did not like the novel, and Achebe used a bit of his poetic license, all of the ideas are plausible, and you should not be so quick to criticize.

A number of students repeated this line of argument, supplementing it with examples from Aztec and Roman society. Another student, Y, gave a number of relevant examples from the text that countered X's reading and concluded his post as follows:

> Expecting the book to conform to the rules of our world will not give us his vision: Respecting other cultures and people.

Pointing to X's presentism and ethnocentrism, this student strategically used the text's own account of cultural conflict and its indictment of violence as a way of critiquing X's post. Y's argument was appropriated and expanded upon in subsequent posts, and several students noted that X's argument was successfully countered by examples from the novel:

> You did not look at all the evidence that clues you in on the 'FACTS' of the story. I apologize if this is too brief and invective, however... what you wrote is a classic example of ethnocentrism.

This insistence upon close reading and cultural sensitivity recurred repeatedly in various forms in the five messages that followed.

The response of Z, a student in Agathocleous' class, was particularly formidable (though in class Z was reticent, shy, and almost never participated). Z argued that she herself was Nigerian and could testify to non-sexist aspects of the culture. Speaking from the privileged position of being both Nigerian, and a woman, Z explained to X that X's anger was hateful (responding, it seemed, to X's unconscious racism, or at least cultural essentialism) and that X was being overly judgmental of Nigerian culture based on a one-sided reading of the novel:

> As an African female [Achebe's novel] is important in dispelling many of the myths that are held about Africans... Achebe did not have the easy task of portraying the complex culture that is ours, but he took on the challenge and in the eyes of many, he has excelled.

Z's response situates Achebe's novel in terms of the representational problems of auto-ethnography and early postcolonial writing. Alluding to the fact that Achebe was one of the first African writers to reach an English-speaking audience, she points out that he faces the formidable 'challenge' of responding to colonial representations, portraying a 'complex' and embattled culture and carving out a new literary space for African writing in a world context. She also defends both her culture and Achebe's representation of it by reminding other students of its complexity. Z's post inspired another rush of students writing in Achebe's defense. Interestingly, her post, perhaps consciously, reproduced some aspects of X's online writing, such as the use of capitals to emphasize her points. Despite Z's resistance to X's reading, she was engaging closely with her writing and with the text.

This exchange, though heated, occasionally unproductive, and not always to the point, turned out to be one of the most stimulating moments in the class. The students were clearly learning from each other, borrowing from both the form and the content of each other's posts. As each student provided evidence supporting her/his point, the next would replicate the argument, and add to the evidence, or adjust the line of reasoning. These exchanges also demonstrated an increasing ability to close-read both the text and each other's postings.

Students' responses were impassioned, but since they were aware that the posts were being evaluated, they took the time to construct arguments and produce examples from the text to correct and provoke each other.

Even when debates such as this one were not raging, students retained this enhanced authority on the Web, posting questions that mirrored the ones we asked them in class and asking their peers to cite page numbers and give evidence in their responses. For example, one thread began:

> [In Bessie Head's 'The Prisoner Who Wore Glasses'] Brille repeatedly calls Warder Hannetjie a child. Giving some examples, explain why he continues to call him this throughout the story.

In posing questions such as this, the students were actively instructing each other, using the perceived anonymity of the Web and the authority it allowed them to assume a far more pedagogical tone with each other than they would have in the classroom. Although this tone sometimes verged on condescension, we were interested in the way the Web seemed to encourage students to position themselves as knowledge-generators. In our other teaching experiences, we have often found it hard to incite students to ask difficult questions; when they do, the teacher is usually the one expected to respond. Without our written presence on the bulletin board, however, students formulated and responded to a range of questions, both ones inspired by class discussion and ones that moved beyond themes covered in the classroom. These questions, and the responses they elicited, convinced us that posting had enhanced the students' level of engagement with texts and with peer-to-peer discussion.

The perception of anonymity on the Web also allowed students to critique each other more openly (particularly when the person they were critiquing was not in their class). Anonymity, however, also had its drawbacks. In the Achebe discussion, for instance, many students ended up drawing upon, and exploiting, the language of identity – as related to race, age, nation and gender – as a strategy for combating anonymity and claiming authority. One student, for instance, writing of 'The Language of African Literature', began her post as follows:

> In Ngugi wa Thiong'o's essay I saw my mother. My family is not from this country...

Another, writing a few posts later, repeated this autobiographical strategy:

> As a person who did not grow up in the US, I can understand why writing in your own language keeps the culture and the meaning of your true heritage in place.

While New Media theory and Cyberfeminists frequently position web identities as free from the constraints of those in real life, the major strategy for many web exchanges in our world literature class relied on the delineation of identity rather than its resistance.[3] The danger of this frequent recourse to identity politics on the Web was that students often took on more essentialized positions than they would have in the traditional classroom, retreating into the kind of facile cultural relativism that had prevailed in the discussion about X's post. X herself had insisted on the moral worth of her position because it was her position, while many other responses – those that supported X, those that wavered, and those who disagreed with her – all tried to achieve some kind of closure by countering X's 'ethnocentrism' with another kind of relativism (in posts such as: 'Our ways would probably seem barbaric to them'). It was easier to challenge these essentialist assertions in the classroom, where we had more control over the direction of discussion, than on the Web. In class, we were able to refer constantly to historical context and to remind students that cultural values, rather than being absolutely relative and therefore universally acceptable, reflect historical circumstances and power relations.

The fact that students' readings, arguments, and ways of talking about identity (one of the class's central concerns) did not always reflect what we were trying to convey in the classroom was sometimes frustrating. However, the web forum *did* give us a constant opportunity to assess the level of misreading going on and to address it in class discussion. In the traditional classroom, misunderstandings often remain undetected until papers are due or journals are collected, by which time the discussion of the text has ended and is difficult to reopen for clarification. The online component of the class provided constant feedback about the effectiveness of our pedagogy, and could better direct classroom time to redress issues and fill in gaps. In the case of the students' use of identity politics, for instance, we were able to generate a conversation about essentialism and its strategic uses and political drawbacks in postcolonial representations. The Web, then, provided us with a more 'uncensored' view of how our students had interpreted the readings and what they had learned from time in the classroom.

Overall, we felt that our bulletin board forum was a stimulating and successful means of generating dialog about world literature's meanings and articulations. One of the most striking effects of the forum was that students produced a lot of text, much more than was required. Their posts were only required to be a short paragraph with a reference to the reading, but most students produced several paragraphs and sometimes as much as five pages of text when discussions were heated. Students were also less afraid to ask 'ignorant' questions about the texts we were reading and the cultures in which they were produced.

Shy students, or non-native English speakers, sometimes found it easier to participate in discussion on the Web, where they had time to compose their responses and felt less self-conscious.

In addition, the web discussions broadened the parameters of the classroom; students in one class would address the comments of those in the other, such as when Z in Agathocleous' class wrote the most powerful response to X, in Enteen's. By extending the space of the class through these conversations (and through the supplemental websites our students were expected to visit), the world literature classroom was no longer situated as a 'minority' or isolated one, as it often is in English departments. Instead, the classroom was positioned as one node in a complex and uneven geography, analogous to the texts we were studying.

Students using the Web were also more willing to stray from the impulse for harmony that we often find exasperating in class: many student threads were based on disagreement than on consensus. Though issues of sexual and racial difference raised in the classroom often met with silence or evasion (because students typically see them as 'impolite' and shy away from discussing them openly), debate and dialog about these issues flourished on the Web, where students seemed far more comfortable with confrontation and controversy. Furthermore, the threaded discussion enabled them to read and address each other directly, something difficult to achieve face-to-face. The asynchronous nature of the forum contributed to this effect. Almost all students participated more in this forum than in class because they could take the time necessary to generate responses and display mastery of the texts. The forum also interacted effectively with what went on in the classroom itself; it was easier to generate discussions because we could constantly refer to residual questions and debates from the online forum, and students could draw on class discussions and activities when designing their bulletin board questions and responses as well. The posted question on 'The Prisoner Who Wore Glasses' (above), for instance, reflected the form of a short in-class writing assignment that we had assigned.

The somewhat undefined genre of the bulletin board post, halfway between speech and essayistic prose, also provided the students with excellent writing experience, not only because they were doing so much writing, but because some students composed notably better posts than they did essays. High school English training, and essays that students are expected to write for classes outside literature departments, often produce a formulaic type of essay – the five-paragraph essay, for instance – that differs dramatically from the critical thinking and close reading that English departments strive for in student writing. In their posts, however, students were more open to being critical and questioning, and we were able to draw attention to this disparity. They also paid closer attention to writing (both each other's and those of the texts) on the Web, partly because the concise nature of the posts was less daunting than the essays they had to write, and partly because the form of the bulletin board made it easier for them to see what we were trying to get them to do: respond to, complicate, and advance ideas.

While the bulletin board format contributed substantially to our classes' work, the fact that our classes were connected in the first place turned out to be equally significant to our students' learning process. Agathocleous' very small, early-morning class felt part of a larger community, and could enter into more varied conversation on the Web than that available to them in an eight-person class; Enteen's class benefited from the sense of a broader audience, and their respect for the reputation of Rutgers created anxiety which translated into more thoughtful contributions. The sense that other English departments teach world literature as Anglophone literature outside the US and UK both validated the canon of ideas and texts we assigned and allowed them insight into a wider range of perspectives. Not only could students sense the political value of our unusual syllabuses, they could also see that that there was not necessarily one 'right' way in which to teach world literature, interpret texts, and conduct a literature class.

The Web as a teaching tool can be a double-edged sword; its more spontaneous, informal and unstructured nature can give rise to the kind of dogmatic and reactive thinking embodied in the post quoted in our title. It can also, however, allow for the thoughtful, detailed and sustained debate that followed it: one that testifies to the pedagogical value of online collaboration, both between student and student and teacher and teacher. Using a web component in a world litera-ture class is not a solution to all the problems that such a class raises, nor is the kind of community that the Web creates any more harmonious than that 'out there,' in the global(ized) space it reflects. But, as the Achebe files demonstrate, the Web allowed us to see learning in process, and to identify the pitfalls and successes of our in-class teaching. More importantly, it allowed our students to see learning *as* process, in all its unevenness, to examine and retrace the roots of conflict and to explore their own agencies and identities through writing – a peda-gogical outcome with particular relevance for the world literature class.

Appendix

Course description and class policy for world literature in English

This course examines world literature in English ('Anglophone' literature) in relation to its historical and cultural contexts. Focusing predominantly on literature of the twentieth century from South Asia, Africa and the Caribbean, we will read novels, drama, short stories and poetry, and also study film and music. Because many of our texts are produced by ex-British colonies, we will engage with issues commonly raised by the study of colonial and postcolonial discourse, such as: how and what 'worlds' are being addressed and con-structed in these texts?; in what ways is literary form used to confront the problems that arise from writing in the colonizer's language?; how do these texts grapple with issues of difference and contend with assimilation and censorship?; what forces shape the selection and distribution of a canon of 'world literature'?

As class and website discussion will function as a vital opportunity to think through, organize and complicate our ideas about these texts, participation in class and on the class website count toward your final grade. It is imperative that you do the scheduled reading before you enter these forums so that you're adequately prepared for discussion.

Required texts	Recommended edition
Conrad, Joseph. *Heart of Darkness* (1902)	Norton
Achebe, Chinua. *Things Fall Apart* (1958)	Bantam Doubleday Dell
Coetzee, J.M. *Waiting for the Barbarians* (1980)	Penguin
Fugard, Athol. *Statements* (1974)	CNS
Rushdie, Salman. *Shame* (1983)	Vintage
Cliff, Michelle. *No Telephone to Heaven* (1987)	Vintage

(Enteen's class, which started earlier in the semester, began with Shani Mootoo's *Cereus Blooms at Night* and substituted Nuruddin Farah's *Maps* for *Waiting for the Barbarians*.)

Recommended reading

Boehmer, Elleke. *Colonial and Postcolonial Literatures* (Oxford: Oxford University Press, 1995). All other reading for the course (such as short stories, poetry and literary criticism) to be distributed in xeroxed form.

Course requirements

- Postings on class website: 15%
- Class participation, short assignments and quizzes: 20%
- Three-page paper: 15%
- Five-page paper: 20%
- Seven-page paper: 30%

Posts to the class website (WebCT)

A bulletin board has been created on WebCT to serve your class and a similar class meeting Tuesdays and Thursdays at the University of Central Florida (taught by Jillana Enteen). Each week you should contribute a substantive comment to one of the threads on the bulletin board. You can respond to any thread or start a thread yourself. Each post must reflect what you have learned from and think about class readings. Substantive responses consist of a paragraph that takes into account previous posts and refers specifically to at least one of the readings.

You may post more than once a week, but a minimum of 15 responses, one each week, is required to receive the full 15 per cent of your grade. One time during the semester, you will be required to start a thread. For this week, you should post a thought-provoking discussion question that shows you have completed the reading and thought about the way the work responds to the goals of the class. I will monitor the bulletin board and delete any responses that I do not consider 'substantive.' I will not delete short responses to other student posts, however. By tracking your substantive posts, you can monitor your own progress towards receiving full credit.

The course site is located at:

> http://reach.ucf.edu:8900/webct/public/show_courses?916345039.

It is listed as Lit 2120, World Lit II (Enteen). I will provide you with guided instructions about how to access this course when we meet in the Douglass Library on Friday, January 21.

Quizzes and short assignments

Reading quizzes will be given every one to two weeks. They will consist of five short factual questions about the reading that will be easy to answer if you have done the reading. Other short assignments will include creating questions for discussion, in-class writing and short take-home writing assignments related to the formal paper assignments.

Essays

Before each essay is due, I will hand out and discuss topics with you in class. Since the essays required for this class make up the highest percentage of your grade, I recommend that you submit drafts to me (by email or in class) at least a week before the due date; I can also look at drafts in my office hours. I also encourage you to test thesis ideas and reading of the texts on the class website (as part of your postings requirement) so as to benefit from the feedback you get there.

Email

You must regularly check your WebCT mail account and the email address you provide for the class for class announcements and correspondence from me. However, please do not write to me on the WebCT site except in response to questions I might post there; instead write to me at the email address provided above, which you can also reach through a link to my name on the WebCT homepage.

Notes

1. Landow's theories of hypertext and his notions of its implications for authorship, analogous to the notions of authorship developed in poststructuralist theories, can be (and have been) dismissed as overly utopic. However, his scholarly websites do indeed complicate notions of authorial agency and textual authority in their presentation of student work alongside the work of literary critics.
2. All students' names, and in some cases their genders, have been changed.
3. Sherry Turkle, Kate Bornstein, and Amy Bruckman, for instance, suggest that gender-swapping may occur unproblematically. Rheingold, more generally, argues that online interaction is conducted by 'personae,' or identities that may have little correlation to the identity of the person utilizing them online.

Works cited

Bruckman, Amy S. 'Gender Swapping on the Internet', in Peter Ludlow (ed.), *High Noon on the Electric Frontier* (Cambridge, MA: MIT Press, 1996), pp. 317–25.

Caws, Mary Ann and Christopher Prendergast (eds). *The HarperCollins World Reader: Single Volume Edition* (New York: Addison Wesley Longman, Inc., 1997).

Landow, George. *Hypertext: the Convergence of Contemporary Critical Theory and Hypertext* (Baltimore: Johns Hopkins University Press, 1992).

Lawall, Sarah N. and Maynard Mack (eds). *The Norton Anthology of World Masterpieces* (New York: W.W. Norton, 1998).

Prasenjit Maiti, 'What is Globalization?'
http://65.107.211.206/post/poldiscourse/maiti/10.html

Rheingold, Howard. *The Virtual Community: Homesteading on the Electronic Frontier* (Reading, MA: Addison-Wesley Publishing Co., 1993).

Ross, Robert L. (ed.). *Colonial and Postcolonial Fiction: an Anthology* (New York: Garland Publishing, 1999).

Sullivan, Caitlin and Kate Bornstein. *Nearly Roadkill: an Infobahn Erotic Adventure* (New York: High Risk, 1996).

Thieme, John (ed.). *The Arnold Anthology of Postcolonial Literatures in English* (London: Arnold, 1996).

Turkle, Sherry. *Life on the Screen: Identity in the Age of the Internet* (New York: Simon & Schuster, 1995).

Appendix 1: Web Resources for Teaching Literature

The following are websites that offer resources for the teaching of literature. Bear in mind when using these links that many websites are ephemeral, or change address and location over time. We have tried to choose websites that are well-established and university-sponsored (therefore likely to have ongoing support and staying-power), but can't guarantee that the addresses listed below will always work (try using the titles provided as search terms in a search engine such as google.com if they don't).

General resources

H-Net Teaching (part of H-Net, extensive humanities and social sciences website; teaching section includes teaching-focused discussion networks, syllabuses, links, conference papers on multimedia teaching, and web-based teaching projects)
www2.h-net.msu.edu/teaching/

Carnegie Foundation for the Advancement of Teaching (see especially under 'Publications' for information on books, articles and reports on teaching published by Carnegie Foundation scholars)
www.carnegiefoundation.org/Resources/index.htm

English Subject Centre (site set up by the Higher Education Funding Council of England as a service to those teaching English at the higher education level; includes resources aimed at those attempting to use teaching and assessment in funding decisions, listservs about teaching and a newsletter with articles about teaching)
www.rhul.ac.uk/ltsn/english/

College Teaching and its Scholarship (site maintained by Craig Nelson at Indiana University, Bloomington)
php.indiana.edu/~nelson1/TCHNGBKS.html

Courses in English and American Literature (course descriptions with syllabuses on Voice of the Shuttle (vos.ucsb.edu), an excellent humanities website constructed by Alan Liu and a development team at the University of California, Santa Barbara)
vos.ucsb.edu/browse-netscape.asp?id = 2737

Teaching Resources in the History of Print Culture (Society for the History of Authorship, Reading and Publishing)
www.sharpweb.org/index.html#teaching

Teaching American literatures

Project Crow (Course Resources on the Web) (website associated with the Associated College of Illinois; a vast 'resource for the online teaching and learning of American literature' with well-organized links to other websites)
www.millikin.edu/aci/crow/

American Studies Crossroads Project (American Studies Association project, sponsored by Georgetown; includes links to syllabuses, online teaching workshops and more)
www.georgetown.edu/crossroads/

Teaching Early American Topics (on Society of Early Americanists webpage; includes syllabuses exchange and other teaching resources)
http://www.lehigh.edu/~ejg1/topics.html

Modern American Poetry (related to Cary Nelson's anthology on the subject; includes syllabuses and poetry criticism targeted at undergraduates)
http://www.english.uiuc.edu/maps/index.htm

Teaching the American Literatures (affiliated with Georgetown's American Studies program)
www.georgetown.edu/tamlit/tamlit-home.html

Teaching British literatures

Medieval Pedagogical Resources (on The Labyrinth: Resources for Medieval Studies, sponsored by Georgetown University)
http://www.georgetown.edu/labyrinth/pedagogical/pedagog.html

General Resources on Renaissance and 17thC Literature (on Voice of the Shuttle website; offers numerous links to web resources)
vos.ucsb.edu/browse.asp?id = 2749

General Resources on Restoration and 18thC Literature (on Voice of the Shuttle website; offers numerous links to web resources)
vos.ucsb.edu/browse-netscape.asp?id = 2738

Romantic Pedagogies Online (part of the Romantic Circles website, an extensive collection of scholarly resources on Romanticism; focuses on incorporating web technology into the Romanticism classroom)
http://www.rc.umd.edu/features/pedagogies/

The Victorian Web (site maintained by George Landow at Brown University; offers links to information about the period and links to sample syllabi under the heading 'Related Courses')
65.107.211.206/victorian/victov.html

Victorian websites (extensive list of online Victorian resources maintained by Mitsuharu Matsuoka at Nagoya University, Japan; see especially section entitled 'Syllabi')
lang.nagoya-u.ac.jp/~matsuoka/Victorian.html#Victorian

Victorian Teaching Resources (from the Victorian Research Web at Indiana)
www.indiana.edu/~victoria/teaching.html

Literary Resources – 20thC British and Irish (collection maintained by Jack Lynch of Rutgers, Newark; see especially 'course syllabi' link).
http://andromeda.rutgers.edu/~jlynch/Lit/20th.html

Teaching World literatures and Postcolonial literatures

Contemporary Postcolonial and Postimperial Literature in English (site maintained by George Landow at Brown University; offers links to information about the subject and links to sample syllabuses under the heading 'Related Courses')
www.scholars.nus.edu.sg/landow/post/misc/postov.html

Postcolonial Studies (site at Emory University, authored by Deepika Bahri; offers students a good introduction to basic terms, issues and authors in postcolonial studies)
http://www.emory.edu/ENGLISH/Bahri/index.html

The Imperial Archive (site at the Queen's University of Belfast; offers students information about the relationship between imperialism and literature in a number of former British colonies)
www.qub.ac.uk/english/imperial/imperial.htm

Combating plagiarism

Student Plagiarism in an Online World (free general information on detecting plagiarism)
www.asee.org/prism/december/html/student_plagiarism_in_an_onlin.htm

Turnitin.com (acclaimed service that tracks down students' plagiarism sources)
www.turnitin.com

Eve2.2: The Essay Verification Machine (like Turnitin.com, this is a purchasable service that locates students' sources for plagiarism)
www.canexus.com/eve/index3.shtml

Appendix 2: Bibliography of Resources on Teaching Literature

Books and articles on pedagogy

Aegerter, Lindsay Pentolfe, 'A Pedagogy of Postcolonial Literature', *College Literature*, 24(2) (June 1997): 142–50.

Avery, S., C. Bryan and G. Wisker (eds), *Innovations in Teaching English and Textual Studies* (London: Staff and Educational Development Association, 1999).

Babiak, Peter, 'The Torture of Articulation: Teaching Slow Reading in the Postcolonial Classroom', *Jouvert: a Journal of Postcolonial Studies*, 3(3) (1999).

Bartholomae, David and Anthony Petrosky, *Ways of Reading: an Anthology for Writers* (New York: St Martin's Press, 2002).

Bassnett, Susan and Peter Grundy, *Language Through Literature: Creative Language Teaching through Literature* (London: Longman, 1993).

Bernstein, Charles, David Bartholomae, Lynn Emanuel, Colin MacCabe, and Paul Bove, 'On Poetry, Language, and Teaching: a Conversation with Charles Bernstein', *Boundary 2: an International Journal of Literature and Culture* 23(3) (Fall 1996): 45–66.

Bevis, Richard, 'Canon, Pedagogy, Prospectus: Redesigning "Restoration and Eighteenth-Century English Drama"', *Comparative Drama* 31(1) (Spring 1997): 178–91.

Bogdan, Deanne, Hilary E. Davis, and Judith Robertson, 'Sweet Surrender and Trespassing Desires in Reading: Jane Campion's *The Piano* and the Struggle for Responsible Pedagogy', *Changing English: Studies in Reading and Culture* 4(1) (March 1997): 81–103.

Bredella, Lothar (ed.), 'The Pedagogy of American Studies', *Amerikastudien–American-Studies* 37(4) (1992).

Burnett, Rebecca E., 'Persona as Pedagogy: Engaging Students in Shakespeare', in Robert P. Merrix and Nicholas Ranson (eds), *Ideological Approaches to Shakespeare: the Practice of Theory* (Lewiston, NY: Mellen, 1992), pp. 243–55.

Burton, Deirdre, 'Through a Glass Darkly – Through Dark Glasses,' in Ron Carter (ed.), *Language and Literature: an Introductory Reader in Stylistics* (London: Allen & Unwin, 1982), pp. 195–216.

Carter, Ron and John McRae (eds), *Language, Literature and the Learner: Creative Classroom Practice* (London: Longman, 1996).

Campbell, Jennifer, 'Teaching Class: a Pedagogy and Politics for Working-Class Writing', *College Literature* 23(2) (June 1996): 116–30.

Cerbin, William. 'Inventing a New Genre: the Course Portfolio at the University of Wisconsin-La Crosse,' in Pat Hutchings (ed.), *Making Teaching Community Property: a Menu for Peer Collaboration and Peer Review* (Washington, DC: AAHE, 1996).

Charles, Casey, 'Was Shakespeare Gay? Sonnet 20 and the Politics of Pedagogy', *College Literature* 25(3) (Fall 1998): 35–51.

Chow, Rey, 'The Politics and Pedagogy of Asian Literatures in American Universities', *Differences: a Journal of Feminist Cultural Studies*. 2(3) (Fall 1990): 29–51.

Collins, Michael J., 'Using Films to Teach Shakespeare', *Shakespeare Quarterly* 46(2) (Summer 1995): 228–35.

Corcoran, Bill, Mike M. Hayhoe and Gordon Pradl (eds), *Knowledge in the Making: Challenging the Text in the Classroom* (Portsmouth, NH: Boynton/Cook, Heinemann, 1994).

Cornwell, Grant, 'Postmodernism and Teaching: Confessions of an Ex-Realist', *Proteus: a Journal of Ideas* 8(1) (Spring 1991): 33–6.

Cranney, Brenda and Gwen Jenkins, 'Feminist Pedagogy: a Short Bibliography', *Canadian Woman Studies (Les Cahiers de la Femme)*. 9(3–4) (Fall–Winter 1988): 121.

Davenport, Doris, 'Pedagogy &/of Ethnic Literature: the Agony & the Ecstasy', *MELUS: The Journal of the Society for the Study of the Multi Ethnic Literature of the United States*, 16(2) (Spring 1989–1990): 51–62.

D'cruz, Glenn, 'Representing the Serial Killer: "Postmodern" Pedagogy in Performance Studies', *Southern Review: Literary and Interdisciplinary Essays*, 27(3) (September 1994): 323–32.

Downing, David, C. Hurlbert and P. Mathieu (eds), *Beyond English Inc.* (Portsmouth, NH: Heinemann, 2002).

Doyle, Brian, *English and Englishness* (London: Methuen, 1989).

Dragland, Stan, 'Poetry and Pedagogy in the Great White North', *Studies in Canadian Literature (Etudes en Litterature Canadienne)* 21(1) (1996): 56–66.

Eco, Umberto, *Travels in Hyperreality* (London: Picador, 1986).

Edgerton, R., P. Hutchings and K. Quinlan, *The Teaching Portfolio: Capturing the Scholarship in Teaching* (Washington, DC: American Association for Higher Education, 1991).

Evans, Colin (ed.), *Developing University English Teaching* (Lampeter: Edwin Mellen Press, 1995).

Fricker, Harald and Rüdiger Zymner, *Einübung in die Literaturwissenschaft: Parodieren geht über Studieren* (Zürich: Schöningh, 1993).

Fong, Colleen, '"From Margin to Center"(?): Teaching Introduction to Asian American Studies as a General Education Requirement,' *JGE: The Journal of General Education*, 44(2) (1995): 108–29.

Gabriel, Susan L. and Isiah Smithson (eds), *Gender in the Classroom: Power and Pedagogy* (Urbana: University of Illinois Press, 1990).

Ghosh, Bishnupriya, 'The Postcolonial Bazaar: Thoughts on Teaching the Market in Postcolonial Objects,' *Postmodern Culture: an Electronic Journal of Interdisciplinary Criticism* 9(1) (September 1998).

Grobman, Laurie, 'Toward a Multicultural Pedagogy: Literary and Nonliterary Traditions,' *MELUS: The Journal of the Society for the Study of the Multi Ethnic Literature of the United States*. 26(1) (Spring 2001): 221–40.

Haynes, Cynthia (ed. and introd.), Jan Rune Holmevik (ed. and introd.) and Sherry Turkle (foreword), *High Wired: On the Design, Use, and Theory of Educational MOOs* (Ann Arbor, MI: University of Michigan Press, 1998).

Hesford, Wendy S., *Framing Identities: Autobiography and the Politics of Pedagogy* (Minneapolis, MN: University of Minnesota Press, 1999).

Hickey Dona J. (ed.); Donna Reiss (ed.) and Kenneth Bruffee (foreword), *Learning Literature in an Era of Change: Innovations in Teaching* (Sterling, VA : Stylus, 2000).

Jernigan, Kim, 'What We Talk about When We Talk about Literature: a Panel on Pedagogy with Stan Dragland, Charlene Diehl Jones, and Robert Kroetsch,' *New Quarterly: New Directions in Canadian Writing* 18(1) (Spring 1998): 138–58.

Johnson, Robert, 'Teaching the Forbidden: Literature and the Religious Student,'*ADE Bulletin* 112 (Winter 1995): 37–9.

Kearns, Michael, 'The Student and the Whale: Reading the Two Moby-Dicks,' *Reader: Essays in Reader Oriented Theory, Criticism, and Pedagogy* 40 (Fall 1998): 1–27.

Knights, Ben, *From Reader to Reader* (Brighton: Harvester Wheatsheaf, 1993).

Kumar, Amitava (ed. and introd.), *Poetics/Politics: Radical Aesthetics for the Classroom* (New York: St Martin's Press, 1999).

Lawall, Sarah, 'Canons, Contexts, and Pedagogy: the Place of World Literature,' *Comparatist: Journal of the Southern Comparative Literature Association* 24 (May 2000): 39–56.

Mann, Harveen Sachdeva, 'US Multiculturalism, Post-Colonialism, and Indo-Anglian Literature: Some Issues of Critical Pedagogy and Theory,' *The Journal of the Midwest Modern Language Association* 27(1) (Spring 1994): 94–108.

McDougall, Russell, 'Post-Colonial Performative: Future Comparative Australian/ Canadian Studies: Research and Pedagogy,' *Australian and New Zealand Studies in Canada* 12 (December 1994): 51–63.

McIver, Bruce and Ruth Stevenson (eds), *Teaching with Shakespeare: Critics in the Classroom* (Newark and London: University of Delaware Press; Associated UPs, 1994).

McRae, John, *Wordsplay* (Basingstoke: Macmillan, 1992).

Morgan, Wendy, *A Poststructuralist English Classroom: the Example of Ned Kelly* (Melbourne: Victoria Association for the Teaching of English, 1992).

Nash, Walter, *An Uncommon Tongue: the Uses and Resources of English* (London: Routledge, 1992).

Nash, Walter and David Stacey, *Creating Texts: an Introduction to the Study of Composition* (London and New York: Longman, 1997).

Newman, Robert (ed. and intro.), *Pedagogy, Praxis, Ulysses: Using Joyce's Text to Transform the Classroom* (Ann Arbor, MI: University of Michigan Press, 1996).

O'Brien, Peggy, '"And Gladly Teach": Books, Articles, and a Bibliography on the Teaching of Shakespeare,' *Shakespeare Quarterly* 46(2) (Summer 1995): 165–72.

Pope, Rob, *How to Study Chaucer*, 2nd edn (London: Palgrave – now Palgrave Macmillan, 2001).

Pope, Rob, *Textual Intervention: Critical and Creative Strategies for Literary Studies* (London and New York: Routledge, 1995).

Pope, Rob, *The English Studies Book*, 2nd edn (London and New York: Routledge, 2002), esp. Part Four: Textual Activities and Learning Strategies.

Pope, Rob, *Creativity* (London and New York: Routledge, 2003).

Scholes, Robert, *Textual Power: Literary Theory and the Teaching of English* (New Haven, CT: Yale University Press, 1998).

Scholes, Robert, *The Rise and Fall of English: Reconstructing English as a Discipline* (New Haven, CT: Yale University Press, 1998).

Scholes, Robert, Nancy, Comley and Gregory Ulmer (1995) *Text Book: an Introduction to Literary Language*, 2nd edn (New York: St Martin's Press).

Selby, Nick, 'Teaching Whitman's "Song of Myself": Radical Poetics in the Classroom,' *Readerly Writerly Texts: Essays on Literature, Literary Textual Criticism, and Pedagogy* 4(1) (Fall–Winter 1996): 63–83.

Sinfield, Alan, *Faultlines: Cultural Materialism and the Politics of Dissident Reading* (Oxford: Oxford University Press, 1992).

Spurlin William J. (ed. and intro.), *Lesbian and Gay Studies and the Teaching of English: Positions, Pedagogies, and Cultural Politics* (Urbana, IL: National Council of Teachers of English, 2000).

Stam, Robert, 'Eurocentrism, Polycentrism, and Multicultural Pedagogy: Film and the Quincentennial,' in Roman de la Campa, E. Ann Kaplan and Michael Sprinker (eds), *Late Imperial Culture* (London: Verso, 1995), pp. 97–121.

Thomson, Jack (ed.), *Reconstructing Literature Teaching* (Norwood, SA: Australian Association for the Teaching of English, 1992).

Treagus, Mandy, 'Australian Literature and the Teaching of "Nation",' *Southerly: a Review of Australian Literature* 59(3–4) (Spring–Summer 1999): 16–21.

Wilson, Deborah S., 'Dora, Nora and Their Professor: the "Talking Cure", Nightwood, and Feminist Pedagogy', *Literature and Psychology* 42(3) (1996): 48–71.
Waldmann, Günter, *Produktiver Umgang mit Lyrik* (Druck: Wilhelm Jungmann, 1996).

Journals

College Teaching. Heldref Publications.
Journal of the Scholarship of Teaching. http://www.iusb.edu/~josotl/
Journal on Excellence in College Teaching. http://ject.lib.muohio.edu/
Pedagogy. Duke University Press.
Readerly Writerly Texts: Essays on Literature, Literary-Textual Criticism, and Pedagogy. Portales, NM.
Teaching English in the Two-Year College. NCTE.
The English Subject Centre Newsletter. http://www.rhul.ac.uk/ltsn/english/

Other teaching resources

Combating stage fright: Some teachers experience a potentially debilitating stage fright when beginning their teaching careers: a course in public speaking or acting can make all the difference. For public speaking, look for a practical course aimed at business people. For either type of course, try the continuing or adult education program at your school or another local one, the YMCA or another neighborhood association, or a company that teaches computer or foreign-language courses.

Conferences: While conferences devoted exclusively to teaching are relatively rare (though Rutgers held one in the spring of 2001), more and more conferences are beginning to include panels on teaching. The 2001 MLA Convention, for instance, had a series of panels on pedagogy in literature and languages and many specialist conferences are including them as well. These panels can often be productive venues in which to develop and exchange ideas about teaching in an ongoing way.

Index

CPSIA information can be obtained at www.ICGtesting.com
Printed in the USA
LVOW132127011112

305521LV00009B/10/P